WOMEN, WORK AND PENSIONS

International issues and prospects

Edited by
Jay Ginn, Debra Street and **Sara Arber**

Open University Press
Buckingham • Philadelphia

Open University Press
Celtic Court
22 Ballmoor
Buckingham
MK18 1XW

email: enquiries@openup.co.uk
world wide web: www.openup.co.uk

and
325 Chestnut Street
Philadelphia, PA 19106, USA

First Published 2001

A catalogue record of this book is available from the British Library

ISBN   0 335 20594 1 (pb) 0 335 20595 X (hb)

Library of Congress Cataloging-in-Publication Data
Women, work, and pensions: international issues and prospects / edited by Jay Ginn, Debra Street, and Sara Arber.
    p. cm.
  Includes bibliographical references and index.
  ISBN 0-335-20595-X – ISBN 0-335-20594-1 (pbk.)
    1. Women–Employment. 2. Women–Pensions. 3. Old age pensions.
4. Sex discrimination against women. I. Ginn, Jay. II. Street, Debra.
III. Arber, Sara, 1949–
  HD6053 .W646 2001
  331.4'252–dc21
                                                            00-050494

Typeset by Graphicraft Limited, Hong Kong
Printed in Great Britain by Biddles Limited, Guildford and King's Lynn

Contents

Foreword

In the now vast comparative literature on the welfare state, one constant across nations has been gender inequality in income in old age. Gender inequality in old age reflects the consequences of the gender division of labour in the household and the effect of women's familial responsibilities on their career paths. Because women shoulder a disproportionate share of household labour, their familial responsibilities frequently disrupt their employment. The costs of a disorderly work history can be high. Women who move in and out of the labour force to care for their families are often penalized by eligibility rules in public and private pension schemes that tie benefit levels to past earnings and employment history. As a result, women always fare more poorly than men.

Many nations have recognized the problem of linking benefits to work history and have succeeded in reducing gender inequality in old age to some degree by adding 'women-friendly' provisions to public systems. Women's increasingly constant labour force participation also has reduced inequality in benefit access and levels. In the past three decades, however, rising public budgets and population ageing have caused many nations to re-examine the eligibility criteria of the programmes created over the twentieth century. The 'liberal' welfare states have begun tightening the link between lifetime earnings and public pension benefits and have instituted measures to encourage expansion of private sector benefits. In *Women, Work and Pensions*, a distinguished group of social scientists examines pension systems in six nations to analyse the effect of changes on women and to determine whether these changes are likely to make pensions less 'women-friendly' in the future. This important book is the first to examine the effect of current trends in welfare state restructuring on gender inequality in old age.

Professor Jill Quadagno PhD
Professor of Sociology, Florida State University
Past President of the American Sociological Association

List of figures

List of tables

Notes on contributors

Sara Arber is Professor and Head of the Department of Sociology at the University of Surrey and a co-director of the Centre for Research on Ageing and Gender. She is well known nationally and internationally for her work on ageing, caring and health. She co-authored *Gender and Later Life* (1991) and co-edited *Connecting Gender and Ageing* (Open University Press 1995), both with Jay Ginn, *Ageing, Independence and the Life Course* (1993, with Maria Evandrou) and *The Myth of Generational Conflict* (1999, with Claudine Attias-Donfut).

Ingrid Connidis is a Professor of Sociology and directs the Interdisciplinary Group on Aging at the University of Western Ontario in London, Canada. She is best known for her work on family ties and ageing, particularly sibling ties and childlessness in later life, and has published numerous articles in this area. She has also written on demographic trends and social policy related to ageing. Her book, *Family Ties and Aging*, will be published later this year. She is currently engaged in a study of multigenerational families with her colleague Julie McMullin.

Mary Daly is Professor of Sociology at the Queen's University of Belfast. A native of the Republic of Ireland, she has previously worked there as well as in Germany and Italy. She has published widely on comparative social policy and is especially interested in how welfare states affect gender relations. Her latest book is *The Gender Division of Welfare* (2000).

Mary Davies is Director of the Pre-Retirement Association of Great Britain and Northern Ireland. She has served on the executive committee of several organizations concerned with ageing and later life, including Help the Aged, Saga (editorial board) and Reach. She has been involved in research on older women's retirement planning and is currently working with companies on a pension education project.

Jane Falkingham is Co-Director of the ESRC Research Group *Simulating Social Policy in an Ageing Society* (SAGE) and Reader in Social Policy and Population Studies at the London School of Economics. Her main research interest is distributional issues in state welfare provision and the implications of demographic change. She has extensive experience in applying computer simulation techniques.

Jay Ginn is employed on an ESRC Research Fellowship in the Sociology Department of the University of Surrey and is a co-director of the Centre for Research on Ageing and Gender. She has published widely on gender differences in the economic and health resources of older people. With Sara Arber, she co-authored *Gender and Later Life* (1991) and co-edited *Connecting Gender and Ageing* (Open University Press 1995).

Brian Gran is an assistant professor of Sociology and Faculty Associate of the Center for Health Services Management and Research, the University of Kentucky. He earned a law degree from Indiana University (Bloomington) and a doctorate in Sociology from Northwestern University. He has received research funding from the National Science Foundation, the Ford Foundation, and the Canadian Embassy. He was a Robert Wood Johnson Foundation Scholar in Health Policy Research at Yale University prior to joining the faculty of the University of Kentucky. He has published in the areas of the sociology of law, comparative social policy, and methodology. Gran's current research focuses on comparative social policy as it is formed in the intersection of the public and private sectors.

Angela O'Rand is Professor of Sociology at Duke University and is affiliated with the Center for Demographic Studies and the Center for the Study of Aging and Human Development as a Senior Fellow. Her research interests focus on how workplace organization, reflected in employee compensation and benefit systems, stratifies the labour force over time.

Kay Peggs lectures on Sociology at Portsmouth University. As part of her PhD study at Surrey University, she conducted qualitative research into women's attitudes to their pension arrangements.

Katherine Rake is Co-Director of the ESRC Research Group *Simulating Social Policy in an Ageing Society* (SAGE) lecturer in Social Policy in the Department of Social Policy, London School of Economics. Her research and publications fall in the fields of pensions; gender and income inequality; the dynamics of old age and European welfare states. She was recently seconded to the Women's Unit, Cabinet Office to direct research on women's lifetime incomes.

Sheila Shaver is Deputy Director of the Social Policy Research Centre at the University of New South Wales. She has published on issues of state welfare, including a book, *Universality and Selectivity in Income Support: An Assessment of the Issues* (1997), and *States, Markets, Families: Gender, Liberalism and Social Policy in Australia, Canada, Great Britain and the US*, (O'Connor, Orloff and Shaver, 1999).

Susan St John is Senior Lecturer in Economics at Auckland University. She has published extensively in the area of pensions and the welfare state. She has served in a variety of appointments to the New Zealand government, including as consultant to the Royal Commission on Social Policy in 1987, to the multi-party talks on Superannuation in 1993, and to Statistics New Zealand on retirement income and savings issues. She has been a consultant to the OECD on private pensions, co-authoring the New Zealand Country Report (1991) and to the Institute of Fiscal Studies, London (1998) on the Comparative Pensions Project. She was the Deputy Chair of the Periodic Report Group in 1997 reviewing retirement incomes policies.

Debra Street is a research scientist at the Pepper Institute on Aging and Public Policy at Florida State University in Tallahassee. She researches pension and health policy issues. She has articles published in several leading North American sociology journals, and is co-editor of *Ageing for the Twenty-first Century* (1996), a widely used social gerontology reader.

Janet Wilmoth is an assistant professor of Sociology at Purdue University. Her research addresses issues related to (1) financial well-being in later life, focusing on the effect of marital history on economic status, (2) social support in later life, with an emphasis on living arrangements and intergenerational relations, and (3) health status among the older population.

Acknowledgements

The editors gratefully acknowledge the expert contributions made by the chapter authors. We have especially appreciated their generosity in providing additional information and responding to the numerous queries that arose as the book developed. Support by the ESRC (Economic and Social Research Council) provided time for Jay Ginn's research and work in producing the book. The support of colleagues, families and friends has also been vital.

CHAPTER **1**

Engendering pensions: a comparative framework

JAY GINN, MARY DALY AND DEBRA STREET

How pension policy should deal with income adequacy in later life has become a highly contentious issue as industrial societies age. Pension policy, and the debate over reform options, may be seen as a barometer for welfare policy more generally, since pensions form the bulk of social security spending. At one extreme, the welfare systems of those European countries which provide relatively generous social protection are widely seen as becoming financially unsustainable as the proportion of older people rises (World Bank 1994). At the other extreme, the liberal model of welfare, with its residual social protection, is approved by the World Bank as fiscally sound. Yet this model, associated mainly with the US, gives rise to 'widening inequality [which] leads to distress and misery for those at or near the bottom and anxiety for those in the middle. Left unchecked it could also undermine the stability and moral authority of the nation' (Robert Reich, former US Secretary of Labor 1997).

Women, who comprise the majority of older people, have a heightened risk of such 'distress and misery'; family caring commitments and gendered pay structures leave women with lower lifetime earnings compared with men. Yet gender is virtually invisible in the copious literature on pension reform. The different circumstances in which women and men participate in the labour market are rarely considered. The economic value of women's unpaid work, and the social consequences if women were persuaded to abandon these tasks in favour of unfettered participation in the labour market, do not enter the debates on pension reform. Instead an ungendered individual is assumed, who can maintain full time employment throughout the working life. Thus economic analysts writing on the problem of 'free-riding' in the welfare system by the able-bodied who are not employed have men in mind, especially men's early retirement. Resulting policy prescriptions generally involve tightening the link between earnings and pension entitlements, ignoring the impact on women's income in later life.

The book aims to redress the male-centred bias of debates on pension reform by providing an analysis, from a feminist political economy perspective, of how women's retirement income is influenced by the interplay of employment histories, marital status, fertility and the design of pension systems. The gender contract (or gender order) – which encompasses gendered relationships of power and gendered emotional/sexual norms as well as the gender division of paid and unpaid labour (Connell 1987) – is central to understanding women's lower lifetime incomes relative to men. Constraints on women's employment due to their performing the bulk of unpaid domestic and caring work, together with gender discrimination in the labour market, leave women less able to accumulate earnings-related pensions. We consider trends in women's paid and unpaid work in combination with shifts in pension policy occurring in key industrialized countries, assessing the likely consequences for women's pension income.

Comparisons are made among six liberal or 'residual' welfare states – Britain, the US, Canada, Ireland, Australia and New Zealand – where an individualistic policy ethos, relatively hostile to redistribution through state welfare, is ascendant. We use the term 'welfare' not in the restricted sense of needs-tested state benefits but more broadly to refer to all social protection organized through the state, whether contributory or non-contributory. The ideology that the market should dominate economic and social life, while the state should merely provide a residual safety net, was most clearly expounded by Hayek (1960, 1982), Friedman (1962) and Friedman and Friedman (1980), informing Thatcherism in the UK and Reaganomics in the US in the early 1980s. This ideology and orientation to welfare is referred to as 'neo-liberal', denoting the marked shift towards New Right thinking and policies since the 1970s.

A common thrust of pension policy has been retrenchment – reducing state pensions and promoting private provision in such a way as to make reversal of the cuts in state pensions difficult (Street 1996). This trend has important implications for women's future pension prospects since current evidence suggests their economic security in later life is closely linked to the adequacy of state pensions. Whether increased reliance on private pensions could improve the outlook for women pensioners of the future, as some proponents suggest, is a claim subjected to critical scrutiny in this book. The precise form of pension reforms implemented over the past two decades varies across the six countries. Pension provision is considered in terms of the development of state welfare in each country and the political climate influencing pension policy. We examine both similarities and differences among the six countries in the interplay between family, labour market and state policies towards women's work and pensions.

The six countries have been selected for two main reasons. First, the residual model of welfare is being promoted internationally by the World Bank and introduced in countries as diverse as Central and Eastern Europe on the one hand and Latin America on the other, making a gender assessment of the model widely relevant. Second, the shared cultural heritage and orientation to welfare of the six liberal countries provides a common background against which variation in women's access to pensions can be compared. Despite similarities among the six countries (apart from the older generation in Ireland) in their social norms concerning gender roles (Braun *et al*. 1998), there is no common way of dealing with women's disadvantages in acquiring pension entitlements. Thus welfare states broadly classified as liberal may vary in the extent to which they are 'women-friendly'. Tensions exist between a neo-liberal approach in which all adults are expected to enter the labour market and conservative family policies based on the view that caring for children and other relatives is the responsibility of women. By examining how the six countries resolve (or ignore) this contradiction, variations in the nature and effects of the residual welfare model can be better understood.

Key concerns for this book are the ways that the gender contract interacts with pension systems and to what extent the traditional gender division of labour is changing. Combining paid employment with raising children has long been a struggle for many women in the early part of the working life. In mid-life, too, demands on women to provide informal care for older relatives have increased, due to both rising longevity and cuts in state welfare services for older people since the 1970s.

We examine whether the apparent revolution in women's employment participation over the past few decades means that working age women will escape the poverty their mothers and grandmothers are experiencing. What are the prospects for reducing gender inequality in later life income in the future?

Women's routes to pension income

The widespread poverty among women in later life, and in particular gender inequality of pension income, can only be understood by examining how women participate in both paid and unpaid work over the life course, together with the structure of the pension system (Arber and Ginn 1991). Women can obtain pension income through three main routes, which are conceptually distinct although often combined in practice. These are:

1 sharing a husband's pension;
2 receiving pensions derived from a husband's (or former husband's) pension contributions (as wives, ex-wives or widows); and
3 living on pensions acquired through their own employment record or citizenship.

Relying on the first route is a risky strategy, especially since an increasing proportion of marriages end in divorce. Of the remainder, most end in widowhood for the woman; about half of British women aged over 65 are widows. While the marriage lasts, equal sharing of pension income cannot be assumed, nor are all husbands successful breadwinners and pension earners.

The second route, through derived pensions based on a husband's contributions to pension schemes, has the drawback that such pensions are often small. For example, British widows' pensions in the private sector are generally only half of the contributor's pension. At divorce, women rarely receive sufficient maintenance for their children and themselves during the working life and are even less likely to obtain any pension settlement for their retirement; financial arrangements at divorce are notoriously complex and difficult.

The third route, in which women acquire pension entitlements based on their own employment (or citizenship) can provide financial security, although the adequacy of employment-related pensions for women depends on how gaps in employment and low earnings are treated in pension schemes.

This book is primarily concerned with women's acquisition of state and private pensions through the third route, since such income implies a degree of security and financial independence. Income provided at the discretion of family members or through means-tested social assistance programmes, in contrast, implies poverty, dependence and loss of autonomy (Sen 1984). However, independent income may also include widows' pensions and spousal benefits (where these are a legal entitlement paid to wives and ex-wives). In assessing the adequacy of women's independent pension income, the main benchmarks are comparisons with equivalent men and with average earnings in each country.

Frameworks for comparing pensions and women's work roles

Welfare through state and market

It is useful to divide welfare states into types in order to capture variations in how they deal with the risks of poverty through unemployment, sickness and old age which arise in labour markets under industrial and postindustrial capitalism. Among the earliest approaches to under-standing intercountry variation in the roles of state and market in insur-ing against poverty was Titmuss's (1974) contrast between institutional welfare states providing comprehensive welfare benefits and residual states offering minimal, contingent social welfare.

Pensions have figured prominently in comparative research on social policy and they go to the heart of welfare state variation. As a result, indicators of pension provision and pension quality for individuals following a male pattern of employment are relatively well-developed (Myles 1989; Esping-Anderscn 1990; Palmc 1990; Kangas and Palme 1992; Doering *et al.* 1994). However, international comparisons of pension systems have focused on institutional characteristics such as the struc-ture and component layers of pension provision; the financing of pen-sion programmes; the scope and coverage of schemes; the method of calculating pension amounts; and the extent of state involvement in the various pension programmes, with little attention to gender. Other com-mon indicators include the closeness of the link to social insurance and the use of income tests, income ceilings and other thresholds for eligibil-ity purposes.

As comparative welfare state research has developed, the need for a more systematic and multidimensional treatment of variation has grown, exemplified in the work of Myles (1989), Esping-Andersen (1990) and Palme (1990). Myles offered a multidimensional index of pension qual-ity, including whether the distributional logic embodied in public pen-sions is primarily income security, income adequacy or need; the indexing formula; and accessibility of pensions. Esping-Andersen analyses pension systems largely in terms of the extent to which they achieve decommodi-fication (freedom from market dependence) in old age. A second criterion used by Esping-Andersen is the social stratification effects of pensions, in terms of the share of private, public and public employee pensions in total pension expenditure and the number of occupationally distinct public pension programmes.

Esping-Andersen's (1990) influential book built on this, identifying three dominant welfare types, or regimes, among advanced industrial democracies: *social democratic/socialist* (Scandinavia), *corporatist/conservative* (European continent) and *liberal* (Anglo-Saxon). In Esping-Andersen's schema, social democratic regimes provide superior social welfare benefits because citizens have social rights to universalist, good-quality benefits that provide a high degree of decommodification. Corporatist regimes provide state benefits linked to employment and earnings, and hence differentiated by class and status. They thus decommodify to a lesser extent. In liberal regimes, like the six countries in this book, residualist social policies are the norm. Liberal states provide only mod-est employment-linked state benefits, with means-tested programmes offering a poverty-level safety net where market and family 'fail'. Low levels of employment-linked state benefits create heavy reliance on the private sector of pensions and other marketized forms of social welfare. Decommodification accomplished through social policy is therefore low. Palme (1990), concentrating specifically on pensions and using the two dimensions of basic security and income security, developed a four-fold typology of pension systems – residual, basic security, income security and institutional.

In these and other studies, inequality and stratification are conceived largely in class terms for men. Their contribution to understanding welfare state policies and outcomes is substantial but incomplete, because the dominant analytic focus is on state/market relations, while gender and family roles are relatively neglected (Orloff 1993). This gap, typical of most conventional scholarship, has given rise to a vibrant body of feminist work on the gender aspects of welfare states. This has included developing conceptual frameworks for how pensions can be gendered in content and outcome, rather than in applying these frameworks across a large number of countries.

State, market and family

Gender and family relations are a crucial dimension of welfare states. Moreover, welfare states condition these relations. As feminists have pointed out, the gendered effects of public policies do not necessarily correspond with welfare state typologies (Lewis 1992; Sainsbury 1994, 1996; O'Connor *et al.* 1999). Within a single regime type, the outcome for women may vary markedly, due to differences in legislation affecting work opportunities, different norms concerning gender roles or specific features of the state benefit system. Among the insights feminists bring to welfare state theorizing is recognition that social welfare regimes can be defined not only by the relationship between state and market but also by the dominant model of gender relations in the family.

Many welfare states were founded on the male-breadwinner model, in which women were primarily seen as wives and mothers, relying on their husbands for financial support. Men were incorporated into the welfare state as workers, expected to contribute to social insurance, while women were included only as family members, whose claims on the welfare state depended on their relationship to a male worker (Lewis 1992; Land 1994).

Changes in patterns of women's and men's employment, the increase in dual-earner households, and evolving trends in family formation and dissolution underscore the inadequacy of the male-breadwinner model for understanding welfare state outcomes. Lewis (1992) offers a typology in terms of the extent to which the male-breadwinner model still dominates welfare provision. Whereas Britain, Ireland and Germany have been strong male-breadwinner regimes, others, such as France, are modified male-breadwinner regimes, in which women's claims as both wives/mothers and workers are recognized. Scandinavian welfare states, such as Sweden, have become weak male-breadwinner societies, their welfare provision treating both women and men as worker/citizens, supporting dual breadwinning and removing the need for benefits as wives or widows. However, British welfare has arguably moved away from the strong male-breadwinner model towards one which places more responsibility on women for acquiring their own social insurance entitlements (Ginn and Arber 1992). Thus welfare states vary (and change) in the extent to which they encourage and enable women to maintain an autonomous household free from financial dependence on a partner. The concept of 'defamilization' has been suggested to capture this gender-sensitive dimension of welfare states, but the key issue is whether women are able to choose freely between marital and other relationships or whether they are coerced by financial need into dependence on private patriarchy (O'Connor *et al.* 1999).

A time-frame approach is suggested by Scheiwe (1994). Welfare states both construct and reward particular uses of time through the rules of public pension schemes. Key features include the eligibility conditions for public pensions, such as minimum working hours thresholds and contribution periods, age thresholds and the treatment of time spent in caring activities. Following this approach, a gender-sensitive analysis of pension systems examines how the rules privilege particular forms of time use. The tighter the link between pension entitlements and employment career, the stronger will be the gender differences in pension access and coverage. Rake's (1999) analysis prioritizes the redistributive mechanisms within the pension system, especially those which loosen the link between past earnings and pension entitlements. Although these features may not necessarily have their origins in gender considerations, they are of signal importance for gender inequalities. Particularly relevant are the existence and amount of minimum pensions, flat-rate provisions and income ceilings for pension purposes, the recognition of care work for entitlement purposes and whether the pension is based on best years, final earnings or average earnings.

A gender-sensitive framework for analysing pension provision

Putting Scheiwe's and Rake's work together combines two distinct indicators of pension quality – the process of gaining access to a pension and the factors affecting the pension amount. Both are vital in a gender-sensitive analysis of pension schemes. Although they are interrelated, treating them as separate is helpful for analytic purposes. In Table 1.1, gender-relevant indicators of pension quality are shown for four sources of income in later life.

Table 1.1   Key components of pension systems from a gender perspective

(a)	*State pensions (individual entitlement)*	
	Access	Earnings or hours thresholds for contributions
		Years threshold for residence-based pension
		The treatment of years of caring
		Age for pension qualification
	Amount	Whether and how pensions are linked to earnings
		The existence of minimum floors and/or ceilings
		Maximum amount as percentage of average earnings
		Duration of contribution/residence period for full pension
(b)	*State pensions (entitlements as dependant)*	
	Access	Married or widowed status required for eligibility
		Provision for pension splitting on divorce
	Amount	Equal or unequal entitlements between spouses
		Percentage allocated to wife, if unequal entitlement
		Percentage 'inherited' by widow
		Arrangements for divorcees
(c)	*State needs-tested* benefits*	
	Access	Unit for needs test – individual or couple
		Basis of test – income, assets or both
		Conditions of withdrawal – tapered or complete
	Amount	Income threshold for receiving the benefit
		Minimum income as percentage of national average earnings
(d)	*Private pensions*	
	Access	Balance of state and private pension provision
		Private pensions mandatory or not
		Earnings or duration of service threshold for eligibility
		Ease of transfer or preservation
	Amount	Defined contribution or defined benefit
		Level of employer's mandatory contribution, if any
		Whether entitlement is inflation-proofed during preservation
		Whether pension in payment is inflation-proofed
		Level of tax relief on contributions, if any
		Widow's pension as percentage of deceased member's pension

Note: *Needs-testing refers to either an income test alone or a means test, in which both income and assets are tested.

The four sources are defined as follows:

(a) state pension entitlements based on the individual's paid employment and unpaid caring work;
(b) state pension entitlements derived from relationship to a husband (alive, deceased or divorced);
(c) state needs-tested benefits; these may result from an income test alone or from a means test, in which both income and assets are tested;
(d) private pensions, including both occupational and individual (or personal) pensions.

A comprehensive examination of the relationship between gender and pensions centres upon the conditions governing entitlement to pensions and factors influencing the amount. This general framework will be referred to throughout the book and used in the concluding chapter to compare the pension quality for women of the six countries.

Plan of the book

Chapter 2 considers how women's work, both paid and unpaid, has been changing over the past few decades in liberal welfare states. We examine the gender gap in pay and how this varies according to women's marital and parental status, their educational level and occupation. The vexed question of why women are often employed part time rather than full time, and how far this is due to structural constraints or is freely chosen, is examined.

Population ageing has fuelled interest in whether public pensions create intergenerational inequity. Chapter 3 explores the validity of this claim and whether switching towards private pensions is therefore desirable. It explores the intersection of demographic trends with the ideology undergirding claims of intergenerational injustice arising from state pension policies. Transfers between generations, and whether these are equitable, has re-emerged as a politicized issue at the end of the twentieth century. The chapter argues that a gender perspective is essential in understanding the generational contract of public pensions, since intergenerational transfers, at the level of families and of society, extend beyond the financial contributions and receipts measured by generational accounting.

Chapters 4, 7, 8, 10, 11 and 12 explore gendered aspects of the pension systems of Britain, Ireland, the US, Canada, Australia and New Zealand, especially features that help or hinder women in building entitlements. Chapters include consideration of trends in pension policy and the political ideas driving reforms, especially the promotion of private pensions. Gender inequality of pension income in later life and the pension arrangements of working age women are examined in order to assess the gender impact of pension reforms implemented or planned, in the light of trends in women's employment patterns.

The effects of pension reforms on women with varying experiences in terms of fertility, employment and earnings are hard to guess, but computer simulation techniques have helped to identify in advance potential problems with planned reforms. In Chapter 5, the effect of recent British pension reforms on women's pension outcomes are modelled, distinguishing according to typical family circumstances and employment patterns.

Pension reforms mean that individuals face a changing and confusing set of pension options. Chapter 6 explores the British pension system through the eyes of women themselves. British women's understanding of pensions and how they made pension choices in the context of reforms are illustrated using qualitative research. The chapter also draws on survey research to assess women's knowledge about British state, occupational and personal pensions.

Chapter 9 uses data from the US Current Population Surveys from 1976 to 1995 to examine private pension income in the US among those aged 50 to 64, in the context of the expansion of defined contribution plans. The analysis shows widening pension inequality between women and men and increasing inequality among women.

In the final chapter, 13, we return to our comparative focus to consider the similarities and differences among the six countries featured in the book. Pension quality is compared in terms of women's access to pensions and opportunities to obtain an adequate amount of pension income in later life. We assess the extent to which the balance of public/ private provision has shifted and the prospects for working age women's retirement income.

Several policy implications arise from our exploration of women's work and pension experiences. We suggest that employee-friendly and women-friendly legislation could ameliorate persistent gender gaps in earnings and the long-term impact of family caring on pension income. We argue that the evidence presented in the six country cases suggests that enhanced public pensions are more likely than private pensions to provide income security for future women pensioners and some liberal welfare states are more successful than others in providing for women's economic security and well-being in later life.

CHAPTER **2**

Cross-national trends in women's work

JAY GINN, DEBRA STREET AND SARA ARBER

The balance of women's paid and unpaid work is crucial to their lifetime earnings and pension entitlements. This chapter sets the scene for the following country-specific chapters on women's pension acquisition by reviewing trends in women's work and pay. We look at trends in women's full time (FT) and part time (PT) employment, the disparities between men's and women's earnings, the gender division of labour and attitudes towards gender roles. Because women's high levels of part time work have far-reaching effects on their lifetime earnings and pensions, we also review the controversy concerning women's choices and constraints in making employment decisions.

Trends in women's employment

Older women, who grew up when the male breadwinner–female carer model of the gender contract was more prevalent, were socialized to marry and bear children, expect financial support from a husband and in turn to meet their family's practical and emotional needs. This traditional gender contract has eroded unevenly across different welfare state regimes in recent decades. In Nordic social democratic countries, the state accepts part of the responsibility for childcare and facilitates mothers' employment, replacing private with public patriarchy (Hernes 1984). In contrast, in the conservative welfare states of Europe, the traditional gender contract remains stronger and reflects the strong breadwinner welfare model (Lewis 1992). In liberal welfare states, policy towards the gender contract has been contradictory, simultaneously encouraging women's employment while providing little support in terms of paid parental leave or publicly subsidized childcare.

Figure 2.1 Percentage of women and men employed* full and part time in the six countries, 1998

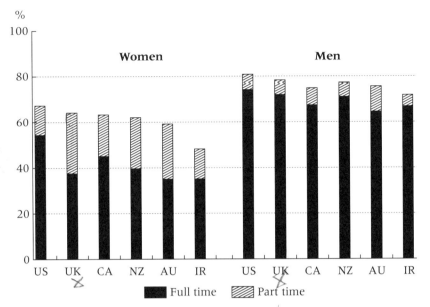

Note: *Employed aged 15–64 (16–64 US and UK) as per cent of population aged 15–64 (16–64 US and UK). FT employment: 30+ hours/week
Source: OECD 1999: calculated from Tables B and E

Although women's employment is increasing, the proportion of working-age women employed in 1998 was still under 70 per cent in the US and under 65 per cent in the UK, Canada, New Zealand and Australia; in Ireland the proportion was just under half (OECD 1999). Thus women's employment rate still lags behind men's, which was over 75 per cent in all the six countries except Ireland (see Figure 2.1).

The impact of the gender difference in employment rates on lifetime earnings and pension acquisition is magnified by two factors. First, women's age profile of employment participation differs from men's, reflecting women's breaks for childrearing, although the gender difference is more evident in some countries than others. Second, part time employment is far more common among women than men.

Effects of age and family roles on women's employment

Australian and British women's employment rates tend to peak in their 20s, when relatively few have had children, and in their 40s, reflecting

Figure 2.2   Percentage of women employed full and part time by age group

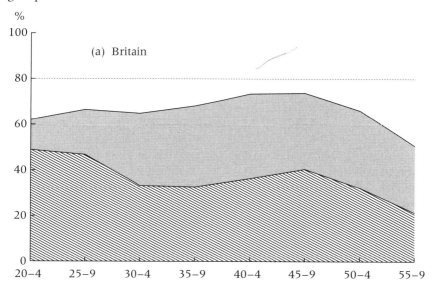

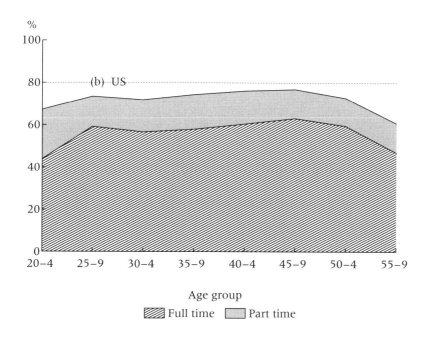

Age group

░░ Full time   ▫ Part time

Note: FT employment: 31+ hours/week in Britain, 35+ hours/week in US
Sources: (a) General Household Surveys 1993–4 (author's analysis)
            (b) Current Population Survey 1999 (analysis by Wilmoth, 2000)

women's return to employment as children become more independent (O'Connor *et al.* 1999). However, in North America women's age profile of employment more closely resembles the inverted 'U' pattern typical of men, although at a lower level. Figure 2.2 illustrates these contrasting age profiles by showing FT and PT employment rates for women in Britain and the US.

Women's economic activity is related to their parental status in most countries. Harkness and Waldfogel (1999) used Luxembourg Income Study data to demonstrate how motherhood affects employment for women aged 24–44. Figure 2.3 shows the 'family gap' in employment for four liberal welfare states. Mothers' employment participation was substantially less than that of childless women in each country, but the effect of children was far greater in the UK and Australia than in North America. For example, 76 per cent of British women without children were employed FT compared with only 26 per cent of women who had children, while the equivalent rates in the US were 73 per cent and 48 per cent.

The age of children and marital status of the mother are also relevant. For example, in Britain, the proportion of women employed increases with the age of their youngest child, for both partnered women (married

Figure 2.3 Percentage of women aged 24–44 employed full and part time by parental status, in four countries, mid-1990s

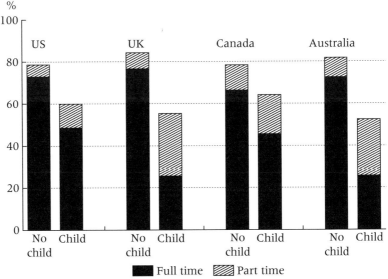

Note: FT employment: 30+ hours/week
Source: Harkness and Waldfogel 1999: Table 1

Figure 2.4   Percentage of women employed[1] full and part time by marital and parental status, UK, 1998

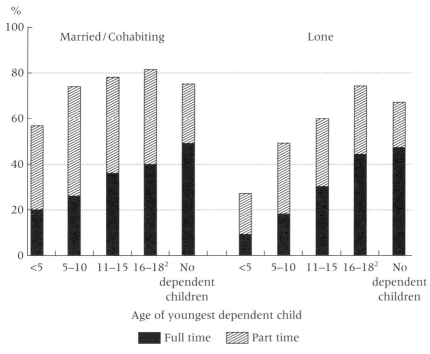

%

Age of youngest dependent child

■ Full time   ▨ Part time

Notes: 1 Aged 16–59. FT employment: 30+ hours/week
2 Those in full time education
Source: ONS 1999a; *Social Trends* 29, Table 4.4

or cohabiting) and for lone mothers (see Figure 2.4). In 1998, the proportion employed among partnered mothers with preschool children was 57 per cent but was only 27 per cent among lone mothers (ONS 1999a). Women's parental and marital status also affects their likelihood of being employed full time. Among British women with no dependent children (childless women and those whose children had left home), nearly half were employed FT but among mothers of preschool children, 20 per cent of partnered mothers and only 9 per cent of lone mothers were employed full time. In the US and Canada, mothers' employment rates have risen rapidly since the 1960s (see Chapters 8 and 10), but still reflect the age of their children.

Motherhood's adverse effects on women's earnings can be far-reaching. For example, research shows that motherhood, especially when followed by a return to PT employment in a different job, increases the chance of women's downward occupational mobility (Dex 1987, 1990). British research shows a divide is emerging between a 'small group of mothers with considerable educational and occupational capital and a much larger group of mothers without such capital' in terms of return to employment after childbirth (Glover and Arber 1995: 169). Rapid return to FT employment in the same job is most common among well-educated, well-paid women, who have enough resources to ease their return to FT employment. This strategy is less available to the majority of women, whose earnings are too low to pay for the long hours of childcare required (Ward et al. 1996). For them, the need to provide care for young children conflicts with maintaining continuous employment, especially full time. This polarization of returner patterns, also evident in the other countries in this book, magnifies the pre-existing occupational pay differentials among women (Dex et al. 1996).

Women's part time employment

Considering overall employment rates conceals women's much lower rate of FT employment (30 or more hours per week) compared with men (see Figure 2.1). In the US, the rate of full time employment for women was 74 per cent of men's. In Canada it was 72 per cent; in the UK, New Zealand and Ireland, it was under 60 per cent and in Australia it was under half that of men.

Part time work is generally associated with poorer working conditions, job insecurity and lack of fringe benefits, as well as lower hourly pay. Moreover, the effects of PT work tend to be long-lasting. In Britain, small scale research on women who entered the labour market between 1946 and 1970 showed that the adverse effect of PT employment on mothers' occupational status (relative to mothers employed FT) applied equally to earlier and later birth cohorts of women, despite the better qualifications held by later cohorts (Jacobs 1999). The timing in the life course of PT working is relevant to occupational status achieved and to earnings. Part time work among women tends to be in the prime earning years between ages 25–54, when opportunities for wage gains and advancement are highest. Part time work among men is rare under age 55.

An important issue is the quality of PT jobs – the extent to which they are low paid, insecure, lacking in opportunities for training and career development and lacking access to fringe benefits. Countries differ in the quality of PT jobs and in the number of hours typically worked (O'Reilly and Fagan 1998). Where hours are longer, PT employment is less strongly linked to low pay, low occupational status and poor long term prospects (Cousins 1994). For example, in 1988, the average weekly hours worked by part timers were 25 in Sweden, 20 in the US and 17 hours in the UK (Sainsbury 1996: Table 5.3). In Britain, there has been a growth in the proportion of 'short' PT jobs (under 20 hours per week). In some countries, PT employment is found in professional occupations and used by employers as a way of retaining valued staff – more a bridge than a trap for women. For example, Swedish mothers of young children have the statutory right to reduce their working week to 30 hours without loss of occupational status. International variation in the quality of PT jobs suggests that although market forces tend to push the most vulnerable workers into the poorest jobs, state intervention can improve the quality of PT employment. The European Union (EU) Social Charter obliges member states to set minimum hourly wages and to ensure part timers have equal access with full-timers to maternity leave, career break schemes, sick leave and redundancy pay. Britain enacted the necessary legislation in 2000, and other liberal welfare states have also enacted legislation to improve pay and benefits for part-timers.

The extent to which women reduce their hours of employment after giving birth varies among countries (Blossfeld and Hakim 1997), highlighting the role of social structure, especially childcare provision and school hours, in influencing mothers' employment. The constraint on mothers' hours of work is far more severe in Britain than in those European countries where affordable quality childcare services are widely available (Joshi and Davies 1992). Public provision of childcare is low in North America, but commercial facilities are better-developed than in Britain (O'Connor *et al.* 1999). Moreover, childcare is relatively expensive in Britain; the net cost for an average income family with two preschool children was 28 per cent of income compared with only 11 per cent in the US (Esping-Andersen 1999). This may contribute to the weaker relationship between employment participation and motherhood seen in the US, although other factors, such as childcare tax credits and the restriction of health insurance to full-timers in the US, also play a part (Dex and Shaw 1986).

Women's hours of employment over time

Figure 2.5 shows the rates of FT and PT employment of working age women in each of the six countries from 1979 to 1998, based on two OECD time series (OECD 1996, 1999). The definition of 'part time' varies among countries, yet within each country the data allow assessment of the time trend.

While there has been a rise in the total and FT employment rates in each country, the rise in FT employment plateaued in the 1990s, except in the US. For example, British women's FT employment rate rose from 35 per cent in 1979 to 38 per cent in 1990 but was no higher in 1998. Women's PT employment rose in all countries except the US.

Figure 2.5 Percentage of women employed* full and part time in the six countries in 1979, 1983, 1990, 1995 and 1998

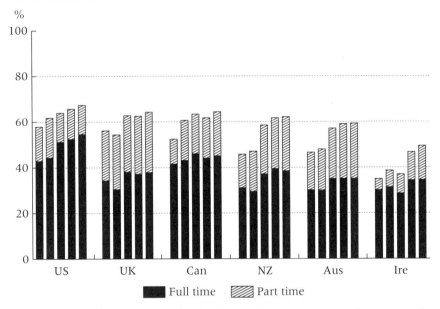

Note: *Women aged 15–64 (16–64 in US, UK) employed as percentage of women aged 15–64 (16–64 in US, UK). FT employment: 30+ hours/week but pre-1990 was 35+ in US and Aus, and self-defined in UK and Ire. Break in series: UK and Ire after 1992; US after 1990, 1993 and 1996
Sources: OECD (1996), calculated from Tables A and E (for 1979, 1983)
OECD (1999), calculated from Tables B and E (for 1990, 1995, 1998)

The gender gap in earnings

Women earn less due to their shorter hours of employment and because of the gender difference in hourly earnings. Employed women's average hourly earnings are substantially less than men's in most industrial societies (United Nations 1991: 88–9). In the mid-1990s, women's average hourly earnings were 88 per cent of men's in Australia, 82 per cent in Canada, 78 per cent in the US and 75 per cent in the UK (Harkness and Waldogel 1999: Table 2). Thus the gender gap in pay for these countries ranged from 12 per cent in Australia to 25 per cent in Britain. Hourly rates of pay are generally lower for part-timers than full-timers, especially where hours are very short or where employers' are using PT work as a strategy of marginalization, rather than as a way of retaining valued employees (Tilly 1992). Even among full-timers, the gender gap in hourly pay was substantial, ranging from 16 per cent in Australia to

Table 2.1   The gender and family pay gaps for full time employed women aged 24–44 in Australia, Canada, the UK and US, mid-1990s

	FT women's hourly wages as percentage of FT men's			
	UK	*US*	*Canada*	*Australia*
All women	81	79	76	84
Women without children	83	83	79	85
Women with children	79	75	73	83
Gender gap	−19	−21	−24	−16
Family gap	−5	−9	−5	−1

Note: Luxembourg Income Study data for 1994 (1995 for UK). Full time employment is defined as over 30 hours per week
Source: Harkness and Waldfogel 1999: Table 2

24 per cent in Canada (see Table 2.1). Women with children had lower average earnings, highlighting the family pay gap (discussed below), another source of heterogeneity in women's labour force experiences.

In each of these four countries, the gender gap in pay is substantial even among FT employed women without children, indicating the gendered nature of labour markets. Labour markets are occupationally segregated by gender, with women mainly confined to lower paid occupations (horizontal segregation). The lower wages associated with 'women's jobs' reflect the undervaluation of work done by women in patriarchal societies. The gender coding of both market work and domestic work has developed historically and represents social practices and assumptions that cannot be justified in terms of biological differences. In addition, women are concentrated at lower levels than men within most occupations (vertical segregation). Much of the gender gap in pay is explained by these two forms of gender segregation, together with women's poorer bargaining position and their fewer years of job experience (Corcoran *et al.* 1984).

The gender gap in pay persists despite legislation in most countries against sex discrimination, which makes it unlawful to pay men and women differently when they do the same jobs. Legal rights to equal opportunities in recruitment and promotion have had only a limited effect in reducing occupational segregation by sex, although women are increasingly entering the professions and management. Many forms of informal sex discrimination in the labour market operate to women's disadvantage (Reskin and Padavic 1994). Traditional gender ideology – the assumption that women are financially supported by men in the

Figure 2.6   Women's paid and unpaid work: relationship between labour market and household

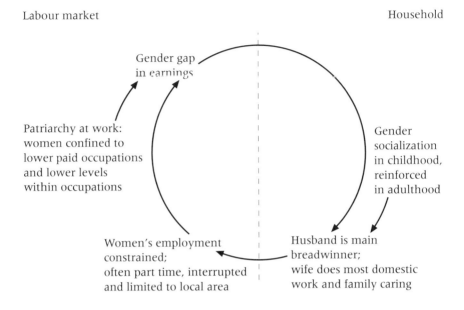

Labour market   Household

Gender gap in earnings

Patriarchy at work: women confined to lower paid occupations and lower levels within occupations

Gender socialization in childhood, reinforced in adulthood

Women's employment constrained; often part time, interrupted and limited to local area

Husband is main breadwinner; wife does most domestic work and family caring

male breadwinner/female carer model of the gender contract (Lewis 1992) – bolsters exclusionary employment practices. Men's higher pay tends to reinforce and perpetuate the gender division of domestic labour (Becker 1981). Thus it is women who are expected to adjust their employment participation, hours of work, occupation and rates of pay to accommodate the family's need for unpaid services, perpetuating the cyclical process connecting the household and labour market (see Figure 2.6).

Links between women's lower pay and their domestic roles are modified by factors such as women's occupational class, educational level, ethnicity, life course stage and family circumstances. Recognizing diversity among women is crucial to understanding variation in the extent of their pension disadvantage relative to men and the pension prospects for later cohorts of women. We discuss each of these factors in turn.

Variation among women in the gender pay gap

Although educational and vocational qualifications are associated with higher pay, neither these nor entry to top occupations guarantees gender equality in pay. Indeed, economists have shown that gender inequality in earnings rises with occupational status and that the relationship between occupational status and earnings is weaker for women than for men in Britain (Sloane 1990) and in Australia (Baxter 1992). Some examples illustrate the point: among textile sewing machine operators in the US, women received 84 per cent of men's pay and in nursing, social work and computer programming, women's hourly earnings were about 80 per cent of men's. In contrast, among university professors, women's earnings were 77 per cent of men's while in sales and financial services, women's earnings were less than 70 per cent of men's (US Bureau of Labor Statistics 1991, 1992, 1993). Among top US executives, women earned only 70 per cent of their male counterparts' earnings (Brooks 1993).

Black and other ethnic minority individuals earn less on average than whites, but the gender gap varies within each ethnic group and among countries. In the US in 1997, white women's median FT earnings were 76 per cent, and black women's 63 per cent, of white men's. Black and Hispanic women's earnings, however, were 85 per cent of men's within each of these ethnic groups (Castro 1998). Overall, British women full-timers earned 80 per cent of men's hourly rate in 1998 (ONS 1998a) but among Black Africans and Caribbeans, women's hourly earnings were 87 per cent of men's, and 88 per cent among Indians (Modood and Berthoud 1997). In New Zealand, similar gaps between and within ethnic groups occur (see Chapter 12).

Age affects gender differences in pay, which are least among the young. In the US women full-timers aged 16–24 earned 90 per cent of men's pay but this decreased to 80 per cent for those aged 25–34, 68 per cent for those aged 35–44 and only 61 per cent for women aged over 44 (Institute for Women's Policy Research 1993). The youngest workers are least likely to be married and have children, and are less segregated in their jobs than older workers. Men's earnings tend to rise with age, while women's decline from their late 30s, especially if they are employed part time (see Chapter 5, Figure 5.1). The widening of the gender pay gap with age is likely to reflect both gendered ageism, in which employers perceive women employees as too old for training or promotion at a younger age than equivalent men (Itzin and Phillipson 1993), and the cumulative effects of women's involvement in family caring work.

Family responsibilities and especially motherhood magnify the gender pay gap, to varying degrees in different countries. Harkness and Waldfogel (1999) explored the 'family gap in pay' for all employed women aged 24–44 in seven countries, including the UK, US, Canada and Australia. The family gap (or loss) in pay (after taking account of age, education and other relevant variables) was largest in the UK, rising from 8 per cent for one child to 24 per cent for two children. The wage penalty for two children was 5 per cent in Canada, 7 per cent in the US and 11 per cent in Australia. In Sweden, however, there was no significant pay penalty for motherhood. Even among women employed full time, the family pay gap for two children remained substantial in Australia and the UK. Intercountry variations are likely to reflect different family policies, as suggested by the association between national childcare services and mothers' employment (Joshi and Davies 1992).

Over the past 30 years, the gender pay gap has narrowed but equality is not in sight, even for full-timers. In Britain, womens' FT earnings improved from 63 per cent of men's in 1970 to 80 per cent in 1998 (ONS 1999b). This trend is also evident in North America, where US women's FT time median annual earnings rose from 60 to 70 per cent of men's between 1960 and 1991 (Reskin and Padavic 1994) and Canadian women's similarly (Drolet 1999).

So far, we have treated the expectation that women will perform most domestic and caring work – and consequently reduce their labour market participation – as a given and as static. Yet attitudes to the gender division of domestic labour have been changing, both in the population and among policymakers. There are signs of some gender convergence in domestic labour, which may have implications for women's ability to undertake continuous FT employment, therefore improving their lifetime earnings.

Trends in women's unpaid domestic and caring work

The gender gap in domestic work

The dichotomized division of domestic work, where husbands are employed and wives restrict their activities to childcare and domestic work has become a rarity. The majority of women combine domestic commitments with paid employment, still assuming responsibility for, and performing, the bulk of domestic and caring work (Murgatroyd and Neuberger 1997). The time women spend in employment is inversely related to time spent on domestic work. Thus women employed FT spend less time on routine domestic chores than non-employed women (Gershuny and Robinson 1988). Women's share of housework increases if there are children in the household and with the number of children (Warde and Hetherington 1993), limiting their time available for paid employment, leisure or civic and political activity.

Cross-national evidence on married men and women shows that women's total workload (paid and unpaid) has been increasing and that women's paid work has increased more than the rise in men's domestic work time (Gershuny *et al.* 1994). Thus employed women come home to a 'second shift' of domestic labour (Hochschild 1989) and the 'Taylorization of family life' as they strive to complete their tasks in ever more limited time (Hochschild 1997).

Time budget surveys indicate some gender convergence in the time spent on domestic work. In Britain and the US, women in the 1980s did substantially less housework than in the 1960s, while men did a little more (Gershuny and Robinson 1988). Similar shifts were evident in other countries for which historical data were available. For example, among British women aged 25–45, the total daily time spent on unpaid domestic work was 6.3 hours in 1961 and 5.7 hours in 1984; the equivalent times in the US (1965 and 1985) were 6.7 and 4.5. Women's 'routine domestic work' (such as cleaning and cooking) declined the most, from about 4 hours per day to 2 hours in the US. Men's time spent increased from about 1.7 to about 2.5 hours per day in both countries.

The gender gap in childcare

Most childcare is performed by mothers, whether employed or not. Significantly, the amount of childcare time has not decreased since the 1960s. Gershuny and Robinson (1988) show that, controlling for employment and family status of women aged 25–45, childcare time actually increased in Britain and the US between the 1960s and 1980s. Moreover, time budget measures may underestimate the constraint of childcare on employment, mainly because respondents often perform other household tasks while minding children and record these tasks as the main activity, even though they are at home primarily to look after their children. Men's childcare time also increased, although remaining only about a quarter of women's. It has been suggested that men spend more time on pleasurable and optional activities with children, leaving daily core tasks to mothers (Lewis 1982; Wheelock 1990), with gender-differentiated implications for employment opportunities.

The intensity and responsibility of the work entailed in the care of young children, in contrast to its invisibility within the term 'housework' and its undervaluation as useful experience by employers, has been highlighted by researchers (Waring 1988; Grace 1998). Feminists, reacting against patriarchal glorification of motherhood and keen to promote women's economic independence, have been ambivalent towards policies supporting motherhood, fearing these could entrench women's difference and be used to legitimate discriminatory treatment of women in the labour market. Yet, as Grace (1998) argues, the exhausting double shift of FT employment combined with childcare could be relieved by policies to enhance women's choices, especially by providing affordable childcare services, removing poverty traps and assisting mothers to return to well-paid jobs. In Britain, the notorious lack of affordable quality childcare constrains mothers' employment. In the US too, childcare costs are an important influence on mothers' employment; the number of children, age of youngest and mothers' perception of the cost of childcare all affect the likelihood of mothers' employment and hours of work (Brayfield 1995). The difficulties of arranging and financing childcare explain much of the pattern of women's differential employment according to the age of youngest child shown in Figure 2.4.

For single, separated, and divorced mothers (growing groups in all countries), the problems of juggling a full time job with children's needs are especially severe. With a single income, paid childcare is often unaffordable. Lone parents also lack the help of a partner and have fewer family members such as grandparents to share childminding. Thus paid childcare must usually be for the full day, including the mother's travel time, increasing the cost and the stress due to separation of parent and child. With school-age children, the mismatch between length of the school day and the working day creates problems for mothers working full time, while school holidays again necessitate expensive full-day childcare. The option of part time hours or part-year jobs, a common solution for married women, is unlikely to provide an adequate income for a lone mother and her children.

Welfare states differ markedly in their policy towards lone mothers' employment, depending on the prevailing model of the gender contract. In male breadwinner states, financial support (often at poverty level) may be provided while childcare precludes employment, whereas social democratic states tend to facilitate mothers' employment. The latter applies to Nordic countries, where generous maternity leave and subsidized childcare give mothers a degree of freedom from reliance on private patriarchy. In contrast, liberal welfare states seldom provide the necessary infrastructural support for lone mothers' employment. In the US for example, lone mothers are extremely disadvantaged; time-limited social assistance programmes in many US states force lone mothers of even very young children into low-paid work, with little childcare assistance. In Britain, Labour's Welfare to Work policy is less punitive, in that lone mothers are not forced into employment. Recent reforms, including the new Working Families Tax Credit and Childcare Tax Credit, together with a National Childcare Strategy, may expand the employment options for lone mothers in future (van Drenth *et al.* 1999).

Although men with employed partners do more 'family work' than those without, mothers with FT jobs still do more domestic and caring work than their partners. Thus the difficulties of coping with a dual earner lifestyle are borne mainly by mothers (Brannen and Moss 1991). Men's contribution to childrearing, in particular, is substantially less than women's and is rarely at the expense of their employment and earnings. Why husbands of FT employed women still do a substantially lower proportion of household work is relevant to women's ability to maintain FT employment in the future. If changes in the gender division of domestic labour do not match women's increased employment, does this represent a 'stalled revolution', as Hochschild (1990) argues? Or is there a process of 'lagged adaptation' (Gershuny *et al.* 1994), where men are merely slow to adjust to new realities by renegotiating domestic responsibilities? Time will tell, but at present it is clear that the persistence of women's disproportionate responsibility for domestic work and childcare impedes their accumulation of human capital while enhancing that of their partners, thus contributing to the gender gap in lifetime earnings. Simulation of lifetime earnings through computer modelling indicates the scale of mothers' earnings losses. For example, estimations using computer simulations show that a British mid-skilled mother of two children would earn 43 per cent less over her lifetime than a similarly qualified man and 22 per cent less than a similar childless woman. The corresponding losses for low-skilled individuals are 66 per cent and 53 per cent (Rake 2000: Table 5.4). These were conservative estimates of the earnings cost of motherhood.

Gender role attitudes

Three models typify the gender division of labour. The traditional model is distinguished by separates roles for breadwinner husbands and home-making wives. In egalitarian models, partners share both breadwinning and domestic work. A compromise model features wives with undemanding jobs who prioritize their family roles. In Britain and Ireland, characterized as strong breadwinner states in welfare policy terms (Lewis 1992), popular support is divided among the three models. Thus the Eurobarometer Survey in 1983 showed that in Britain 39 per cent favoured the egalitarian model, 37 per cent the compromise and 24 per cent the traditional; in Ireland, where conservative values are stronger (see Chapter 7), the corresponding figures were 32, 26 and 42 per cent. Taking the EU as a whole, support for the egalitarian model was higher among women than men and among younger than older age groups – 45 per cent of women aged 25–39 compared with 31 per cent of those aged 55 and over (Hakim 1997).

Attitudes to mothers' employment, and to gender roles as a whole, have been changing slowly. The overwhelming majority of men and women in Britain and the US approve of women's employment when childcare is not an issue but most disapprove of employment for mothers of preschool children (Alwin *et al.* 1992). Women are more likely than men to approve of mothers' paid employment, especially if employed themselves, if from a younger cohort and if highly educated.

The reasons for inter-country differences in attitudes to maternal employment are far from clear. Scott's (2000) research on attitudes in European countries, using the 1994 International Social Survey Programme, shows that Swedes and Britons were more likely to reject the notion that maternal employment harms preschool children or family life, compared with respondents in Ireland and five other European countries. However, approval of maternal employment in Britain was far higher where children were of school age, 91 per cent, compared with only 38 per cent in the case of preschool children. This distinction according to child's age was less marked in Sweden. Inter-country differences in attitudes to maternal employment were strongly linked to gender-role ideology (whether mainly traditional or egalitarian) and to differences in institutional support for mothers' employment (Scott 2000). The striking variation in British attitudes to mothers' employment according to the child's age is consistent with a lack of preschool childcare and with the wide availability of PT work that is compatible with school hours. State financing of childcare not only increases women's employment through reducing childcare costs; it is also associated with positive attitudes to maternal employment (Alwin *et al.* 1992).

Social and economic value of women's unpaid work

The ways in which men and women negotiate domestic roles is often presented as a private matter within the family; orthodox economists tend to treat women's unpaid work as a voluntary activity irrelevant to the economy. Yet women's domestic labour, especially their role in reproducing and socializing children, is crucial to the survival of society, an obvious point but one which is rarely discussed in economics or sociology. As feminist economists have argued, the formal (exchange) economy is dependent on women's unpaid work in the private sphere of the family (Himmelweit 1998). Time budget data for Britain indicates that unpaid household work exceeds paid work and would cost up to 120 per cent of GDP if paid at average wages (Murgatroyd and Neuberger 1997). Yet there is no formal accounting of the value of women's unpaid work in countries' measurement of GDP. In fact, the only time that women's unpaid work is valued in financial terms is when, through accident or death, an insurance claim must establish the cost of replacing it with paid services.

Women's kin-keeping, caring and supportive roles benefit society as a whole, while adequate parenting promotes the physical health, emotional stability and creativity of each new generation. Rossi warns that an employment-dominated society threatens not only fertility rates but also the quality of life:

Nor is it in the interest of the nation, or the well-being of individual men and women, to diminish the time and energy invested in parenting; or to crowd out of their lives the time available to enjoy marital intimacy and quiet self-reflection, as so often demanded by busy work lives, with the result of stressed marriages, psychological depression, or cardiovascular disease.

(Rossi 1993: 208)

Other writers have pointed to stress and fatigue among mothers of preschool children employed full time, or to long-term adverse effects on children. Recent research by Joshi and Verropoulou (2000) suggests that mothers' employment during a child's early infancy may impair child development and educational attainment, although maternal employment when children are older may enhance outcomes.

Clearly, few would wish to defend traditional family forms in which women are treated as childbearing chattels, excluded from education, employment and political life. Yet the benefits of FT continuous employment, in terms of occupational achievement and lifetime earnings, must be weighed against possible adverse effects for women themselves, their children, and society as a whole.

Choice and constraint in women's employment

Given the major impact of reduced hours on women's lifetime earnings and pension income, it is worth exploring whether women's preferences or structural constraints are more important in influencing their hours of employment.

Hakim (1991, 1995, 1996, 1998) argues that women's part time employment reflects their preferences. She categorizes women into three types: the 'committed', who prioritize their career, the 'uncommitted' who prioritize domestic responsibilities, and a residual category of 'adaptives' or 'drifters' with unplanned careers. This implies the orientations towards career or family are stable, steering women into one of these categories. Because 'uncommitted' women have chosen to work part time, Hakim argues, their disadvantaged labour market position arises from preferences associated with their attitudes and values. She suggests they are not, therefore, 'victims' of institutional factors when they experience all the adverse conditions associated with PT employment.

Although sociologists agree on the heterogeneity of women's orientations to employment, Hakim's thesis has aroused controversy. Bruegel (1996) argues that women's employment choices are not made in a vacuum but reflect opportunities and constraints which vary with life cycle stage. Constraints include exclusionary practices in the labour market, including the preferences of and discrimination by employers (Walby 1986), family caring responsibilities (Brayfield 1995; Ginn *et al.* 1996), and the institutional regimes of welfare states that assist or impede women's labour market participation.

Joshi and Davies (1992) showed that mothers' patterns of employment in four European countries in the 1980s were associated with the level and type of subsidized childcare, quality of parental leave and length of the school day. Worldwide, over three-quarters of all care for elders is informal (Chappell 1993) and done mainly by women, affecting their ability in midlife to work full time (Arber and Ginn 1995; Martin Matthews and Campbell 1995).

While women who care for children or adults do choose their hours of employment, their options are limited by locally available jobs and satisfactory affordable alternative care. Lone mothers' choices are particularly restricted, as discussed above. Perception of available options colours people's attitudes and choices (Rees 1992). Thus it is unsurprising that part-timers are satisfied with their jobs as short hours minimize the conflict between employment and family obligations. Once caring responsibilities diminish, part-timers may be trapped in this type of job, limiting opportunities to move into higher status or more lucrative FT jobs (Jacobs 1999).

A qualitative study of two groups of young British women – the first single, childless and employed full time and the second partnered mothers with at least PT employment – casts further doubt on the utility of Hakim's categorization of women and on whether orientation to employment is stable (Procter and Padfield 1998). The single FT workers were not simply oriented to either family or career; the two aspirations were intertwined. The mothers were oriented towards their family, but this was as much due to constraints on developing a career as to the exercise of choice. A longitudinal element of this research showed that single, childless women's orientation to work changed with the social structural context.

Women's orientations to work are fluid, shifting with family needs and labour market opportunities. Even women strongly oriented towards a career, as indicated by their investment of time and effort to qualify as a doctor, often reduced their hours of employment when children were young (Crompton and Harris 1998). Survey research showed that among professional and managerial staff in social services, women with children aged under 12 and working full time were much more likely to report feeling rushed and overloaded compared with similar women working part time (Ginn and Sandell 1996). Ferri and Smith (1997) reported marital tension and stress among some mothers, particularly those who were employed for long hours, shouldering what were effectively two full time jobs.

The segmentation of mothers' labour supply according to work orientation, educational level and earning power is evident in Britain (McRae 1993; Glover and Arber 1995; Dex *et al.* 1996) and the US (Desai and Waite 1991). Yet this may only reflect the fact that those mothers whose advantaged position allows them to escape or minimize the constraints of motherhood are able to make a greater commitment to a career, compared with other mothers.

Choice and structural constraint need not be seen as opposed alternatives. We suggest that choosing implies taking account of the availability, cost and quality of the childcare and eldercare arrangements required for FT employment, as well as assessing whether the total workload is tolerable. Women tend to respond to their family's immediate needs while neglecting the long-term consequences of their employment decisions for their pension income. We concur with Walby (1997: 25) that, 'Women make choices, but not under conditions of their own making.'

Conclusions

Women's employment has expanded alongside changing family structures, including rising rates of cohabitation before marriage or instead of marriage, delayed childbearing, higher rates of childlessness and of lone parenthood (Ermisch 1990b; Dex *et al.* 1996). Increasing employment of women reflects considerable shifts in attitudes and life experiences, and is often taken to imply progress towards gender equality and hence in women's financial independence. Certainly women's need to earn and build their own pensions is greater than in the past. Yet it is not clear that the changes in women's employment patterns will enable the majority of women in liberal welfare states to achieve pension incomes comparable with men's.

Women's rates of FT employment in the liberal welfare states have remained stable through the 1990s, increasing consistently only in the US. The differing rates of women's PT work in the six countries suggest that historically contingent social policies and labour market conditions are influential, although inter-country variation in gender role attitudes may also play a part. In all six countries in this volume, the gender gap in pay is substantial, even for highly qualified women, despite some improvements following equality legislation.

Time spent on unpaid routine domestic work has declined since the 1960s, with a marginal redistribution from women to men. Caring work however, including the physical tasks and emotional labour involved in responding to family members' needs, is not amenable to efficiency gains in the same way as routine domestic work where convenience foods and cleaning equipment can cut the time spent. Although many women do manage to combine FT employment with motherhood, this is most likely where household income is high and/or where relatives (partners, grandparents or siblings) are willing and able to help with childcare. Ageing populations will tend to increase the demand for women's unpaid caring work.

New divisions among women are emerging as women's family caring responsibilities become increasingly decoupled from marriage. Since it is mainly motherhood, rather than marriage, which now restricts women's employment, lifetime earnings are likely to be highest in future for childless women, married or not, and lowest for lone mothers. Thus although there has been some improvement in the position of women in the labour market relative to men, the gains have been unevenly distributed. The proportion of women with high educational and professional qualifications is increasing and such women are more likely than others to maintain FT employment and receive better pensions. However, for the majority of women who have children and for those who care for frail elders, periods of PT employment and gaps, albeit shorter than in the past, remain common. Working PT can have long-term effects, trapping women in low status, poorly paid jobs and substantially reducing their lifetime earnings and pensions.

This chapter has focused on common challenges women encounter in paid and unpaid work across liberal welfare states. High quality, subsidized childcare or eldercare is rare, gender differences in unpaid work are large, women's pay and extent of employment are less than men's, all of which contribute to women's risk of inadequate pensions in the future. These challenges, however, are played out within particular institutional arrangements in six different countries, each with different implications for women's future pension incomes. Chapter authors examine how gender differences in employment and earnings in each country translate into gender inequality of pension income from state and private sources; how this varies according to class and race; and the outlook for women's pensions in the future.

CHAPTER 3

The demographic debate: the gendered political economy of pensions

DEBRA STREET AND JAY GINN

Among liberal welfare states, there are many similarities in the foundational values, the rhetorical frames, and the problem solutions that comprise their pension politics. Collectivists propose one set of potential solutions for dealing with the challenges of population ageing and societal change.[1] However, in recent years it has been neo-liberals who set the parameters of pension reform debates.

Because public pensions represent the largest single public expenditure item in most national budgets, the 'old age welfare state' (Myles 1989) merits special attention. By the late 1970s, the vista of guaranteed financial security in old age and political consensus about the appropriate role for public pensions were overshadowed by a variety of perceived social and economic crises that halted the expansion of state welfare systems and called their legitimacy into question. Neo-liberals asserted that population ageing would overwhelm public pension systems, creating unsustainable and unfair tax burdens on working-age citizens (World Bank 1994). These claims were often reported uncritically in the mass media, influencing the understandings and expectations of mass publics (Street 1996). Right-leaning political parties, think tanks, coalitions of business and financial interests, academics and the media advanced a neo-liberal agenda to retrench public pensions and increase reliance on private pensions. Governments everywhere have sought to rein in state pensions in response to demographic trends. A revitalized neo-liberal ideology promoted the supremacy of markets for meeting individuals' economic needs, challenging whether government could, or should, provide pensions above a subsistence minimum. The neo-liberals' solution was compulsory personal pensions versus occupational pensions, on the grounds they would maximize individual choice and flexibility in retirement planning. In each country, both academic researchers and oppositional groups have resisted the neo-liberal challenge to current pension arrangements.

We argue that the severity of the demographic challenge has been exaggerated, especially in Britain (where the transition to an 'aged' population has already occurred) but even in the other five countries where national populations are ageing more rapidly. We contend that claims of intergenerational inequity ignore gender differences in the nature of contributions to society's welfare and that the gender implications of neo-liberal pension retrenchment are poorly understood. Women pay for pension regimes, both through their employment and social reproduction, yet often gain inadequate benefits in later life (see Dominelli 1991; Langan and Ostner 1991; Taylor-Gooby 1991; Ginn and Arber 2000a). Thus the political economy of demography which is used to justify neo-liberal pension reforms has profound gender implications. This raises two important questions: Do the arguments made by neo-liberals support their prescription of public pension cuts? Why has the doctrine of retrenchment and privatization achieved ascendancy, more in some countries than others? We explore answers to these questions in this chapter.

The gendered development of pension regimes

Public pension systems typically arose in the historical context of universal *male* suffrage (although New Zealand is an exception) and the male breadwinner/female homemaker pattern of employment/family relations. Pensions addressed one of the risks of industrial capitalism – the risk of *men's* unemployability in old age (Myles 1989). Factory owners demanded young workers, whose physical strength and endurance were required to maintain productivity. Older people were doubly displaced, since factory work replaced the family production in which older people had been able to work at their own pace (Graebner 1980). Most pension regimes still reflect these patterns of paid work and family relations, and a gender ideology that relegates women to a 'private' role in the family (Harrington Meyer *et al.* 1994). Thus pension systems were 'developed by men with men in mind' (Hill and Tigges 1995: 100), overlooking women's unpaid work and constrained employment and resulting in the concentration of poverty among older women.

However, such an explanation oversimplifies, in so far as it treats a close linkage of pension entitlements to participation in the formal economy as inevitable and fails to account for variation across countries in the adaptations since made to address women's pension needs (detailed in country-specific chapters). But the Golden Age of welfare state improvement ended in the mid-1970s, with most pension reforms since then aimed at retrenching public pensions. Since the neo-liberal position represents the dominant political challenge to adequate public pensions, the remainder of this chapter considers the main neo-liberal arguments from a feminist perspective.

Neo-liberal arguments against PAYG public pensions

Concerns about population ageing have been integrated with neo-liberal ideological perspectives on the welfare state to problematize continued support for public pensions. For two decades, neo-liberals have claimed that public pensions are a drain on deficit-ridden public economies, are wasteful extravagances in an era of economic uncertainty, create untenable tax burdens for working age individuals (Longman 1987; Johnson *et al.* 1989; Kotlikoff 1992; Peterson 1993; Courchene 1994), limit national savings needed for capital investment (Feldstein 1974, 1982; Morgan 1984; Ferrara 1985) and are less efficient than the market for providing future pensioners' retirement incomes (World Bank 1994).

Notwithstanding differing national economic conditions and demographic age structures, neo-liberal reformers often cited twin structural imperatives of deteriorating demographic and economic conditions as compelling new constraints in all public pension programmes. Crisis metaphors linking the number of older people and the economic cost of providing pensions have become dominant shorthand rhetoric used to legitimize the neo-liberal retrenchment project. We next examine the demographic and economic arguments neo-liberals commonly use to justify reducing public pensions, in order to inject balance into the pensions debate and to highlight the gender dimension.

The demographic argument: rising dependency ratios

An assumption that is central to the politics of pension reforms is that increases in the proportion of elderly people in national populations necessarily lead to increased and unsustainable state expenditures. Yet these are only weakly related in OECD countries (Castles 2000). Demographic determinism – or the belief that demography is destiny – identifies demographic change as the major engine of social change, with political choices and economic influences having only secondary importance. Demographic projections have been used to imply an increasing 'burden' of older people amounting to an impending 'crisis' (World Bank 1994). The assumption is that dependency ratios tell us most of what we need to know about the dynamics of population ageing (Street and Quadagno 1993).

Table 3.1 Dependency ratios in the six countries, 1960–2030, and fertility rates

(a) *Elderly dependency ratios* (population 65+/popn 15–64)

	1960	1990	2000	2010	2020	2030
US	15.4	19.1	19.0	20.4	27.6	36.8
UK	17.9	24.0	24.4	25.8	31.2	38.7
Ire	18.6	18.4	16.7	18.0	21.7	25.3
Can	13.0	16.7	18.2	20.4	28.4	39.1
Aus	13.9	16.0	16.7	18.6	25.1	33.0
NZ	na	16.7	17.1	18.9	24.6	30.5

(b) *Overall dependency ratios* (population 0–14 and 65+/popn 15–64)

	1960	1990	2000	2010	2020	2030
US	67.4	51.7	52.0	50.5	57.4	68.0
UK	53.7	52.9	54.0	52.3	58.3	68.0
Ire	70.6	61.4	49.8	51.3	52.6	54.5
Can	70.5	47.5	48.3	47.5	56.3	69.0
Aus	63.2	48.9	48.0	47.6	53.7	62.6
NZ	na	50.9	51.9	50.2	54.7	61.6

(c) *Fertility rates* (number of children per woman of childbearing age)

	1990–95
US	1.8
UK	2.1
Ire	2.0
Can	1.9
Aus	1.9
NZ	2.1

Note: Projections in italics
Source: Bos *et al.* 1994

Overall dependency ratios measure the proportion of the dependent (children and pensioners) population to the number of working-age individuals in a society, while old-age dependency ratios measure the ratio of the pension age to the working-age population. Across the developed world, old age dependency ratios have increased since 1960 and are projected to continue doing so (see Table 3.1a).

There are several reasons to question the claims of a looming demographic crisis. First, projections are uncertain because it is decreasing fertility rates, rather than increasing longevity, that are the major reason for population ageing (Ermisch 1990a). The birth rate could stabilize or increase with state support for childcare and more family-friendly employment practices. For example, in Sweden, where such policies operate, the birth rate has remained higher than in Britain.

Second, in North America, Ireland and the Antipodes, overall dependency ratios in the forseeable future are actually slightly lower than in the 1960s, when the baby boom flooded national demographic structures (see Table 3.1b). Although the composition of the dependent population has changed, fewer children means that resources previously needed to meet their needs are available to meet the needs of more pensioners.

Third, old age dependency ratios are crude measures of the 'productive' and 'dependent' populations in that they implicitly assume that all those of working age are employed and contributing to tax and social insurance, while all those of pension age are not employed. Important factors such as rising women's employment, the rate of pensioners' employment and the extent of unemployment and of early exit from the labour force are all ignored in calculating the old-age dependency ratio.

Fourth, Britain made its transition to an 'aged' population in the 1970s and experienced no public pension spending crisis from this source.

Finally, if boosting the working age population is required, a ready solution presents itself in welcoming, instead of attempting to prevent, immigration of working-age individuals from countries with high fertility rates and young populations (Vincent 1996). If it is lack of jobs which justifies efforts to limit immigration, then the 'problem' of population ageing is revealed as stemming from the failure of postindustrial capitalism to generate sufficient employment.

For all these reasons, dependency ratios, often presented as an objective measure of the 'burden' of population ageing, tell a demographic story that is partial, uncertain and shorn of the sociopolitical ones underlying it. Demographic determinism, by casting the issue as a population problem and the major driving force behind social change, depersonalizes pension issues, overshadowing the implications of pension reform for the welfare of individual pensioners and their families. Women 'disappear' when populations are considered in the aggregate, yet are intrinsically linked to population ageing.

The economic arguments

The 'crisis' rhetoric associated with population ageing has contributed to a more general perception of crisis within welfare states when economic uncertainty exists or state revenues are particularly constrained (Quadagno 1989). Demographic 'crisis' is then translated into economic 'crisis'. The 'demography of despair' (Walker cited in Marshall 1993: 156) alleges that nations have (or soon will have) more old people than they can afford, with projections ranging from pessimistic to apocalyptic. In its pessimistic variant, 'the evolution of public pension schemes is likely to put a heavy and increasing burden on the working population in coming decades' putting intergenerational solidarity 'at risk' (OECD 1988). 'Apocalyptic demography' goes further, arguing that fewer workers cannot support more pensioners and that elderly citizens are an unaffordable burden (Robertson 1991). Thus, 'If no action is taken to deal with the incipient crisis of population ageing, then it seems certain that western societies will experience major social and economic dislocation, and they may experience this relatively soon' (Johnson *et al.* 1989: 13). Media accounts amplify this message, perpetuating the assumption that population ageing causes an abundance of social problems, current and future (Walker 1986; Marshall 1993; Moon and Mulvey 1996).

Neo-liberals have exploited these concerns to promote privatization of pensions, combining demographic determinism with economic reductionism (Marshall 1993) in which all issues are framed as a matter of costs and in the case of pensions, the volume of financial transfers through the state. However, moral claims have also been invoked in support of pension privatization. We consider the claims that pension privatization would benefit individuals and the economy and that it is necessary to avoid injustice between generations.

Will pension privatization bring economic benefits?

Neo-liberals argue that shifting the mix of pension provision towards the private sector, and thus from PAYG (Pay-As-You-Go) to funded pensions, will avoid the impending crisis due to population ageing. A further claim is that public pensions undermine individual thrift and saving, while private pensions would boost national savings rates, providing necessary capital to finance economic growth. Chile is often held up as a successful model for mandated privatized individual pensions and subsistence public pensions (World Bank 1994). A number of counter-arguments have been advanced.

First, it is now widely acknowledged that current production must support current consumption so that population ageing affects *all* pensions, private funded as well as public PAYG. There is no inviolate 'pot of gold' in a funded pension, since population ageing will affect returns on the capital fund and also annuity rates. Meeting pensioners' needs will always depend on what a given society produces at a specific time, irrespective of the particulars of the arrangements (Myles and Street 1995).

The high rates of return on private pensions promised by neo-liberal advocates depend on the assumption that past investment returns will be maintained in the future. Yet economists have pointed out that population ageing will adversely affect private pensions, tending to reduce interest rates and to bring diminishing returns on capital (Mabbett 1997). It has been suggested that private pensions can only meet their future liabilities by increasing recruitment of new contributors, an example of Ponzi finance, or in common parlance the chain letter, or pyramid selling, scenario (Toporowski 1999). No one can predict with any accuracy when there will be a serious and sustained fall in investment returns. When this does occur, individuals with private pensions will risk having much of their pension wealth wiped out. Smaller pensions than expected will be especially serious for the low paid and those with intermittent labour market attachment. Thus privatization strategies are especially risky for women. The retirement of the baby boom will bring a synchronous dissaving in financial markets, increasing their instability (Toporowski 1999). Public systems, where risks are broadly shared, appear more likely to weather such demographic bulges in retirement timing than will financial markets.

Second, empirical evidence that expanding personal pensions increases national savings is lacking. To achieve such an increase, the amount of savings would have to exceed the value of the tax subsidies that support private pensions (a public dissaving) and individuals would have to save more than in the past, and not merely shift between types of savings to take advantage of the tax subsidies (Orszag *et al.* 1999). Mabbett (1997) finds that the case for pension funding based on its potential to increase savings is weak, while the double burden of taxation during the transitional period is likely to reduce economic performance. If increasing national savings is a virtue in and of itself, public pensions can be shifted from strictly PAYG financing to some level of prefunding, since, by definition, the national savings rate is the sum of public and private saving. The idea of prefunded public pensions, however, is anathema to neo-liberals, because it represents democratic control over capital (Myles 1988).

Third, individual private pensions entail diseconomies that are downplayed by neo-liberals. Millions of individuals starting and stopping pension plans and adjusting contribution levels is an expensive proposition in terms of administrative fees and charges, reducing rates of return on contributions by up to 45 per cent (Murthi *et al.* 2001). This contrasts with the administrative efficiencies gained under public systems operating under a single set of funding and benefit criteria (Myles and Street 1995).

Fourth, Chile seems a peculiar case for advanced democracies to emulate, given that the privatization of pensions in 1981 was imposed by a dictator, whereas citizens in the six countries in this volume generally support public pensions. Moreover, the 'success' of the new Chilean pension system may be overstated. An estimated 50 per cent of Chileans work in the grey economy to avoid participation, and may therefore become reliant on state support in the future (see Barrientos and Firinguetti 1995; Ghilarducci 1997; Williamson 1997). As outlined in Chapter 5 (this volume) the Chilean model of pension provision widens income inequality in retirement, disadvantages women whose employment was restricted by raising children, and leads to expansion of means-tested assistance in old age (Evans and Falkingham 1997).

Do public pensions create intergenerational inequity?

A claim combining moral and economic elements is that affluent older citizens are willing (and able politically) to impoverish younger generations in order to maintain lavish public pensions for themselves, which will be unavailable when working-age individuals retire (Quadagno 1989; Street and Quadagno 1993; Binstock 1994). The public largesse of Pay-As-You-Go pensions, it is argued, places intolerable tax burdens on the working young, provoking generational conflict (Johnson et al. 1989; Peterson 1993). Moreover, whereas public investment in children's education and well-being will pay off in terms of productivity of the next generation of workers, support of older people is not warranted since they are past their productive potential (see Myles and Street 1995). Thus the welfare of age groups are presented as opposed and older people 'blamed' for absorbing a disproportionate share of public expenditure (Binstock 1983; Minkler 1991). Private pensions, it is claimed, would avoid these adverse and inequitable effects.

As with many other cultural fads, intergenerational inequity pronouncements started in the US, and spread like a virus to other western countries (see Street 1996; Arber and Attias-Donfut 2000). Among the first promoters of the intergenerational equity cause was the US group 'Americans for Generational Equity' (AGE), well-funded by the US financial industry (see Quadagno 1989). Its spokesman, Paul Hewitt, claimed Social Security expenditures harmed younger age groups, and that 'we need to get parents and grandparents concerned about the future of their children and grandchildren' (quoted in Keister 1986: 41). Such claims, given the empirical reality of mothers' and grandmothers' commitments to family care, could be dismissed as absurd, were the unfounded claims of impending public pension bankruptcy and generational conflict not reported as news in the mainstream media (see Jacobs and Shapiro 1995; Street 1996).

The intergenerational inequity argument was formalized by US economist Laurence Kotlikoff (1992), in 'generational accounting' models promoting a political agenda of Social Security privatization. This has been influential in US and international policy circles. An important argument underpinning the claims of intergenerational inequity and of economic crisis is that public pension systems are Ponzi schemes, potentially benefitting only those joining early. This claim is based on two premises: first, high and unrepeatable returns on public pension contributions for early cohorts; and second, inevitable bankruptcy of public pension systems as the pool of new contributors diminishes. By implication, it is suggested that funded private pensions are fairer and will avoid the risk of national bankruptcy (but see above). Claims of intergenerational inequity have been challenged on several fronts.

First, affluence among pensioners is rare and statistics on average pensioner incomes obscure gender and class inequalities, as the country chapters in this volume demonstrate. For example, in Britain affluent pensioners are mainly younger, middle-class, male pensioners (Falkingham and Victor 1991), while the gender gap in pensioner income is rising (see Chapter 4). Poverty remains widespread, especially among older women who have raised children. Britain's retirement income profile, where recently retired men have the highest incomes and where women, minority people, and the oldest-old have a high risk of poverty, is mirrored in other countries. Moreover, the claim that pensioners determine pension policy overstates the influence of 'grey power'. It is demonstrably untrue in Britain (Walker 1999) and suspect in Canada and the United States (Street 1996).

Second, claims that public pensions will become unaffordable for future generations do not take into account productivity gains, thus understating the capacity for the working aged population to support the 'dependent' population (Street and Quadagno 1993; Binstock 1994; Mullan 2000). While the rapid postwar growth of national economies that contributed to welfare state expansion in the 1960s and early 1970s is unlikely to recur, all liberal welfare states are forecast to experience growth in the future. As national workforces become more productive, societies become wealthier. Barring a depression (which would also reduce private pensions), working aged citizens will be able to afford to pay the modestly higher rates of taxes or pension payroll contributions to support public pensions, while still making gains in their own standards of living (Baker 1998). When economic downturns do occur, public pension benefits are much more predictable and secure than private ones, since they depend on the political capacity of national governments to tax and spend rather than solely on the vagaries of the market (Myles 1988).

Third, contrary to the chain letter scenario, there is evidence that PAYG social insurance can achieve an equilibrium, in which a high degree of intergenerational equity is assured. For example, although the first generation to enter the British public pension scheme gained higher returns on their contributions than are available for later cohorts, all subsequent cohorts are projected roughly to break even in terms of net transfers into and out of the welfare system (Hills 1995). If benefits are cut, however, the next generation to retire will lose out (Hills 1995: 61). Moreover, the first generation required to switch from current PAYG arrangements to funded pensions would have to pay twice – once to finance past public pension obligations and again to fund their own private pensions. If working-age citizens cannot afford to pay once for public pensions, it is hard to imagine how they can afford to pay twice. Thus reducing public PAYG pensions would have the perverse result of *creating* intergenerational inequity. Because women's levels of employment and pay are less than men's, they would be particularly hard hit by this double payment problem. Public pension schemes usually provide additional benefits of value to citizens of all ages, such as insurance against early death (through survivor's benefits for dependents) and disability (expensive to insure privately).

Finally, many mainstream economists have critiqued the assumptions and model Kotlikoff used, which were concerned only with public sector taxes and expenditures (see Baker 1995). Generational accounting disregards the many social contributions pensioners made in the past (which are notoriously difficult to value), including the built environment, the foundation of healthy economies, a legacy of democratic institutions, and their own investment in current generations. It also overlooks the productive contributions older citizens continue to make to civic life, social institutions, and families, because they are not monetized (Street and Quadagno 1993; Myles and Street 1995; see also Bakker 1998; Arber and Attias-Donfut 2000). Generational accounting can only be a partial measure of equity between generations since this depends on more than just the welfare state and formal monetary transfers (Hills 1995: 61). Intergenerational equity is also about social transfers.

In common with other strictly economistic critiques of public spending, generational accounting overlooks the essential social and productive contributions of women. Through *the gendered generational contract*, in which women reproduce and nurture the next generation of wage earners and taxpayers at the expense of their own earnings and pensions, a chain of solidarity links both family and economic generations (Ginn and Arber 2000). As Attias-Donfut and Arber (2000: 15) observe:

> The gender contract is implicit and self-evident: it is women who undertake the largest part of domestic tasks, the education of their children and the care of others. In undertaking this role, often in combination with paid work, they allow men more time to pursue their careers. The unpaid work of women brings a double contribution to welfare systems: on the one hand it increases the availability

of men for paid work, and on the other hand it relieves the state of part of its obligation towards children, the elderly and the sick. More fundamentally, the physical reproduction of society depends upon women upholding the gender and generational contracts, since women are the guarantors of procreation. This demonstrates the profound injustice towards women: generational accounting ignores the contributions women make and the wealth they produce.

When flows of resources between generations in families are considered, the dependent/independent dichotomy of demographic ratios disappears, to be replaced by interdependency within the ongoing generational contract (Kingson *et al.* 1986; Phillipson *et al.* 1986; Street and Quadagno 1993; Bengston and Harootyan 1994; Marmor *et al.* 1994; Attias-Donfut and Arber 2000).

The generational contract perspective rejects the idea of a zero–sum game in which age groups are pitted against each other in competing for welfare resources. Age groups (and other groups) with the greatest needs because they are outside the formal economy receive the largest public transfers. When citizens can (because they are in paid work or have substantial wealth), they pay taxes to support public expenditures, and when they cannot, they receive support from the state. Similar transfers (economic and social) to those most in need also occur within families. In supporting such transfers, states and families participate in a generational contract predicated on social justice, one that attempts to ensure adequate resources in times of need. As Vincent (1995: 147) puts it, 'the question of generational equity and the position of elderly people in society is not simply a demographic or economic one. It is essentially a political and moral question.'

In sum, the neo-liberal argument for public pension retrenchment is endowed with a seeming sophistication through its use of economic models based on assumptions about demographic trends, the future performance of financial markets, and individual behaviour. Yet claims about the unaffordability of public pensions, consequent intergenerational inequity and the superiority of private pensions can be effectively countered. An interesting paradox is that Britain, where the increase in the older population is gentler than in most of Europe, has implemented the most severe retrenchment (see Chapter 4) and the most vigorous promotion of private pensions. This suggests that neo-liberal pension policy is not driven by demography or economics but, as some have argued, by a desire to protect the profits of the financial sector (Shutt 1998) and by an ideological *belief* among policymakers that most people should rely on the market for income, with the state stepping in with subsistence level benefits only as a last resort. Neo-liberals often imply that relying on social insurance is less 'responsible' than private saving, conflating contributory schemes with social assistance in order to obscure the moral rights to benefits generated through the contributory principle.

The foregoing discussion does not suggest that public expenditure levels of nations are unimportant, that meeting the future pension needs of ageing populations does not require creative thinking, nor that private provision is unnecessary in pension regimes. These are legitimate areas of concern. However, crisis constructions of population ageing compounded by misleading information about the economic consequences of continued public provision forecloses possibilities for balanced examination of the strengths and weaknesses of both public and private pensions, and for all citizens (Street 1995; Quadagno 1996; McDonald 2000).

Conclusions

Following the Golden Age of pensions, those who had hoped to improve the women-friendliness of pensions found themselves resisting a neo-liberal onslaught which threatened the very existence of collective social insurance. Neo-liberal individualists claimed that welfare states were fatally flawed, public pensions could not be afforded and private pensions should be expanded. Governments pursuing a retrenchment agenda invoked strategies (see Pierson 1994) to obfuscate policy changes by making arcane or technical adjustments that cut pensions, or to divide the public by cutting public pensions and extending tax reliefs to private pensions. Individualists portrayed pension reform as a zero–sum game, with stark choices between greedy affluent pensioners and a demographic 'time bomb' on one hand (see Binstock 1994), and reduced taxes and generous private sector benefits on the other.

Such neo-liberal framings of pension issues are necessary to make the assertion 'this policy choice and no other' appear plausible (Edelman 1977, 1988). This sense of inevitability was embedded in the pronouncements of many government leaders, but quintessentially by Margaret Thatcher, who was fond of reminding the public about her broad array of public sector cuts; 'there simply is no alternative' (Thatcher 1993). Retrenchment advocates argued that governments could not simultaneously fight inflation and maintain or expand public sector pensions; provide comprehensive public pensions and still compete in a global economy; promote self-sufficiency while providing more than subsistence income; meet the needs of elderly citizens and those of other age groups. Sweeping neo-liberal claims about unaffordable public spending and the alleged macroeconomic disutilities of public pensions were used to legitimate retrenchment. Demographic determinism combined with economic reductionism emphasized the economic needs of a capitalist economy above social welfare.

These arguments overlook the human face of the generational contract expressed in collective state provision and within families. The gendered generational contract, in which women's unpaid work accommodates the immediate needs of market economies and ensures the longer-term survival of society, is not treated analytically as having economic value. To women, whose unpaid work impedes their participation in the labour market, social welfare is of critical importance. Macroeconomic research and policies are typically gender blind, yet their focus on economic rather than social values tends to have deleterious effects on women's social welfare (Bakker 1998). Unpaid work does not 'count' as productive in national accounts, nor usually, in gaining much access to pension credits or savings, particularly in private pensions. Because women have the deepest stake in maintaining adequate public pensions, they are usually harmed most when pension retrenchment occurs. Beck (1992) has commented that an economically rational society would be a childless one, but a socially rational society could not be. The reasons why more women are choosing childlessness, delaying starting a family and having fewer children may be connected with both the neoliberal emphasis on the (paid) work ethic and increasing awareness among women of the earnings and pension costs of children.

Population ageing and economic constraints were common challenges faced by all six countries considered in this volume, but yielded distinctive country-specific pension reforms in the aftermath of the Golden Age of public pensions. Despite strong public support for social insurance, Britain travelled furthest along the retrenchment path, although Canada and New Zealand tested the water as well. In Britain, particularly, the pension future for women appears grim. The reforms adopted, and the effects they are likely to have on current and future generations of women, are explored in the following chapters.

Note

1 We use the terms 'collectivists' and 'individualists' to refer to the dominant conceptual frameworks and value clusters consistent with progressives and the Left in the first instance, and libertarians and the Right in the second. Collectivists generally conceive of the state as an appropriate site for intervention into problems that plague social life. Individualists, in contrast, see the state as a coercive and misguided site of intervention in social problems, preferring the market as the favoured site for improved social welfare. We suggest that there are identifiable clusters of values that characterize each position's mobilization of normative beliefs in symbolic politics favouring dominance of either collective welfare provision or individual responsibility.

CHAPTER 4

A colder pension climate for British women

JAY GINN AND SARA ARBER

The British pension system is distinctive in the large size of its private sector and the low value of public provision. Pension fund assets are equal to nearly 80 per cent of GDP, compared with nearly 60 per cent in the US, 40 per cent in Ireland, and 20 per cent in the EU as a whole (PPG 1998). State pensions provided only a third of all pensioner income in the late 1990s, while occupational pensions and investment income together provided 40 per cent. While state provision is redistributive towards women and others disadvantaged in the labour market, private pensions translate low lifetime earnings into low or zero pension income. Thus most British women, whose caring responsibilities have constrained their employment and earnings, have low personal incomes in later life.

The Conservative pension reforms since 1980, maintained by the Labour government elected in 1997, have markedly shifted the balance towards private provision, giving rise to concerns about increasing gender and class inequality of later life income.

This chapter outlines British state and private pension provision, highlighting features affecting women's opportunities to gain adequate entitlements. Because current older women's incomes reflect pension policies in place up to 50 years ago, we indicate the major changes over time, especially the trend since 1980 towards privatization. By examining older women's pension incomes and younger women's private pension coverage, we highlight the interplay between women's family circumstances, paid work and the structure of the pension system. We distinguish among women according to marital status, fertility, ethnicity and occupational class. Finally, we outline the likely impact on women of reforms planned by the Labour government.

State pension provision

A common concern for British feminists has been the gender assumptions which shaped the social security system (Land 1989, 1994; Lister 1992, 1994) and its consequences for women in later life (Ginn and Arber 1994). The Beveridge system of National Insurance (NI) contributions and benefits, set up in the 1940s, represented the 'strong-breadwinner' model of welfare (Lewis 1992). A gendered division of labour in lifelong marriage, childbearing confined to marriage and full employment of men were assumed. It was considered unnecessary to enable women with caring responsibilities to obtain a pension independently of a husband and state pension provision until the mid-1970s reflected these assumptions. The Basic Pension and State Earnings Related Pension Scheme are funded by NI contributions on a Pay-As-You-Go (PAYG) basis. NI contributions (excluding the portion earmarked for the NHS) are 18 per cent of relevant earnings (between a Lower and Upper Earnings Limit, LEL and UEL), shared roughly equally between employee and employer.

Basic Pension

The main component of state pensions in Britain is the flat-rate Basic Pension (BP), which pays full benefits to individuals with full contribution records. This is currently 39 years for women and 44 years for men, reflecting the state pension age of 60 for women and 65 for men. When an individual's average annual earnings are below the LEL (£67 per week in 2000), as is the case for some 2 million women each year, they are excluded from contributing to the NI system (McKnight *et al.* 1998).

   Before 1978, married women who were employed could opt for a reduced NI contribution which carried no BP entitlement. Instead of encouraging married women to obtain their own state pension, wives aged over 60 were (and still are) entitled to a spousal benefit at 60 per cent of their husband's entitlement, paid when the husband reaches age 65. Since married women can receive either this derived pension or one based on their own NI contributions, they had little incentive to make full contributions. Married women were further discouraged from seeking an independent BP by the 'half-test', whereby *all* their contributions were void unless covering at least half their married life (Joshi and Davies 1994). Widows over state pension age receive a BP equal to their deceased husband's (if better than their own entitlement) and divorced women can use their ex-husband's contribution record for the period of the marriage if this improves their entitlement. Thus the postwar welfare state 'compensated' married women for limited opportunities in the labour market through derived benefits – that is, benefits based on their husband's contributions. It served 'to reduce most married women to the status of appendages in the social security scheme' (Joshi and Davies 1994: 236).

Derived benefits raise issues of equity (Cuvillier 1979). First, married women who have paid contributions for most of their life may feel their contributions have been 'wasted' since their BP is often no higher than that of wives who ceased employment on marriage. Second, all other contributors, including employed women raising children, subsidize non-employed wives and widows, even those who had no children. Attaching pension rights to marital status rather than carer status also means that single (never married) mothers had no help until the 1970s in building a BP. Cohabiting women are still excluded from rights to derived pensions received by wives. As marriage and motherhood become increasingly separated, the rationale for derived benefits linked to marriage has become increasingly anachronistic.

The British pension system has undergone many changes since 1948. Second wave feminism, increased female employment participation and a relatively progressive Labour government in the mid-late 1970s combined to bring significant changes for women, manifested in equality legislation and women-friendly reforms to state pensions. Feminist research provided justification for these reforms, challenging the assumptions that married women have no need of an independent income and that married couples share family resources equally (Brannen and Wilson 1987; Pahl 1989).

Women's need for their own pension income was first addressed by the Labour government's Social Security Benefits Act of 1975. The 'half-test' and reduced contribution option were removed. A major advance for women was the introduction of Home Responsibilities Protection (HRP) in the BP. Those not in paid employment or who earn less than the LEL qualify automatically for HRP if they are caring for a child aged under 16 (or 18 if in full time education). Carers of a frail or disabled adult may also be covered by HRP. HRP reduces the number of contribution years required for entitlement to the BP so that, provided NI contributions have been paid for at least 20 years, a woman may still qualify for the full amount if the remaining years are covered by HRP. By protecting pension rights during caring years, HRP has helped to accommodate women's dual family and employment commitments.

Also important to women was the provision in the 1975 Act indexing the BP to the higher of national earnings or prices. This enshrined a longstanding practice of ad hoc uprating to follow earnings; since 1948 the BP approximated to 20 per cent of male average earnings (Johnson and Falkingham 1992). Such uprating was particularly valuable to those with no access to occupational pensions – predominantly women and the low paid.

Second tier state pension

A new State Earnings Related Pension Scheme (SERPS) was introduced for employees in 1978, as provided on the 1975 Social Security Act. All employees earning above the LEL must contribute to the scheme, unless they are contracted out into a suitable private pension scheme. The original SERPS was intended to be based on the best 20 years of earnings, a formula which, unlike private second-tier schemes, promised a dramatic reduction in the pension cost of years spent caring for children or other relatives. The pension matured in 1998, with an accrual rate of 1.25 per cent of revalued average pensionable earnings, reaching 25 per cent for individuals who had contributed for the full 20 years. Although the maximum possible SERPS for a new pensioner in 1998 was £125 per week, the average received by those who had been continuous contributors since 1978 was £44 for men, £22 for women (PPG 1998). Widows would receive all their husband's SERPS pension as well as their own, up to the maximum for a single earner.

The BP was never intended to prevent poverty on its own, but until 1980 provided a secure platform at around 20 per cent of male average earnings on which second tier pensions could be built. The combination of BP and SERPS provides a very low income by international standards – an average £51 per week for women and £73 for men in 1997 (77 per cent and 106 per cent respectively of the official poverty level for a non-married pensioner). For a person with average male earnings, the replacement rate was only 37 per cent in 1997 (PPG 1998). However, this state pension package is redistributive towards the low paid, providing a maximum replacement rate of 50 per cent for a female full time (FT) manual worker (Groves 1991).

Private pensions

The main type of private pension in Britain is occupational (supplementary, group-based pension schemes operated by employers), with the addition since 1988 of personal (individual) pension plans. Unlike NI contributions, private pension contributions attract tax relief on contributions, up to 15 per cent of earnings in the case of occupational pensions. Private pensions are a major source of income inequality in later life, structured according to gender, class and ethnicity.

Occupational pensions

Beveridge expected men to supplement the BP with private pension provision. Generous tax relief, compulsory membership in occupational pension schemes (OPs), combined with a meagre BP, encouraged the expansion of OP coverage among employees in the 1950s and 1960s (Shragge 1984; Hannah 1986). By 1996 over 11 million British employees belonged to OP schemes, whose total assets exceeded £500 billion (Ward 1996). Since 1978, OP schemes have usually been contracted out, replacing SERPS, so that an NI rebate from both employer and employee is paid into the occupational scheme. An advantage of OPs is that employers usually provide an additional contribution above this minimum. Designed for middle-class men's patterns of employment and to encourage company loyalty, most OPs are defined benefit schemes, basing the pension on 'final salary' and years of pensionable service. A minority are money purchase (defined contribution, DC) schemes. Although OPs generally represent a worthwhile investment, the Maxwell fraud in the 1980s (the most infamous of many cases of pension fund mismanagement or abuse) has dented confidence in these schemes (Ward 1996).

OP schemes discriminate against women in two main ways, both stemming from the constraints which women's family roles place on their employment (see Chapter 2). First, because such schemes are provided voluntarily by employers, they are less available to some employees than others. Part-timers, the low paid, those with casual or temporary jobs, those in small organizations and those employed in the private sector are all less likely to have access to a scheme (Ginn and Arber 1993). In the mid-1990s, jobs being done by women were only half as likely to offer an OP scheme as those done by men (Walker *et al.* 2000). Second, the return on contributions in Final Salary schemes is maximized for those whose earnings rise with age and who remain in the scheme until retirement. Women's typically flatter earnings profile (see Chapter 5, Figure 5.1) yields a poorer return on their contributions. Thus women have lower coverage rates than men and those who do join an OP scheme tend to receive poorer benefits than men due to lower earnings, fewer pensionable years and the penalties of early leaving (Groves 1987; Ginn and Arber 1991, 1993, 1996). The mix of private pensions with women-friendly state provision under a Labour government in the 1970s was short lived, overtaken by neo-liberal reforms under the Thatcher administration which came to power in 1979.

Pension retrenchment from 1980

The neo-liberal ethos of Thatcherism in Britain, like Reaganomics in the US, brought all aspects of the welfare state under scrutiny. In pension policy, as in other areas, the aim was to curb public spending and promote the private sector. Cuts to state pensions have serious implications for older women, who rely more heavily than men on this source of income.

Cuts in value of Basic Pension

BP indexing was limited to prices in the Social Security Act 1980. Since then, its value for a non-married pensioner has fallen from 20 per cent of average male earnings to about 15 per cent in 2000, well below the level of means tested Income Support (IS). The full BP for a non-married pensioner in 2000 was £67.50 per week, nearly £11 below IS, over £28 lower than it would have been under the original indexing formula and £30 below the minimum income considered necessary for a lone pensioner woman to avoid poverty (Parker 2000).

Cuts in SERPS

The 1986 Social Security Act brought major cuts in SERPS, to apply from 1999. The basis of calculating average earnings changed from the best 20 years to the whole working life, so that periods out of paid work or on low pay reduced the pension that women could expect. Provision was made for HRP to apply to SERPS from 1999 but this has never become law. From 2000 to 2010, the maximum SERPS will fall from 25 to 20 per cent of the individual's average revalued assessable earnings. The legislation halved the widow's pension for those widowed from 2000 (a change now delayed until 2002).

As a measure of state pension retrenchment, between 2000 and 2050 the cost of the BP and SERPS is projected to fall from £34 billion to £26 billion (in 1997 earnings terms); combined NI contributions to fall from 18 to 14 per cent; and the replacement rate of the BP and SERPS together to fall from 37 to 20 per cent of average male earnings (PPG 1998). The government hopes that the shortfall in older people's incomes will be met by an expansion of private pensions.

New personal pensions – APPs

Appropriate Personal Pensions (APPs), like the personal pensions that were already available to the self-employed, are individual portable defined contribution (DC) accounts whose fund must be annuitized (converted to an annual income for life) at or during retirement.

The 1986 Social Security Act removed the right of employers to require membership in their OP scheme, opening the way for the notorious mis-selling scandal. Commission-driven sales techniques, combined with overgenerous financial incentives, persuaded many people to contract out of an OP or SERPS into an APP when they would have been better off in their existing scheme (Ward 1996). Far surpassing the half a million predicted by the government, 5 million employees contributed to an APP by 1993 (DSS 1994: 9). By 1995, APP coverage among employees was 28 per cent for full time men, 22 per cent for full time women and 11 per cent for part time women (ONS 1997).

APPs provide poor value for most women and for the low paid (Davies and Ward 1992; Waine 1995). In any DC scheme, contributions made early in the working life have a disproportionate effect on the fund at retirement; yet women's ability to contribute is often very limited until their children have become independent. Charges for administration, investment management and annuitization may reduce the value of contributions by 45 per cent, according to pensions experts (Murthi *et al.* 2001). The charging structure, with flat rate charges paid predominantly in the first year of membership, penalizes the low paid and those with breaks in contributions, making APPs a very poor option for women who have gaps in FT employment when their children are young. Employees and employers may make extra contributions above the minimum required to replace SERPS but employers rarely do so. Annuity costs are required to be sex neutral for the part of the fund which replaces SERPS but the cost for any extra portion of the fund is higher for women than men due to women's longer life expectancy. Like occupational DC schemes, APPs are subject to the risk of poor investment performance. It remains to be seen whether the return on contributions to APPs will be better than even the scaled back SERPS, and for which population groups.

Raising the state pension age

A final blow to working-age women was 1995 legislation raising women's state pension age from 60 to 65 for those born after 1950, phased in from 2010 to 2020. For a full BP, the number of qualifying years (contributions and HRP credits) will increase from 39 to 44 years. The cost to women will be considerable (Hutton *et al.* 1995). First, waiting an extra five years could deprive each woman of over £17,000 (at 2000 prices). Second, women will lose the current option to obtain an enhanced BP (up to 37.5 per cent higher) by deferring it until age 65. Third, including the additional five years in the calculation of average earnings will reduce women's SERPS by up to £20 per week at 1995 prices (Hutton *et al.* 1995: Table 7.3). Thus raising women's pension age to 65 will magnify gender inequality in state pension income unless there is a dramatic rise in women's employment from age 60–4. However, currently only a quarter of women aged 60–4 are employed, mainly part time (PT). Moreover, many employers raised women's pension age to 65 in their OP scheme, reducing the pension payable at age 60.

Supporting private pensions, undermining state pensions

The Conservatives' pension reforms escalated the public subsidy to private pensions while reducing the capacity of National Insurance to provide higher state pensions, a process of 'reverse targeting' (Sinfield 1993: 39). Tax relief for private pensions grew from £1.2 billion in 1979 to £8.2 billion in 1991 (Wilkinson 1993), while the net cost to the NI fund of tax and other incentives to transfer from SERPS to APPs was estimated as £6 billion (in 1988 prices) for the five years 1988–93 (National Audit Office 1990). For 1994/95, tax expenditures, rebates and incentives to occupational and personal pensions had risen to £20 billion (Glennerster and Hills 1998).

The shift towards private pensions since 1979 undermined state pensions fiscally and politically. Low and declining state provision has made increased private provision necessary, eroding middle-class support for state pensions. Reforms, although ostensibly gender-neutral, disproportionately affected women, threatening their autonomy in later life. It is women who rely most heavily on the BP; who lost most from the 1986 SERPS reforms; and whose state pensions will be reduced by raising their age of eligibility to 65. Yet women remain disadvantaged in private pension schemes designed primarily to ensure men's replacement income in later life. Table 4.1 summarizes the current British pension system.

The second part of this chapter draws on our research using national survey data to show how older British women's and men's income is related to their marital status, class and ethnicity; and how private pension coverage among working-age women depends on their family roles.

Gender inequality of later life income

The gendered effects of the British pension system are evident in older people's income. Older women are twice as likely as men to have incomes below the poverty level. Few older women have yet benefited substantially from Home Responsibilities Protection (HRP), introduced in 1978. Thus only 28 per cent of women pensioners receive a full BP on their own NI contributions (Johnson *et al.* 1996). Over 70 per cent of IS recipients among pensioners are non-married women (Johnson *et al.* 1996). Married older women often have very low personal incomes but are rendered ineligible for IS due to their husband's income, since means-testing for couples (married or living as married) is based on joint income and savings. IS is withdrawn pound for pound in respect of any additional pension income above the threshold of £78 per week (in 2000 for a non-married pensioner aged up to 74) and is reduced if savings exceed £3000, with complete withdrawal where savings exceed £8000.

Table 4.1   British pension regime

Public pensions: Basic (BP)	
Per cent receiving	Almost all over state pension age
Eligibility	Age 65 (men), 60 (women)
	NI contributions for 10+ years
	HRP, provided 20+ years contributions paid
	Through spouse and survivors' benefits
Financing	PAYG: NI contributions from employees and employers
Public pensions: State Earnings Related Pensions Scheme (SERPS)	
Per cent receiving	Most pensioners have only modest amounts of SERPS
Eligibility	Age 65 (men), 60 (women)
	NI contributions[1]
	Through survivors' benefits
Financing	PAYG: NI contributions from employees and employers
Social assistance: IS, also called Minimum Income Guarantee (MIG)	
Per cent receiving	Of non-married, 15% of women, 7% of men
Eligibility	Age; low income and low assets
Financing	General taxation
Private pensions: Occupational pensions (OP), mainly Defined Benefit	
Per cent receiving[2]	Among those aged 65+, 33% of women, 61% of men
Eligibility	Employees in organizations operating a scheme
Financing[3]	Contributions from employee and employer + tax subsidy
Private pensions: Appropriate Personal Pensions (APP) and self-employed personal pensions	
Per cent receiving[2]	Among those aged 65+, 3% of women, 8% of men
Eligibility	All with earnings
Financing[3]	Contributions from members + tax subsidy

Notes: 1 Self employed are not eligible for SERPS
2 In 1993–94, authors' analysis
3 For employees contracted out of SERPS, NIC rebates are paid into OPs or APPs in respect of SERPS rights forgone

Older women's personal income is less than two-thirds of men's, on average. For example, in 1993–94, the median gross personal income of women aged over 65 was £68 per week, compared with £110 for men. Older women are more likely than older men to live alone, with all the diseconomies entailed in solo living; the gender difference in incomes thus under-represents the gender difference in living standards (Arber and Ginn 1991).

In Britain, personal income in later life is a mix of state benefits, earnings, interest on savings and private (mainly occupational) pensions. Income

Figure 4.1   Personal income in pounds per week (median, gross) – women and men aged 65+ by marital status

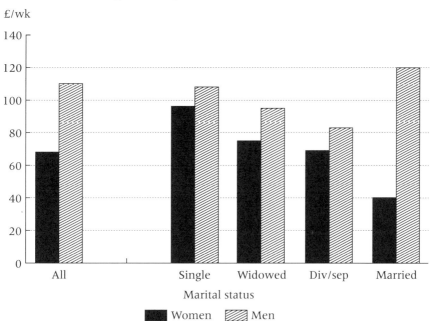

£/wk

Source: General Household Surveys 1993–94 (authors' analysis)

from the state may include the BP, SERPS, various disability-related benefits and IS. Figure 4.1 shows how older people's personal income in 1993–94 varied with marital status. For those who were widowed, survivor benefits are included. Among women, those who were never married (single) had the highest income, a median value of £96 per week. Women who had ever been married had a lower income; married women's median income was just over £40 per week. Among men, in contrast, those who were married had the highest median income, nearly £120 per week.

Because of the extremely low level of state pensions, a substantial income from private pensions is necessary to avoid personal poverty in later life.

Inequalities in private pensions

Older women are less likely than men to have any income from a private pension and for those who do, the amounts are less than for men. As Figure 4.2 shows, two-thirds of older women in 1993–94 had no private pension income at all and were therefore heavily reliant on state bene-fits or on members of their family.

Figure 4.2 Percentage with a private pension – women and men aged 65+ by marital status

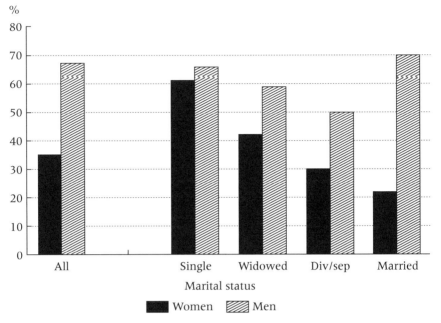

Source: General Household Surveys 1993–94 (authors' analysis)

Older women who had ever been married were far less likely to have a private pension than men, whereas among single (never married) older people the gender difference in private pension receipt was very small (see Figure 4.2). Just over 40 per cent of widows had a private pension (including survivors' pensions inherited from deceased husbands), compared with nearly 60 per cent of widowers. Among women who were divorced or separated, only 30 per cent had any private pension. The gender difference was greatest among the married, where only a fifth of women had a private pension compared with 70 per cent of men.

The amounts of private pension women received (including survivor pensions), were much lower than for men; the median amount for all women with any income from private pensions was £26 per week, compared with £46 for men. Significantly, single women with a private pension had a median amount of £54 per week, exceeding even married men's, which was £51 per week. This suggests that in this generation, many of the single older women with a private pension were exceptionally advantaged in their employment and lifetime earnings, having prioritized their career over marriage and a family.

The class bias of occupational pensions is well documented (Sinfield 1978; Hannah 1986; Arber 1989; Ginn and Arber 1991). Figure 4.3 shows the percentage of older men and women receiving any private pension in each of seven socioeconomic categories based on the individual's own last main occupation, with an eighth category for those who had never been employed.

Within each socioeconomic category, older women are much less likely to have any private pension than men. Yet the inequalities among women are also substantial. Women in the highest occupational group (1 – professionals and managers in large organizations) were three times as likely as those in the lowest group (6 – unskilled manual workers) to

Figure 4.3 Percentage with a private pension – women and men aged 65+ by socioeconomic category

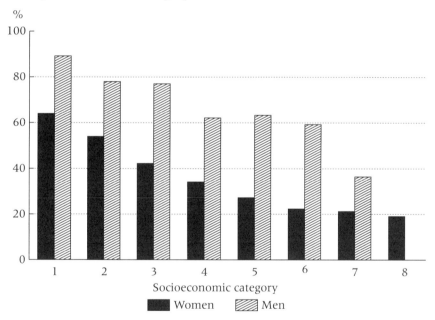

Key: Socioeconomic categories
1 Professionals/managers in large organizations
2 Intermediate non-manual/managers in small organizations
3 Routine non-manual
4 Skilled manual/supervisory
5 Semi-skilled manual/personal service
6 Unskilled manual
7 Employers/self-employed
8 Never employed
Note: Excluded: Armed forces/FT students/inadequate description
Source: General Household Surveys 1993–94 (authors' analysis)

have any private pension income. Amounts of income from private
pensions showed a similar class gradient.

A further dimension of social differentiation is ethnicity, reflecting
migration patterns as well as the disadvantaged labour market position of
ethnic minorities compared with whites. Figure 4.4 shows the proportions
of older women and men with any private pension income in each of
five ethnic groupings – white, Indian, black, Chinese/other and Pakistani/
Bangladeshi. Black (African and Caribbean) women were as likely as
white women to have some private pension income but such income
was rare among Indian, Pakistani and Bangladeshi women. In each
ethnic group, women's pensions were lower than men's but women's
disadvantage was least for blacks and greatest for whites and Indians.

Comparing older people's income in the mid-1990s with that in the
mid-1980s (before the 1986 Social Security Act), gender inequality had
increased. Older women's median total income as a proportion of men's
fell from 77 to 62 per cent. Receipt of private pensions increased, with
narrowing gender and class differences in coverage. However, gender
inequality in the amount of private pension income widened over the
period. Among all older women, private pension income rose from 7 to

Figure 4.4   Percentage with a private pension – women and men aged
60+ by ethnicity

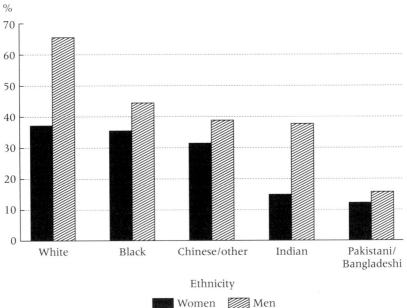

Source: Family Resources Surveys 1994–96 (authors' analysis)

11 per cent of total personal income and among men from 17 to 25 per cent. Among those with a private pension, women's median income from this source fell from 65 to 56 per cent of men's (Ginn and Arber 1999). This suggests that the extension of pension coverage has included women with relatively low earnings and/or few years of pension scheme membership.

The income of those aged over 65 reflects the experience of particular birth cohorts, the result of their gendered employment patterns interacting with past state and private pension schemes. In the next section, we examine working-age women's private pension arrangements in order to understand how the pension income inequalities described above are generated during the working life and the extent to which low pension income arises from parental, as distinct from marital, roles. An important issue is whether younger cohorts of women will acquire better pension entitlements than those of the current generation of older women.

Working-age women's private pension coverage

The dramatic increase in women's employment since the 1950s may be deceptive in terms of the implications for women's pension acquisition. Many extra years of paid work are in PT and low paid employment, due to the disruptive effect of caring responsibilities on women's employment histories, combined with gender discrimination in employment (see Chapter 1). PT employment contributes little to private pension entitlements (Ginn and Arber 1996, 1998). Those who are low paid tend to remain so and there is a high turnover between being in low paid jobs and being out of employment (McKnight *et al.* 1998). As noted earlier, in Britain avoiding poverty in later life requires a substantial private pension income, which depends on being employed FT for most of the working life. Women's FT employment is closely related to their marital and parental status (see Chapter 1).

All employees who are paid over the Lower Earnings Limit (LEL) must contribute to a second-tier pension as well as to the basic NI pension. They may join an occupational pension scheme (if their employer operates one), contribute to an Appropriate Personal Pension (APP) or remain in SERPS. While SERPS may provide better value than personal pensions for certain groups, the maximum pension will be modest following retrenchment in the 1980s. We therefore focus on private pension coverage.

Just over half of adults aged 20–59 contributed to some form of private pension in the mid-1990s, 64 per cent of men but only 38 per cent of women (see Table 4.2a). A third of adults contributed to OP schemes

Table 4.2 Current membership of an occupational or personal pension scheme – percentages of men and women aged 20–59

	(a) All Adults			(b) Employees		Women		
	All	Men	Women	All	Men	FT	PT	All
Has private pension:	**51**	**64**	**38**	**69**	**81**	**72**	**34**	**56**
Employee, occupational pension	32	40	25	52	61	56	23	42
Employee, personal pension	11	13	9	17	20	16	11	14
Self-employed, personal pension	6	9	2					
Not employed, personal pension	2	2	2					
No private pension:	**49**	**36**	**62**	**31**	**19**	**28**	**66**	**44**
Employee	19	12	27	31	19	28	66	44
Self-employed	4	6	3					
Not employed	26	18	32					
Col %	100	100	100	100	100	100	100	100
N=	24,069	11,756	12,313	15,056	7,603	7,453	4,260	3,175

Note: Emboldened figures are the %s which sum to 100%
Source: General Household Surveys 1993–94 (authors' analysis)

and 19 per cent to some form of personal pension (Ginn and Arber 2000b). Among employees, less than half of women belonged to an OP scheme, while 61 per cent of men did (see Table 4.2b). The lower membership among women was mainly due to part-timers, of whom only 23 per cent were OP scheme members. A fifth of men employees contributed to an APP compared with 14 per cent of women.

Women's domestic roles and private pension coverage

Membership of private pension schemes is related to both marital and parental status. Contributions to private pensions were most likely among single women, and least among previously married women (Figure 4.5). Among men, those who were married were most likely to contribute to a private pension, in all age groups. Membership of an OP scheme was associated with being single for women, but with being married for men, while rates of contribution to the less advantageous personal pensions were more evenly spread across marital statuses.

Figure 4.5   Percentage of women contributing to a private pension, by marital status and age group

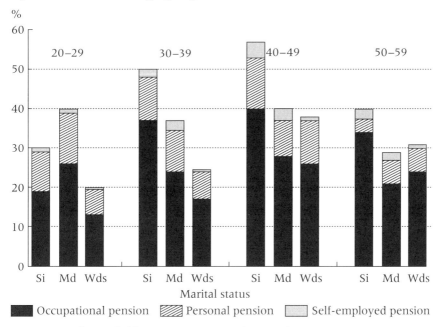

Source: General Household Surveys 1993–94 (authors' analysis)

Figure 4.6 Percentage of women contributing to a private pension, by parental status and age group

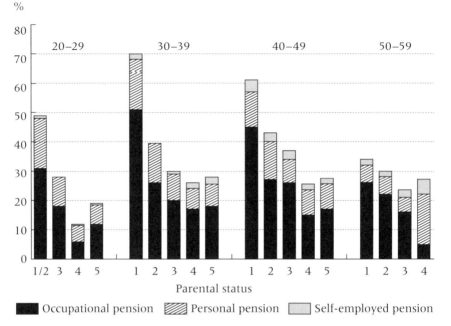

Key
1 No child ever born
2 No dependent child still at home
3 Youngest child aged 10–15
4 Youngest child aged 5–9
5 Youngest child aged 0–4
Source: General Household Surveys 1993–94 (authors' analysis)

Figure 4.6 shows the proportions of women with private pension coverage by parental status. Childless women were substantially more likely to have pension coverage than other women. Among women of all ages, increasing parental responsibility was accompanied by a decline in pension coverage (see Figure 4.6). In contrast, parental status had no consistent effect on men's private pension coverage.

Relative impact of parental and marital roles on private pensions

Because marriage and motherhood are often associated, their effects on the employment and pension opportunities of women tend to reinforce each other. With rising lone parenthood and married childlessness, however, it is important to disentangle the effects of marital and parental roles. In a multivariate analysis of the GHS 1993–4, we found that the chief constraint on women's private pension acquisition is parental, not marital, status. Indeed, for women with children aged under 15, marriage improves their chance of private pension scheme membership. Lone mothers of children aged under 10 were least likely to have pension coverage, with odds of coverage less than one-tenth of the odds for childless married women. Whereas single (never married) older women tend to have better pension income than women who ever married, our analysis of working-age women suggests that single women's advantage will be less in later cohorts, especially for those who have had children.

Longitudinal research using retrospective pension histories from the Family and Working Lives Survey confirms that it is children rather than marriage which create a gender gap in private pension rights (Walker *et al.* 2000). Half of working-age women had never contributed to a private pension. The chance of having no years of private pension cover was increased by 37 per cent if they ever had a child, by 24 per cent if they were ever divorced, by 53 per cent if they were ever out of employment and by 68 per cent if they ever worked PT. In practice, these effects would tend to overlap, since women's non-employment and PT employment are strongly associated with responsibility for children. These authors also showed that among women aged over 60 who had ever belonged to an OP, their average membership was 16 years, compared with men's 24 years. The corresponding figures for women and men aged 16–69 were 10 and 15 years. Thus among those with any OP entitlement, a shortfall of one-third in years of coverage, compared with men, applies to both older and younger generations of women.

Widening pension choices

If the Conservatives' 1986 reforms widened pension choices, they also increased the opportunities to choose unwisely. For those without access to occupational schemes, the advisability of opting out of SERPS into an APP is deemed a better risk for men than women, for younger than older employees (Dilnot *et al.* 1994) and for the higher paid. Experts have estimated that opting out of SERPS into an APP was not advantageous for those earning below £200 per week (in 1993) (Durham 1994). Applying this criterion, 70 per cent of women and 28 per cent of men who opted for an APP over SERPS were unlikely to benefit from this choice (Ginn and Arber 2000b). For those with low lifetime earnings, a misguided switch to an APP can be disastrous. Although this estimate of mis-selling is inevitably crude, since the outcome depends on the quality

Table 4.3 Women-friendly and adverse features of the British pension regime

---

Women-friendly features

Public pensions: Basic (BP) and SERPS
- Flat-rate BP, based on years of contributions or allowances
- BP protects years of childcare or eldercare, through HRP
- Wives can receive 60 per cent of husband's BP
- Widows receive 100 per cent of husband's BP
- Divorcees can use husband's BP contribution record for period of marriage
- SERPS is portable between jobs and across employment gaps
- SERPS provides earnings-related defined benefit pension

Private pensions: Occupational (OP) and personal (APP)
- Some survivor benefits mandatory
- OPs must provide some inflation proofing of pensions (since 1995)
- OPs must provide some inflation proofing of preserved entitlements (since 1975)
- APPs are portable between jobs

Adverse features

Public pensions
- Very low BP, 15 per cent of national average earnings
- SERPS has no protection for childcare or eldercare years
- SERPS has relatively low accrual rate
- Those earning under £67/wk excluded from both BP and SERPS
- Self-employed excluded from SERPS

Private pensions
- OPs less available to the low paid and part-timers
- Early leavers from OPs receive a poorer return on contributions
- Lower employer contributions to OPs in female-dominated occupations
- Transfer between OPs difficult or impossible
- Flat/falling age profile of earnings brings worse return in Final Salary OPs
- High charges in APPs, especially for the low paid
- Financial penalties for gaps in APP contributions
- Lower annuities for women from APPs

---

of the APP, the individual's future earnings and future macroeconomic performance, it is clear women are particularly vulnerable to the additional risks associated with widening pension choices (see Chapter 6).

The women-friendly and adverse features of the British pension system are summarized in Table 4.3.

Pension prospects for later cohorts of women

Expectations of a better pensions deal for women from a Labour govern-ment elected in 1997 have crumbled. Despite promises in the Labour Party's *Policy Review for the 1990s* (1992) to restore the cuts in state pen-sions, by 1996 those plans had been abandoned. Labour's policy (see Chapter 5 and DSS 1998a) continues to promote private pensions and to reduce spending on state pensions – projected to fall from 4.4 to 3.4 per cent of GDP between 2000 and 2050 while the number of pensioners rises by about a third. Means-tested IS for pensioners, which carries passported housing allowances, was renamed the Minimum Income Guarantee (MIG), a misleading name as the benefit is not 'guaranteed' but must be claimed. The MIG is generally considered insufficient to prevent poverty (Birch *et al.* 1999; Parker 2000).

Crucially, the BP will remain indexed only to prices, continuing the decline relative to average living standards. SERPS is to be replaced with a new State Second Pension (S2P), which provides a higher pension for the low paid and will include some carer protection. This reform repre-sents some improvement for women given the impact of Conservative cuts on the value of SERPS. After a transitional period, those earning over £9500 per annum will be offered financial incentives to join a private Stakeholder Pension (SHP), a more regulated form of personal pension, operated on a group basis. Since SHPs will replace SERPS as the only earnings related pension available for the moderately paid, many women are expected to opt for this form of pension. The reform package has numerous drawbacks for women.

First, failure to raise the BP substantially or to index it to average earnings – 'a covert way of phasing it out' (Parker 2000) – means that those without private pension income (most older women) will experi-ence declining relative living standards. For older women living alone, the gulf between the MIG and the BP (nearly £11 per week in April 2000 and widening each year) will draw more of them into dependence on means-tested benefits. The MIG will not help married women pen-sioners on low incomes if they are ineligible due to their husband's income or savings. Moreover, an estimated 2 million older people enti-tled to MIG fail to claim (DSS 2000a). Those with modest second-tier pensions or with savings over £3000 (the current threshold) may be caught in a poverty trap, disqualified from claiming MIG but living at poverty level and no better off financially as a result of their efforts to provide for their retirement. Without an adequate BP, well above the level of MIG, the rationale for saving or investing in a private pension is undermined. This is particularly so for those whose lifetime earnings are low, which is often the case for women.

Second, the credits for childcare in S2P will be restricted to those with a child under age 6, unlike HRP in the BP. Many women will be unable to obtain the full S2P, which will require 49 years of contributions or credits.

Third, SHPs share the drawbacks of personal pensions in terms of charges and risks, although to a lesser extent. Like all private pensions, they cannot avoid the crux of the pension problem for women – the adverse impact on lifetime earnings of periods of non-employment or PT employment while raising children and providing care for the frail and disabled.

Fourth, the new pension system will be regressive, placing disproportionate burdens on the low paid. Opting out of the S2P into a private SHP will attract NI rebates, as is currently the case for those opting out of SERPS into an APP or OP. The rebates will be higher than the amount of SERPS/S2P saved however, so that every £1 of rebate handed over to the personal pension providers will cost 22p in public subsidy (PPG 1998: Table 7.1). Those remaining in the S2P will have to pay higher NI contributions than otherwise needed for a given level of benefits, to finance rebates for the higher paid who opt out. Thus any redistribution in favour of carers and the very low paid will come from those who are themselves low paid. The effect of the planned reforms (compared with an approximation to the existing pension system) is quantified in Chapter 5, using computer simulations of pension incomes for women with alternative employment histories.

A widely supported alternative policy is to increase the BP substantially and index to rises in national prosperity. This would be simpler, cheaper to administer and easier to understand than the S2P and would lift most pensioners out of means-testing. The net cost to the National Insurance fund of an increase of £20 per week in the Basic Pension has been estimated as £5.8 billion per annum in 1997, or only £2.1 billion if the Upper Earnings Limit on NI contributions were abolished (Hancock and Sutherland 1997). Given the substantial surplus held in the NI Fund above the prudent level, £6 billion and projected to rise each year (GAD 2000), an increase in the Basic Pension is certainly affordable (Birch *et al.* 1999).

Conclusions

Older British women's low income stems from both past constraints on their employment associated with family commitments and a pension system that penalizes deviation from the typical male employment pattern. For working-age women, the need to build an adequate pension entitlement of their own is increasingly urgent with the high and rising rates of divorce, cohabitation and lone parenthood. Reliance on receiving pension income from a husband or as a widow is a more risky strategy than in the past.

Prospects for women's private pension income in the future are not encouraging. In spite of women's growing participation in the labour force, most of the increase has been in PT employment, whereas continuous FT employment is needed to ensure a good occupational pension. While marriage no longer restricts working-age women's career opportunities, motherhood does. For the majority of women, PT employment enables them to retain an attachment to the labour market while raising a family, but often in jobs where earnings, prospects and fringe benefits are relatively poor, with adverse effects on private pension entitlements. Although private pension coverage among women has increased, this may not translate into gender convergence of pension income, because of women's lower lifetime earnings and the way private pension schemes penalize gaps in contributions. There is evidence that as coverage extends to include lower-paid women the gender gap in amount of private pension received is likely to widen. Much of the increased private pension coverage is accounted for by personal pensions, which are likely to provide poor value for money to most women.

Yet it is important to recognize that women's pension prospects will increasingly reflect their educational and occupational status, as the minority of highly qualified women who are able to maintain FT continuous employment receive markedly higher private pension income than those who cannot. Moreover, because individuals with similar levels of human capital tend to marry or cohabit, partnered women with better than average pensions of their own will tend to inherit better widows' pensions based on their husbands' employment. The divide between work-rich and work-poor households that has accompanied the rise in women's employment will lead to increasing polarization among older married couples in their combined pension income.

Since it is mainly motherhood, rather than marriage, which restricts women's employment and pension acquisition, future women's pension advantage is likely to be greatest with childless marriage, while lone mothers will be the most acutely disadvantaged. We suggest that a historical change is underway in Britain, where career success for women is less strongly related to single status than in the past but remains constrained by childbearing. The growing divergence of wifehood and motherhood may create a different pattern of private pension advantage among older women in the future, compared with the 1990s.

As the contribution of state pensions to later life income declines, income inequality between women and men, by class and ethnicity and also among women is likely to grow. British pension policy since 1980, although profitable to the finance industry and offering wider choices, is likely to exacerbate women's pension disadvantage. Gradual privatization of the pension system leaves those with low lifetime earnings, mainly women whose employment has been constrained by caring respons-ibilities, severely disadvantaged. The Labour government's planned Stakeholder Pensions share many of the weaknesses of personal pen-sions; unlike an improved SERPS, they do not offer a means of ensur-ing that periods of family caring count towards the pension. The State Second Pension, although ostensibly women-friendly, will be effectively undermined unless the Basic Pension is raised substantially. Privatization has diverted resources from the National Insurance Fund and incurred substantial costs to the Exchequer in tax reliefs. Such tax expenditure, which mainly benefits men, is often overlooked, while the cost of improv-ing state pensions has been portrayed by governments as unaffordable, despite evidence to the contrary. Compared with other OECD countries, 'the UK pension system is currently one of the "cheapest"' (Hutton *et al.* 1995: 15) and most welfare analysts agree that there is no ageing crisis facing Britain (Hills 1993; Disney 1996; and see Chapter 3).

State pensions can ensure that the enormous pension costs of caring are fairly shared between those who undertake this task and those who do not. Private pensions, on the other hand, allow the costs to lie where they fall, mainly on women in later life. They cannot fulfil the social function of protecting the pensions of those who raise the next genera-tion. As the balance of provision shifts towards the private sector, the power of the Basic Pension to equalize between carers and non-carers is diminished.

A reassessment by policymakers of the way pension systems treat those who provide family care is essential if the pattern of the past is not to be repeated. Allowances for women in respect of their marital roles, in both state and private pensions, need to be replaced by arrangements that protect periods of family caring – but for this to be effective, state pensions must be substantially improved and the drive towards pension privatization reversed.

Acknowledgements

We are grateful to the ONS and DSS for permission to use the General House-hold Survey and Family Resources Survey, and to the Data Archive at Essex University and Manchester Computing Centre for access to the data. The data analysis is the responsibility of the authors alone and was part of a research project funded by the Leverhulme Trust (ref: F/242/4).

CHAPTER 5

Modelling the gender impact of British pension reforms

JANE FALKINGHAM AND KATHERINE RAKE

Introduction

In 1998, in the foreword to the new Green Paper *A New Contract for Welfare: Partnership in Pensions*, the Prime Minister of Britain promised a radical reform of the whole pension system to deliver 'dramatically better pension provision for . . . those unable to work because they are caring for children or a relative who is ill or disabled', and to ensure that 'everyone can look forward to a secure retirement' (DSS 1998a). Given that the majority of those who are involved in caring are women, the rhetoric appeared to offer hope that the reforms would improve the pension position of women in old age.

The failure of current pension systems to provide an adequate income for women in later life – the 'pensions problem' for women – emerges starkly from virtually every report on pension income. The high risk of poverty that women pensioners face has been well documented. The World Bank, in its 1994 report *Averting the Old Age Crisis* stated that 'old age means something quite different – and more troubling – for women than for men' (World Bank 1994: 29). In Australia, where the public Age Pension is means-tested, it is received by 85 per cent of older women compared with 65 per cent of older men (Mitchell 1993), while in Britain 1.2 million women over 60 claim means-tested Income Support compared to 561,000 men (DSS 1998b).

In this chapter, we argue that the pensions problem for women stems from their different life course experiences in combination with a pension system that was not designed to meet women's needs. Governments have been quick to identify how behavioural differences between women and men, in labour market participation and in the division of caring labour, impact upon income in old age. They are, however, more reluctant to examine those features of pension systems that perpetuate the economic advantages and disadvantages experienced during the working life into inequality in old age.

A comparative analysis of six countries – Australia, Chile, Italy, Poland, Sweden and Britain – (using computer simulation) showed how the structure of the pension system affected the pension incomes of women with different employment histories (Evans and Falkingham 1997). The performance of each country's mandatory pension system was measured in terms of the amount of expected pension at retirement as a proportion of average gross male earnings, computing the value of 'relative income' for seven hypothetical employment histories of women. For part time low-paid work with childcare gaps, women's income in retirement relative to average male earnings was about 50 per cent in Sweden and Poland, 37 per cent in Italy, 23 per cent in Britain and Australia but only 11 per cent in Chile. The authors conclude that a pension system dominated by private defined contribution pension schemes perpetuates and widens income inequality in retirement. In particular, women whose labour market experience has been interrupted by raising children are disadvantaged where there is a strong link between earnings and income in later life while the existence of a minimum pension, if this is above the level of assistance safety nets, mitigates the pension consequences of childrearing for women (Evans and Falkingham 1997). Simulations such as these are valuable in indicating the gender impact of a range of pension reforms.

In the first part of the chapter we explore the factors which give rise to gender differences in pension income. In the second, we look at the proposed reforms to the British pension system. In the third we use computer simulation techniques to estimate the effects of these reforms on women's pension incomes, illustrating how pension systems may mitigate, replicate or compound gender differences in lifetime experiences. Will the proposed pension reforms deliver for women, as British Prime Minister Tony Blair promised, 'the security we all want, now and for the future'?

The 'pensions problem' for women

Women's participation in the labour market is distinct from men's in several respects. Overall, women are less likely to be in paid employment. Where women are in the labour market they are more likely to be working part time, especially if they have young children or care for a dependent adult. This generalization holds across Anglo-Saxon countries (see Chapter 2, Figures 2.1 and 2.3).

Women, especially mothers, tend to experience greater discontinuity of employment compared to men. These discontinuities accumulate across the lifetime so that women have a shorter employment record than men at retirement. For older women and men the differences in lifetime employment are dramatic – for example, Rake estimates that the 1924–29 cohort of British women had an average of 27 years in employment (compared to 47 years for men), of which 7.5 years were spent in part time work (Rake 1999: 232). This cohort of women would have had to increase their employed years by a full 74 per cent to match the *lifetime* labour market activity of men. It is uncertain what the lifetime totals for younger generations of women will be. Although gender differentials are set to narrow, there is plenty of evidence (see Chapter 2) of continuing differences both among women, and between the sexes, which are likely to accumulate into a larger differential over the whole lifetime.

Employment discontinuity, in combination with women's greater tendency to be in temporary or casual employment, has a further knock-on effect in terms of the length of time women and men spend in any given job. Job tenure may be interrupted by caring duties, while the type of work women perform means they are more likely to be in temporary employment (see below). The duration of employment is important where time requirements are placed on joining a company's pension scheme and may affect promotion and pay. Among British employees, almost three times as many men as women have been with their employer for 20 years or more, while at the other end of the spectrum 35 per cent of women (and 39 per cent of those with a child under 5) have been with their employer for less than two years, compared to 30 per cent of men (ONS 1998b).

The pay gap between men and women

Recent analysis of women and men's pay (discussed in Chapter 2) shows that the pay penalty experienced by women includes both a gender gap (affecting all women) and a family gap (resulting from women's experience of motherhood) (Harkness and Waldfogel 1999; Rake 2000) which both vary across Anglo-Saxon countries.

Women's pay is affected by segmentation of the labour market (see Chapter 2), which adversely affects women's careers and earnings mobility and hence their earnings profile over their working life. Men's earnings profile is 'humpbacked', suggesting that men benefit from an age/experience premium in their middle years, whereas women have a much flatter earnings profile, reflecting the impact of interrupted employment patterns and labour market segmentation (see Figure 5.1 for an illustration using the British case). The gender differences illustrated

Figure 5.1 Earnings by age. Men and women in Great Britain, 1998

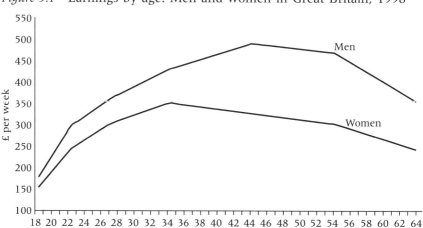

Notes: Data on earnings are drawn from the New Earnings Survey and refer to all full time employees in 1998 (ONS 1999)

in Figure 5.1 understate lifetime gender differentials, since pay gaps accumulate throughout a woman's working life.

Women are concentrated in parts of the labour market with less access to occupational pensions

As mentioned above, women are concentrated in certain sectors of the labour market. In Australia, Canada, Britain and the US, more than 60 per cent of employed women work within the 10 most feminized occupations (OECD 1998a). Low pay and a high concentration of female workers tend to go together. This has important implications where there is an earnings-related element in the pension system.

Where occupational pensions are a major part of overall pension provision, occupational segregation of women is important. Small firms and those in certain sectors – such as retail – are less likely to offer occupational pension coverage. Further, where employers limit the membership of schemes and exclude part time workers or those on short-term contracts, women are disproportionately affected (see Chapter 4). In Britain from 1994–96, 54 per cent of women in full time work and 23 per cent of those in part time work were members of an occupational scheme compared to 59 per cent of men working full time (Rake 2000: 160). Cross-sectional figures underplay the lifetime differentials, as women are more likely to leave occupational schemes before they reach retirement.

The British Retirement Survey shows that over 30 per cent of women aged 60–74 in 1994 who had joined an occupational pension will never draw a pension from it, compared to 14 per cent of men (Disney *et al.* 1997: Table 5.4).

Women live longer than men

Finally, women outlive men in most developed countries (see Chapter 3). Women's greater longevity means that women are more likely to be widowed in later life and to live alone, losing the spouse's contribution to household income *and* the principal source of caregiving. Greater longevity means income is needed to cover a longer period, recognized by insurance companies who use sex-based annuity rates. Only pensions that are indexed to earnings will maintain the prosperity of pensioners, relative to the whole population. Given women's greater longevity these issues of indexing are of particular importance in determining well-being in later life.

In sum, the 'pensions problem' for women arises from differences in both longevity and labour market experiences. Women are less likely to be in paid employment than men and more likely to work part time and/or in low paid occupations. Consequently women have lower lifetime earnings than men and are also less likely to have access to privileged occupational pensions. Women's longer lives make them particularly vulnerable to inadequate pension indexation. Below we discuss the current and proposed British pension systems and evaluate the extent to which the regimes perpetuate or ameliorate in old age differences between men and women accumulated across the working life.

The current and proposed British pension system

The current pension system in Britain (see Chapter 3) consists of three basic elements:

1 First is the flat-rate *Basic Pension* (BP) payable in full to those who have fulfilled the contributory requirements. Home Responsibilities Protection (HRP) covers years of caring.
2 The second element is a *state-run secondary pension*. This is currently provided by SERPS (State Earnings Related Pension Scheme), designed to supplement the BP for low earners who are unable to benefit from private pensions.
3 The third element is *private provision*: occupational and personal pension schemes and also income from personal savings and investments.

Alongside these contributory pensions, a means-tested state benefit, previously called Income Support but relabelled the Minimum Income Guarantee (MIG), may be claimed by older people.

In November 1998, the British government published the Green Paper *A New Contract for Welfare: Partnership in Pensions*, one of a series of papers on welfare reform (DSS 1998a). These reforms have been largely adopted by Parliament at the time of writing, although minor amendments may yet be made. Under the proposed reforms the new pension system will consist of:

- the contributory BP whose rules are untouched.
- The State Second Pension (S2P) which will replace SERPS. S2P will be targeted at those earning under £9000 per annum.
- Private pensions, significantly expanded through the new Stakeholder Pensions (SHPs), which will be targeted at those earning between £9000 and £18,500 per annum who do not have alternative private cover.

How well do the current and proposed pension systems address the 'pensions problem' for women discussed above? Do they mitigate, replicate or compound differences in the lifetime experiences of women and men?

Women spend fewer years in the labour market – pension systems reward long working lives

Rights to a final pension may be earned by contributing time, as well as contributing money, to that scheme. Time requirements may be placed on access to the pension system – pension rights may be conditional on spending a certain minimum time, while long periods of service may be rewarded by higher pensions. Where a pension scheme operates either of these time requirements it is likely to penalize women. The BP is reduced for those with a short contribution record so that women receive lower amounts (see Chapter 4).

The 1998 Green Paper proposals attempt to compensate women for their shorter working lives by offering credits, but there are major concerns about the effectiveness of the proposed credits. Firstly, S2P credits are *less* generous than those offered in the BP. Currently, those registered as unemployed get credits that count towards their BP, while S2P offers no coverage to the unemployed. In addition, S2P credits provide coverage only until the youngest child reaches age 6 and, as such, offers 11 fewer years of coverage for childcare responsibilities than are available under HRP. According to our estimates this could affect 6 million individuals (mainly women) at some stage in their lifetime. For carers of adults, the credits apply to S2P in the same way as HRP.

Second, the proposed credits will operate within S2P only. They will not be transferable to other parts of the pension systems, and will do nothing to enhance entitlements to SHPs, occupational or private pensions. If individuals accumulate entitlements across a number of parts of the pension system (for example, S2P combined with some SHP), then the value of the credits to S2P may be limited. In addition, the operation of a means-tested Minimum Income Guarantee paid regardless of years of earnings or credits means that, contrary to government claims, credits to S2P will *not* give carers an extra £50 of income a week when compared with the income they could receive from MIG.

Third, even if a woman did gain full entitlement to S2P, there are questions about its adequacy. As Rake *et al.* (1999) show, even those women with full S2P entitlement are very likely to fall into income-testing at, or soon after, retirement if they are not in a couple.

The pay gap: the pension system may operate an earnings threshold or pay earnings-related pensions

The majority of pension systems incorporate a link between earnings and final pension entitlement. This may take the form of a minimum earnings threshold which has to be passed for contributions to count and/or the payment of an earnings-related pension.

In Britain, a Lower Earnings Limit (LEL) operates for the BP and SERPS. When earnings fall below the LEL, contributions are lost for that year (unless covered by HRP), reducing pension entitlements. Evidence points to the persistence of low pay – spells below LEL are likely to accumulate across the lifetime with serious consequences for income in later life. The proposed reforms do nothing to address this, as the LEL also operates for S2P.

Payouts of all current second tier schemes in Britain (SERPS, occupational and private pensions) are related to earnings, so that low earnings in the working life translate into low income in old age. In contrast, S2P will be a flat-rate benefit once it has matured and this *will* work to the advantage of low paid women. It is forecast that S2P will outperform SERPS for low earners. The flat-rate nature of the benefit means that anyone with earnings above the LEL but less than £9000 per annum is treated as if they earned £9000 (DSS 2000a).

However, the change signalled by the Green Paper in the overall pensions mix through the introduction of SHPs (targeted at those earning between £9000–18,000 per annum) also has an important effect on women's pension incomes. By continuing the shift away from a pension system that relies on public Pay-As-You-Go pensions towards privately funded individual pensions, the government's ability to use the pension system to redistribute between high and low lifetime earners is further eroded.

Women are concentrated in different parts of the labour market, with less access to occupational pensions

As discussed above, a smaller proportion of women are members of an occupational pension. Moreover, those with such a pension receive smaller amounts which may bring little or no financial gain (see Chapter 4). A small private pension may merely disqualify the recipient from entitlement to means-tested benefits and with them all the other passported benefits – the so-called occupational pensions trap (Walker and Huby 1989). To address women's exclusion from occupational pension schemes, Barbara Castle introduced SERPS in 1975 as an alternative second-tier pension. This promised to minimize the adverse effect of interruptions to women's working lives but reforms in the 1986 Social Security Act have since reversed this advance for women, resurrecting the very institutional structures that work to the disadvantage of women (see Chapter 4).

S2P has been presented as a replacement for, and an improvement on, SERPS. However, the SHP has better claims to being a second-tier pension, but like the occupational and private sectors will exclude many women. The government itself states that 'Those in today's workforce who are most likely to join SHPs are predominantly in full time work . . . Roughly two-thirds are men and a third are women' (DSS 1998a: 49). This shows that the government's expectation is that the gender imbalance of the existing private pension coverage will be mirrored by SHPs. The ability of higher paid workers to opt out of S2P means that S2P risks being a residualized system populated principally by low paid women. Any part of the welfare system in which the middle classes do not have a vested interest carries significant political risk – when cuts have to be made, such parts of the welfare system are vulnerable, and even more so if they are feminized, given women's lack of political voice.

As we illustrate below, SHP also perpetuates the problems inherent in other private pensions in that women who contribute for relatively short periods are disadvantaged. Those who switch between different kinds of pension scheme as their circumstances change may find their pension entitlements from all these sources are worth less than if they had remained within one scheme.

Women live longer than men – inadequate indexing of pensions
affects the oldest most

An effective pension system needs to provide protection from inflation throughout an individual's period of retirement. Women's greater longevity means that they are particularly vulnerable to the erosion of the value of their pensions through inadequate indexation. Since 1979, the BP has been indexed only to prices, effectively excluding older people from sharing fully in the benefits of economic growth. It is expected that S2P in payment will also be linked to prices, raising similar questions about the adequacy of this pension through the period of retirement (see Falkingham and Rake 1999; and Rake *et al.* 1999 for a full examination of these issues).

Women are also disadvantaged in annuities (see above). Women require a larger fund in any money purchase pension, including SHP, to provide an adequate income in retirement. Furthermore, annuities rarely, if ever, provide full inflation proofing. Many women and men who draw an annuity income may find their incomes dropping below that of the means-tested Minimum Income Guarantee. This will send a signal to younger workers that there is little reward to thrift.

As a consequence of all these factors, women are likely to find themselves reliant on the state, and on means-tested benefits, as a source of income in old age. This makes the level at which such benefits are payable especially important to women.

An illustration of the 'pensions problem' for Britain

So far we have discussed the 'pension problem' for women and how the current and reformed British pension systems accommodate, or fail to accommodate, lifetime patterns of labour market participation more typical of women. We now extend this discussion by comparing pension entitlements for different individuals using a simulation model, Pensions and Hypothetical Lifetime Income Simulation model, or PHYLIS (for detailed explanation of the programming of PHYLIS see Evans and Falkingham 1997; Johnson and Rake 1998; Rake *et al.* 1999). PHYLIS is updated to match changes in the British pension system and the version used here has been programmed with both the current pension system and the proposed reforms discussed above (see Appendix, this chapter). This allows us to compare the outcomes for a hypothetical individual if the current system remained constant through her lifetime and the outcomes if the same hypothetical individual lived her entire lifetime under the reformed system.

This type of simulation modelling does not, of course, produce representations of real outcomes since it assumes two alternative 'steady states', in which policy, economic and demographic change are left out of the equation so that the 'pure' impact of the two pension systems may be compared. In the first of these steady states, the current BP is combined with a lifetime's contribution to SERPS under the current rules. The second illustrates the operation of the Green Paper's proposals – the BP, S2P and the SHP in the year in which these are due to be fully matured (2050). We use a number of assumptions which are set out in the appendix to this chapter. To aid comparison between the two steady states, all figures are expressed in 1999 prices. In modelling the proposed reforms, we assume that the BP will continue to be uprated in line with prices so that its worth relative to earnings will continue to decline by 2050 to 7.5 per cent of male average earnings (or £32 per week in 1999 prices). In modelling the current system, however, the BP is not allowed to deteriorate further and is maintained at its 1999 value of £66.75 (15.7 per cent of male average earnings). The differential between these two rates demonstrates very clearly the long-term impact, especially on women, of the decision to continue to index the BP to prices only.

We calculate pension outcomes using gender-based age-specific profiles (see Figure 5.1) derived from the 1998 *New Earnings Survey* (ONS 1998a: Table F13). This is not an accurate representation of any actual individual's lifetime earnings profile but is, however, consistent with our steady-state assumption that the policy world remains unchanged throughout the working life.

The hypothetical cases have been chosen to illustrate the impact of a range of experiences common to many women, rather than to represent the full diversity of women's lives. The first simulation uses a simple whole working lifetime for women and men – continuous employment on average wages from the age of 18 through to pensionable age at 65 – to explore how the gender differential in lifetime earnings translates into differential pension income under both systems. We then explore the pension outcomes for women who experience persistent low pay but remain in the labour market continuously, to see whether penalties are attached to low pay in and of itself. The remainder of the analysis explores the effect of interrupted employment histories. We examine how employment gaps of differing lengths are treated where there is a subsequent return to full time work and then analyse the combined impact of employment gaps and a spell of part time working on final pension income.

Scenario A – the full time, continuously employed, average wage woman and man

Scenario A is the simplest of the cases and operates as a baseline with which to compare the variations in the hypothetical lifetimes that follow.

Table 5.1   Pension incomes in pounds per week under Scenario A. Britain.

	Man	Woman
(i) *Pension entitlement under the current system*		
BP (Basic Pension)	66.75	66.75
SERPS (State Earnings Related Pension Scheme)	66.76	45.07
Individual total	133.51	111.82
Household total		245.33
(ii) *Pension entitlement under the proposed reforms*		
BP	32.00	32.00
S2P (State Second Pension)	–	–
SHP (Stakeholder Pension)	84.88	54.67
Individual total	116.88	86.67
Household total		203.55

In Scenario A, the woman works full time from age 18 to 64 earning 100 per cent of average female wages (for her age group) across her working life. She is compared with a man with an identical labour market pattern, earning 100 per cent of average male wages continuously. This allows us to isolate the impact of the lifetime gender pay gap from other potentially confounding factors such as gaps in employment. The results for this pair are given in Table 5.1.

According to our age-earnings profile, the woman's earnings amount to 71 per cent of the man's over her lifetime. Under both pension systems, a gender gap in pension entitlements is also apparent. However, if we look at SERPS alone the gender differential is actually wider – the woman's SERPS entitlement amount to 67.5 per cent of the man's. This slight widening of the differential is a result of SERPS taking into account only those earnings above the Lower Earnings Limit (discussed above). Even though, in this scenario, the woman's earnings never fall below the LEL, her earnings above the LEL represent a smaller proportion of her total earnings than they do of his, leaving her slightly more penalized by the operation of an earnings threshold. Looking at total individual pension income, the gender differential under the current system is somewhat narrower – women's pension entitlements being 84 per cent of men's – than that in lifetime earnings. Hence, the reduction in the gender differential is being driven entirely by the flat-rate BP, demonstrating the importance of a flat-rate pension for reducing gender differentials, even for those women who are continuously employed.

Under the proposed reforms, the package of pensions is less effective at reducing the gender gap. The woman's total pension income is 74 per cent of the man's. Although the BP maintains its equalizing effect, its relative value has withered so much by the time the reformed pension system reaches maturity that it has less impact on the differential overall. The estimated gender differential in entitlement to the SHP is wider than SERPS, standing at 64 per cent. This reflects both the lower fund that the woman has built up over time (worth about 75 per cent of his), and gender differentials in annuity rates. Our model assumes that men purchase an annuity at a rate of 7 per cent, and women 6 per cent, in line with current practice (see Appendix, this chapter). In other words, a woman would need to build up a fund of around 117 per cent of a similar man's in order to compensate for the differential in annuity rates.

Scenario B – woman experiences persistent low pay

For this we vary the woman's profile to illustrate the experience of those with persistently low earnings. Under this scenario, the woman is continuously employed full time, earning the National Minimum Wage of £3.60 for a 37.5 hour week (£135 per week).

Comparing individual pension incomes, it is clear that S2P outperforms SERPS for those with continuous employment and long periods of low pay. The woman's continuous employment means that she has full entitlement to S2P, which is worth more than three times what she would receive under SERPS. However, the low-paid woman has a slightly *lower* income overall under the proposed reforms compared with the

Table 5.2 Pension incomes in pounds per week under Scenario B. Britain.

	Man	*Woman*
(i) *Pension entitlement under the current system*		
BP	66.75	66.75
SERPS	66.76	12.69
Individual total	133.51	79.44
Household total		212.94
(ii) *Pension entitlement under the proposed reforms*		
BP	32.00	32.00
S2P	–	44.00
SHP	84.88	–
Individual total	116.88	76.00
Household total		192.88

current system, resulting from the lower value of the BP. As the relative value of the BP withers, it will be a growing challenge for S2P to plug the ever-widening gap between the price-linked BP and the means-tested MIG, which is planned to rise in line with average earnings. Because of this, many low-paid workers will find themselves dependent on means-tested benefits in later life.

Scenario C – woman has gap in employment, returning to full time employment

We again adopt the assumption that the woman earns 100 per cent of average female wages for her age group (as in Scenario A), but here introduce breaks in employment. Since the impact of a break to care for older relatives would be similar under the current and reformed system, this event is not modelled here. We assume that the couple have two children, the first when the woman is aged 27 and the second at age 29 (based on 1997 data for women's ages at first and second births, ONS 1998b). Three different patterns of labour market absence following the birth of these children are investigated:

1 *the short gap* – in this scenario the woman takes just one year out of paid employment following the birth of each child;
2 *the medium gap* – here the gap following childbirth lasts until her youngest child enters primary school at age 5, a total absence from employment of seven years;
3 *the long gap* – in this case, the woman returns to paid employment when her youngest child enters secondary school at age 11, a total absence of 13 years.

As a result of HRP coverage in the BP, gaps in employment have no impact on final entitlement. In this scenario, all the women have over 20 years of contributions and so qualify for the full amount of BP. Assuming HRP also applies to SERPS (as was provided for but never enacted), it reduces the period over which earnings are averaged so that the effect of gaps is very small compared with the woman without gaps (Scenario A). Thus SERPS with HRP is very effective in protecting women's pension entitlements against the risk of an interrupted employment history. Furthermore, if the years of earnings 'lost' are years when earnings would have been below the woman's lifetime average, HRP serves to improve average lifetime earnings. In these circumstances, SERPS entitlements may be higher for women with gaps than women without gaps.

  Turning to the proposed reforms, there are interesting variations in outcomes according to the length of gaps in employment. All women remain members of a SHP scheme as their earnings fall within the

Table 5.3 Pension incomes in pounds per week under Scenario C. Britain.

	Man	Woman (short gap)	Woman (medium gap)	Woman (long gap)
(i) *Pension entitlement under the current system*				
BP	66.75	66.75	66.75	66.75
SERPS	66.76	43.93	43.82	41.64
Individual total	133.51	110.68	110.57	108.39
Household total		244.19	244.08	241.90
(ii) *Pension entitlement under the proposed reforms*				
BP	32.00	32.00	32.00	32.00
S2P	–	1.05	1.19	1.29
SHP	84.88	51.68	44.32	36.10
Individual total	116.88	84.73	77.51	69.39
Household total		201.61	194.39	186.27

income band (£9000–18,500) for which the government recommends opting out of S2P into a SHP. However, SHPs offer no credits by way of contributions for years out of the labour force and therefore cannot compensate for gaps in employment. For a short gap there is a correspondingly small drop in the SHP, although, in common with all other cases, the woman is worse off overall under the new system because of the smaller BP. The woman experiencing a medium length gap of seven years is in an interesting position. Although her earnings while in work will mean that she 'qualifies' for SHP, her final entitlement under SHP is very close to that she would have obtained had she opted to remain a member of the S2P, receiving credits for her gap years.

For the woman with the longest gap, 13 years (shown in the far right-hand column), the income from her SHP fund is significantly lower than income she would have received from S2P (the flat-rate £44 per week). This example illustrates that earnings at any one point in time may not be a reliable guide to suitability for a SHP. Those considering starting an SHP will need to take into account not just their current earnings but their likely *lifetime* pattern of earnings. A perfect decision about pension scheme membership requires perfect foresight about lifetime earnings and any absences from the labour market. Obviously, perfect foresight is impossible and for the majority of women, whose lifetime employment and earnings are especially hard to predict, the risk of unwittingly making a wrong decision is high.

Furthermore, differences in the inflation proofing of the different components of the proposed reforms mean that the decision to opt out of the State Second Pension may be misguided for many women. The government promises that S2P in payment will be increased at least in line with prices. By contrast, the annuity income purchased from SHP funds may not incorporate adequate inflation proofing. Any inflation proofing is purchased at a cost, in terms of a lower annuity rate, than would otherwise have been obtained. Moreover, annuity providers usually place an upper limit on the price adjustment. This will be a particular problem for women given their greater longevity.

Scenario D – woman has gap in employment, returning to part time employment

The assumption that women return to full time work after a break in employment is, of course, rather unrealistic. Many British mothers are employed part time (see Chapter 2) so this example assumes that the women with the medium and long gaps return to work part time for the remainder of their working lives. Earnings at 50 per cent of average hourly wages are assumed for the part time employment, an optimistic assumption since part-timers' hourly rates are on average lower than for full-timers.

Returning to work part time has a distinct impact on women's pensions under both the current system and the proposed reforms. As SERPS

Table 5.4 Pension incomes in pounds per week under Scenario D. Britain.

	Man	*Woman (medium gap)*	*Woman (long gap)*
(i) *Pension entitlement under the current system*			
BP	66.75	66.75	66.75
SERPS	66.76	20.67	20.47
Individual total	133.51	87.42	87.22
Household total		220.93	220.73
(ii) *Pension entitlement under the proposed reforms*			
BP	32.00	32.00	32.00
S2P	–	32.11	33.65
SHP	84.88	16.50	11.56
Individual total	116.88	80.61	77.20
Household total		197.49	194.08

is earnings related, part time work reduces average lifetime earnings and roughly halves the SERPS pension for the hypothetical women. Under the proposed reforms, part time work means that both the illustrative women accumulate S2P entitlements, rather than remaining in an SHP. Credits in S2P for gaps due to family caring result in these women actually getting a *higher* pension income than if they had returned to full time work and continued membership of the SHP scheme. This applies particularly to the woman with the 13 year gap, whose simulated pension is 11 per cent higher compared with the full-timer with the longest gap in Scenario C. From the point of view of pension income alone, once a woman has experienced a lengthy gap in employment her incentive to return to full time work and membership of SHP will be limited. In such cases, pension income will be maximized where full benefit is drawn from the S2P credits. This means relinquishing membership of the SHP or never becoming a member.

Towards a gender sensitive pension regime?

A number of conclusions stand out from the above discussion. First, *none* of the illustrative women gets a higher total income from the state under the proposed reforms. Although S2P and SHP outperform SERPS in many cases, in the overall pension package the decline in the relative value of the BP offsets any improvement in these second-tier pensions. The reforms do not include any proposals to change the current system of price indexation of the flat-rate BP, projected to be worth only 7.5 per cent of average male earnings by 2050 when the new pension system is fully matured. If the government were serious about raising the pension income of the low paid, then a better approach would be to index the BP to earnings *and* provide a decent second-tier pension.

Second, the reforms will result in a change in the balance between the elements of the pension system. Where previously women were reliant on an already ungenerous but non-means-tested BP, in future increasing numbers will be reliant on mean-tested benefits. This has consequences for pensioner poverty if such means-tested benefits are stigmatized and not fully taken up. Additionally, those who have saved over their lifetime may find little reward to their earlier thrift.

Third, in changing the balance between the elements of the pension system, the proposed reforms will introduce a greater degree of earnings-relatedness in final pension entitlement. Given women's lower lifetime earnings, such a shift means that gender inequality in lifetime earnings will be reproduced in the period of old age. With such a system in place, policymakers need to be aware that the gender pay gap has important consequences for poverty in later life.

Fourth, the proposed reforms do address an existing difficulty. As discussed earlier, gender-based occupational segregation results in women's lower access to occupational pensions. The SHP offers an alternative second-tier pension, with open access and full portability. These are very positive features for women in particular. However, unlike occupational pensions, which generally pool risks through a defined benefit formula, the risks in an SHP (like a personal pension) are individualized. Thus individuals are vulnerable to poor fund performance or a bad day on the annuity market which can significantly reduce their pension entitlement. Additionally, the introduction of the SHP will add another layer to an already highly complex pension system. This renders the decision-making process complex also, and without perfect foresight many, not least women with their complex working lives, may make the wrong decisions.

Fifth, women's greater longevity combined with an increasing emphasis on funded pensions means that it is timely to consider reform in the annuity system and a review of survivors' benefits across all elements of the pension system. The practice of offering sex-based annuities is currently under legal challenge and eliminating this practice will clearly work in women's favour. As for survivors' benefits, until women are guaranteed a decent pension income of their own, attention needs to be paid to inconsistencies in the current system. For example, while the State Second Pension (S2P), will offer survivors' benefits at 50 per cent of the former spouse's entitlement, there is currently no legislation to enforce similar coverage within SHP.

One way to minimize the numbers of women reliant on means-tested benefits is to enhance entitlements to a decent BP. In the British case, this would require both an improvement in the level of the BP, and the maintenance of a comprehensive crediting system such as Home Responsibilities Protection (HRP). The existing British pension scheme demonstrates the effectiveness of HRP in overcoming the 'problem' of interrupted work histories and women's shorter working lives. Any gender-sensitive pension scheme needs to ensure that all parts of the system incorporate carer credits, if it is to avoid perverse outcomes. Within an increasingly earnings-related system, the case for introducing earnings-related credits for periods of caring becomes stronger. For example, a credit could be set at some percentage of average wages.

It is clear from the British pension reforms that solving the 'pensions problem' for women was not a priority. While there are some positive features of the proposed reforms – such as the enhanced access and portability of SHP and the higher earnings replacement for low earners within S2P – the analysis highlights how much remains to be done. If the 'pensions problem' for women is to be resolved, policymakers in Britain, as elsewhere, need to give detailed consideration to how institutional features of the pension system may perpetuate or ameliorate the economic disadvantage experienced by women during their working lives. There are clear principles – all that remains is the political will.

Acknowledgements

This research was funded by the ESRC research group on Simulating Social Policy in an Ageing Society (SAGE), grant number M-565-28-1001.

Appendix

The key rules written into PHYLIS about the current scheme are:

1 Full BP for an individual was £66.75 per week in 1999.
2 SERPS entitlement is based on the current rules, i.e. 20 per cent of lifetime earnings between the lower and upper earnings limits averaged over 49 years (except where there is entitlement to HRP which reduces the denominator).
3 HRP is assumed to apply to SERPS as well as the BP. This assumption reflects the legislative framework provided, although the provision for HRP in SERPS has never been enacted, and given current reforms is unlikely to be so.

The key rules written into PHYLIS about the reformed scheme are:

1 Following the Green Paper (DSS 1998a), benefits are paid at the following weekly rates: full BP of 7.5 per cent of average male wages (the equivalent of £32 per week in 1999 prices); full State Second Pension (S2P) of 10.4 per cent of average male wages (£44 per week); Minimum Income Guarantee (MIG) at age 65 at 17.5 per cent of average male wages for a single individual (£75 per week and £117 for a couple). We follow the Green Paper's example by expressing benefit rates as a percentage of 1999 average earnings.
2 We assume S2P entitlement is calculated in the same way as entitlement to SERPS with no minimum contribution period required.
3 As with the current BP, we assume that S2P credits for care reduce the number of contributory years needed (e.g. 5 years of credits reduces the contributory requirement for full S2P from 44 to 39 years).
4 Contributions to the SHP are set at the rate of National Insurance (NI) rebates for those opted out of S2P. Following the outline given in the Green Paper, on the tranche of earnings between the Lower Earnings Limit (LEL) and £9000 we assume a flat-rate contribution of £524 (equivalent to a 9.2 per cent rebate); for the tranche of earnings between £9000 and £18,500 the rate of contribution is 2.3 per cent; while for earnings above £18,500 the rate is 4.6 per cent. After management costs, the real rate of return is assumed to be 1.75 per cent and the default annuity rate is set at 7 per cent for men and 6 per cent for women (in line with the differential which currently prevails in the British annuity market).

5 The LEL is assumed to rise in line with earnings. The level of the LEL is a policy choice, so we cannot accurately predict the future level. We examined the impact of changing this assumption on simulations where earnings fell below LEL and this was not found to have a significant effect on overall income.

6 Our age-specific lifetime earnings simulations lead us to model hypothetical cases where incomes across the working life are both above and below the £9000 ceiling for S2P. This means that we had to assume rules about entry and exit from S2P and SHP. Since any one-way exits from S2P for low earners would be inherently unjust if their earnings later fell to a level that was better covered by S2P, we assumed free flows between schemes would be allowed.

CHAPTER **6**

Women and pensions: perspectives, motivations and choices

KAY PEGGS AND MARY DAVIES

Introduction

The disadvantage faced by most women in Britain in terms of private pensions has been considered in the previous two chapters. A good defined-benefit occupational pension is the key to more adequate finances for most in later life, yet women are much less likely than men to have this source of income (Evandrou and Falkingham 1993; Ginn and Arber 1999). Thus women have not shared equally in the increase in private pension income in the 1990s due to the maturation of occupational pensions whose base has expanded since the 1950s (Falkingham 1998). Appropriate Personal Pensions (APPs) are often unsuitable for women (Davies and Ward 1992 and Chapter 4). Women consequently have to rely to a greater extent than men on state pensions. However, little is known of women's own perceptions about pensions. In this chapter we aim to illuminate how women themselves view their pension arrangements and the pension options available to them.

Women's pension decisions depend on the options available in a changing pension system. Legislative changes in Britain in the 1980s and 1990s have encouraged private provision and reduced state provision yet events in the pensions industry have undermined trust in private schemes. Government changes to state pensions, the mis-selling of private pensions, and the theft and misuse of occupational funds have highlighted the risks we take as consumers of pensions (Ward 1996; Peggs 2000). The increasing marketization of pensions in the UK is part of the more general rolling back of the welfare state, with risks and costs being passed on to individuals (Aldridge 1998). Thus UK governments in the 1980s and 1990s have been less willing to guarantee financial security during pensionable years (Falkingham 1998).

In this chapter we consider mid-life women's decisions about their pension arrangements, their understanding of the pension options available, the financial constraints on them and the effects of pension policies and life events on their perceptions of pensions. The chapter begins with a brief review of research on individuals' expectations and knowledge about state, occupational and personal pensions. We then present results from two empirical studies of women's views about pensions. The data lead us to conclude that state pensions need to be improved to enable women to achieve a more financially secure retirement.

Perceptions of pension options

Perceptions of pension options depend on the ideologies associated with financial provision for retirement. Choices are constructed within a moral climate that emphasizes that individuals should take increasing responsibility for their welfare (Aldridge 1998). This 'rhetoric of responsibility' (Smart 1999) has asserted a moral distinction between state and private welfare (Ginn and Arber 1999: 323) suggesting that relying on insurance through the state is less responsible than taking out private insurance. Such shifts in ideology have been accompanied by an emphasis on consumer power and choice, and choice has been linked to notions of good and evil and right and wrong (Gabriel and Lang 1995; Phillips 1998). The second-tier pension options open to employees have increased since 1988 (see Chapter 4) and employees may be able to choose between an occupational pension scheme, an APP, or to remain in the State Earnings Related Pension Scheme (SERPS).

The private pension industry and both the Labour and Conservative governments have promoted the belief that private provision is the better option both financially and morally. Individuals are encouraged to think about their future financial needs; 'we need to help people understand how they can ensure that they have the level of income in retirement that they want and which type of pension is best for them' (Secretary of State for Social Security 1998: 85). Such statements skate over the fact that choice is not equally available to everyone. Women, especially, often have very little choice about pension scheme membership. Some earn too little, below the Lower Earnings Limit (LEL) and so cannot contribute to even the state scheme (Hutton *et al.* 1995; National Council of Women of Great Britain 1998), while many lack access to an occupational pension (Ginn and Arber 1993; Peggs 1995) and others lack sufficient earnings for contributions to an APP to provide good value (Davies and Ward 1992). Since second-tier pension options are restricted to those who are employed, women are further disadvantaged. Only 76 per cent of women aged 30 to 49 are economically active compared with 96 per cent of men of the same age (National Council of Women of Great Britain 1998: 13).

Low membership levels in private pension schemes are not due to lack of interest in pensions among women. A survey by the National Council of Women of Great Britain (1998) showed that most women agreed that women should be responsible for their own financial planning for retirement and most disagreed that they would rather spend now than save for retirement. Respondents' perceptions of the need to plan for retirement fell into three distinct categories. The first comprised women who were 'financially unconscious' and thus had given little consideration to pension planning. The second comprised those who were 'financially conscious but fiscally unempowered', too poor to contribute to the pensions they felt they needed. The third group were 'financially conscious and fiscally empowered' and thus able to make pension contributions at the level they felt necessary (National Council of Women of Great Britain 1998: 27). Age was a major factor, since concern about financial planning for retirement grew as interviewees approached pension age, with lack of forethought being most common amongst women under 25 years old and those not in paid employment. Mid-life women had a greater expectation that their income would decline in retirement than younger women, but a fifth of women with no current pension plan or who had not considered their retirement thought that they would have a higher standard of living during retirement than at the time of interview (National Council of Women of Great Britain 1998: 15). Thus the researchers concluded that a sizeable proportion of women had unrealistic expectations about their retirement finances. A major problem is the lack of knowledge that people have about pensions.

Pensions are complicated and understanding of the different options is often very limited. Research has revealed that occupational pensions are often taken up with very little thought, as scheme members have little knowledge about them (Field and Farrant 1993; Williams and Field 1993), and the complexity of accompanying written material does little to assist understanding (Field and Farrant 1993). Only a minority of APP members feel they have a very good understanding about them (Williams and Field 1993) and advice to women takes little account of their often disrupted employment patterns (Davies and Ward 1992). Research by Claire Hawkes and Andrea Garman (1995) highlights gender differences in perceptions of and knowledge about state, occupational and personal pensions among the employed. Among those who were not members of an occupational pension scheme, women were more likely than men to cite ineligibility as the main reason. Also, more women than men felt that they did not know enough about pensions or had not given enough thought to the matter to join: 13 per cent of women compared with 4 per cent of men. Of those with a personal pension of any type almost

4 in 10 incorrectly thought that their eventual pension would be a guaranteed amount based on their contributions. Men were more likely than women to make this error, 45 per cent of men compared with 29 per cent of women.

There is also a lack of understanding about SERPS. For example, many full time employees who reported that they were not in any contracted out scheme said they were not contributing to SERPS (42 per cent) even though SERPS is the default scheme for all employees earning over the LEL (Hawkes and Garman 1995). A higher percentage of men than women were confident that they would receive a retirement pension from the state (54 per cent compared with 46 per cent). Comparing all types of pension scheme, men were more likely than women to say occupational pensions were the most secure and women more likely to say personal pensions were most secure but women were also more likely than men to say they were not sure.

In summary, the majority of working-age people do give some thought to financial arrangements in retirement, especially those who are over age 50 and have private pension arrangements. However, knowledge of the different pension options is limited, so that choices are often made with inappropriate information, especially among women. Since the current moral climate in Britain emphasizes individual responsibility for retirement income and state provision of pensions is declining, women's perceptions of pensions and the decisions they make in this respect are crucial. This chapter builds on the above research by describing more fully women's experiences of making pension choices. Qualitative data from two empirical studies by the authors is used (Peggs 1995; PRA/HtA 1997).

Data and method

Two sources of data on women's perceptions and experiences of pensions are used. The first is a series of interviews with mid-life women carried out in 1992 about pensions (Peggs 1995) and the second is a postal questionnaire survey carried out in 1996 (PRA/HtA 1997). These are described below.

The interviews

The interview sample consisted of 45 women aged 40–59 and was obtained by the snowball method of gathering further contacts from each interviewee. This age range was chosen because there is a higher level of labour market participation among women of this age, many of whom have had children who have left home. The majority of the women, 30, were employed full time and 15 were employed part time (30 hours per week or less). The sample was stratified according to part time and full time employment since previous research on womens' pension membership had shown that private pension scheme member- ship varies markedly between the two groups (e.g. Arber and Ginn 1991). Twenty-six of the interviewees were married. The majority (43) of the interviewees identified their ethnic origin as white, one woman as Asian and one as black. All the interviewees had lived in the South of England for at least three years. The taped interviews ranged between 30 minutes and two hours in length and were conducted over a six month period in 1992. The interviews provided a wealth of information leading to the emergence of several major themes.

The questionnaires

At the end of 1995, the Pre Retirement Association (PRA) and Help the Aged (HtA) invited readers of SAGA magazine, which is distributed to older people throughout the UK, to take part in a survey entitled 'Women and Pensions'. A total of 223 people responded to a small advertisement placed in the magazine, a mix of retired and not yet retired. Following a pilot survey in 1996, each respondent was sent a questionnaire that included questions addressed to the following groups of women

1 never married women;
2 married women;
3 divorced women;
4 widowed women;
5 women who were cohabiting.

Two hundred and twenty-three people responded, 207 women and 16 men. Many women clearly felt very strongly about the issues and wrote comments on the questionnaires. The survey was addressed to all women aged 50 and over whether or not they were retired. The majority were retired. Although the survey was aimed at women, 16 men responded and they are included in the analysis presented in this chapter.

A profile of the readership of SAGA magazine, obtained from a National Readership Survey of 1998–99, indicated that most readers (71 per cent) were middle class and had been in non-manual occupations. Seventy-four per cent were car owners, 87 per cent owned their homes and 52 per cent took at least two holidays each year. The readership was also concentrated among those living in London and the southeast who made up 44 per cent of the total. Because the sample comprised a self-selected group responding to a magazine advertisement there is likely to be bias towards those who felt strongly about the issue of pensions.

The themes emerging from the interviews and the questionnaires re-late to three main areas:

1 women's perceptions of the choices and constraints they had in pensions;
2 their knowledge about pensions;
3 their views on the adequacy of advice given relating to pensions.

Women's perspectives on pension choices and constraints

Each interviewee was asked about her pension arrangements. All 30 full-timers had been offered an occupational pension but only 15 had joined, while none of the part-timers belonged to such a scheme. Thus at the time of the interview, 30 women had the option of belonging to an occupational scheme, an APP or SERPS as a second-tier pension. Four of the 15 who were occupational pension scheme members said that membership had been a prerequisite of employment at the time they had joined (before legislative changes in April 1988 prohibited this practice).

> You had to go into superannuation I think, the only time you didn't is if you were under a certain salary.
>
>> (Dora; occupational scheme member for 16 years)

> When I started I was forced to join and I've never stopped since.
>> (Sally; occupational scheme member for 15 years,
>> in Peggs 2000: 355)

Among those who were compelled to join their pension scheme some complained that they had received little information about the benefits of joining (discussed below). However, all now felt grateful that they were members. Among respondents to the PRA questionnaire, 67 per cent reported that they had some form of private pension scheme and most members of an occupational pension scheme were pleased that membership had been automatic.

> When I started working the existence of a compulsory occupational pension seemed irrelevant! It was only years later that I realised how lucky I was to have chosen a career with a good pension.

> I am so pleased I had no choice in the matter. Without the pension now, I would be really miserable.
>> (PRA/HtA 1997: 23)

None of the part-timers were offered an occupational scheme. The interviews were undertaken before legislative changes prohibiting the

exclusion of part-timers from occupational pensions. Part-timers therefore had, at most, two pension options, an APP or SERPS. Those on
earnings below the Lower Earnings Limit for National Insurance (NI)
contributions could not pay into SERPS and would have been ill-advised
to contribute to a personal pension (Chapter 4). The insecure nature of
many part time jobs also makes personal pensions an unsuitable choice.

> Even if I wanted one [a pension], which I do, I haven't got one –
> I've got no choice.
>
> > (Sarah; no second-tier pension, working part time
> > in the informal economy)

Such 'no choice situations' (Bauman 1998) are usually the province of
the poor. Constraints such as the expectation that women's primary role
is located in the home often limits the range of job options and thus
pension options for women. Since women's employment histories are
often characterized by career breaks and job changes due to domestic
responsibilities, their employment is often perceived as short term and
as restricting their pension options. The following response was typical.

> At that particular time, I'd only been here a couple of months, and
> they brought out the scheme, and at that time I didn't know whether
> I wanted to commit myself, and really I thought I wouldn't be
> there long enough to be thinking about things like that. But on
> reflection I should have joined then – I would have been two and
> a half years down the road, but I didn't.
>
> > (Clare; offered an occupational pension, stayed in SERPS,
> > in Peggs 1995: 171)

It is difficult to predict the future. Although a job might seem temporary, it could turn out to be relatively long term. Valuable years of pension contributions can be lost for women who perceive their jobs to be
temporary, and the problems associated with transferring pension entitlements (discussed below) compound the dilemma. The temporariness of
jobs is an issue that affects many women who have either had children,
or envisage having children, and modify their careers accordingly (Hewitt
1993; Newell 1993). Expected future job changes can also affect attitudes to joining an occupational pension scheme.

> Yes, I have considered it [joining the occupational pension scheme].
> It's partly because I'm not sure about my future in [her job], and
> I don't know if there's the commitment there to spending. I'm not
> going to spend years there anyway, but I'm actually thinking about
> leaving in the near future, which is one of the reasons why I
> haven't gone into it. That was the choice I made really.
>
> > (Yvonne; offered an occupational pension, stayed in SERPS,
> > in Peggs 1995: 172)

Women's perceptions can be affected by the expectation of sharing their husband's pension, a risky strategy given divorce rates in Britain.

> I didn't actually take it up, mainly because I don't intend to work until I retire. In fact, I hope I won't work full time for much longer, plus my husband is in a very good pension scheme, and if anything happens to him, I would get half of his pension, plus a lump sum, so that's why I decided not to.
>
> (Fiona; offered an occupational pension, in SERPS,
> in Peggs 1995: 172)

Pension planning involves long-term commitment, but an uncertain future can deter women from joining an occupational pension scheme. This was a particular issue for part-timers since for many, part time employment was viewed as a temporary stepping stone to a full time job.

> I would [join] now . . . if I had a full time job now, I would be somewhat better off. But I think because I regard this job as temporary, I know even if I start paying a personal pension, I won't have a massive pension and I won't be able to maintain the same standard of living I had beforehand. Employment has always been conditional, and therefore it's always been very difficult to plan for the future, when it's like that.
>
> (Liz; no second-tier pension, earnings too low for SERPS,
> in Peggs 1995: 173)

Conditional and sporadic employment makes pension planning virtually impossible and part time employment is generally less secure than full time. The issue of transferability of pensions between jobs was central to women's perceptions of pension options. Personal pensions were seen as providing the best means of transfer out of an occupational pension scheme, thus making career moves easier.

More attention needs to be given to providing information about transfers, and about possible benefits and losses, since personal pensions are often the worst pension option for women (Davies and Ward 1992 and Chapter 4) and SERPS the best option in terms of portability. Very few (3) of the women interviewed saw their occupational pensions acting as 'golden chains', keeping them in their present job rather than moving to a job without an occupational pension. This minority view was expressed by Ava and June, although they differed in their reasoning.

> I wouldn't ever go into jobs that didn't have unions, didn't have pension schemes and didn't have health and safety. It had to be total, not just the money. The money was important but everything else

had to be right . . . if they're offering you rubbish money then their attitude to women in general is bad.

(Ava; occupational scheme member for 19 years,
in Peggs 2000: 355)

Even where shorter membership of an occupational pension scheme meant there was less to lose, some women valued the security offered by membership, while regretting the constraint on job options.

I have a friend who's setting up doing a market research agency and I thought to myself, if I was 30 I might go into it, but I'm 40, and I started to think of my pension, and in some ways that disgusts me, because I've got another 20 or maybe 25 years if they let me . . . and here am I considering security to such an extent that I might miss out on what could be very exciting. I could get a personal pension, I suppose, but then it's a very risky business . . . I was only talking to someone today about the desire to do something disreputable with one's life.

(June; occupational scheme member for one year,
in Peggs 1995: 188)

Pensions were seen to be part of whole job package. In Ava's case, without a 'career', it may be that job change is difficult, especially where age restrictions may make getting another pensionable position impossible. Awareness of future prospects without an occupational pension may result in feeling cornered into staying in a job, or thwarted opportunities, as in June's case.

Effects of pension reforms

In 1988 occupational pension membership became voluntary in Britain so that members had the option of contributing to SERPS or to a new personal pension (APP). Those who had been compelled into occupational pension membership spoke about the choices they had made regarding this change. It is unlikely that a personal pension will provide as good a return as an occupational pension scheme. Some women were more aware than others that leaving an occupational pension scheme would be a bad move, although uncertain why.

I was already paying into it [occupational scheme] here then, it was just an automatic thing and it didn't seem worth changing when it wasn't compulsory.

(Sheena; occupational scheme member for five years who
did not opt out)

They had this big thing, didn't they, about opting out. To be honest with you I can't remember why it wasn't worth it for me.
(Dora; occupational scheme member for 16 years who did not opt out, in Peggs 2000: 356)

Women who took the newly available option of an APP and subsequently had the opportunity to join an occupational pension scheme would generally have benefited financially from joining. Some seemed unaware of this, however. This particular choice is affected by the operation of heavy financial penalties for leaving a personal pension, in the form of front-loaded charges. Individuals are often conservative when making choices; perhaps particularly so in the complex area of pensions. In the absence of additional or clear information, or because they are used to the scheme they already belong to, individuals are likely to avoid change.

Nevertheless, discussion about pensions resulting from the introduction of APPs increased awareness of the need for pension planning, especially for those without the option of occupational pension membership. Moreover, a lack of trust in successive governments to honour their state pension promises encouraged many people to transfer to private schemes (Vincent 1995). Concerns about government policies on state pensions had influenced several women to choose a private second-tier pension instead of SERPS, even though most of the women had little or no understanding of SERPS.

The way the law goes on pensions, it's disgusting . . . The government keeps taking away benefits and when I get to retirement age I think they'll have got rid of pensions altogether. A lot of people don't join pension schemes because they think they can rely on SERPS but I don't think you can.
(Tessa; occupational scheme member for two years)

In the first few years of the introduction of APPs many people were ready to be persuaded to take out a personal pension plan.

I took out the pension scheme [APP] and it was one of my patients that persuaded me that this really was a good thing to do, and in fact it was one of my older patients. She'd taken one out and it was when they first came out. I thought it sounded like a good idea.
(Kirsty; not offered occupational scheme, member of APP, in Peggs 1995: 182)

Public confidence in private pension schemes has subsequently been eroded by revelations about the mis-selling of personal pensions and by the Maxwell scandal, which generated grave doubts about the safety of money invested in occupational pensions (Ward 1996). Information and persuasion are inextricably linked in the world of personal finance (Aldridge 1998), with pension providers competing for consumers. Some women recognized the lack of impartiality, where 'advice' was provided by salespersons.

> When a man comes round from the insurance company and he's selling pensions you know he's trying to do his bit to make a living and not necessarily what's good for you.
>
> (Kit; not offered occupational scheme, member of APP)

Thus problems with occupational pensions and APPs meant that most of the interviewees had misgivings about choosing a private scheme. Polly articulated this dilemma:

> I doubt whether I'd take out a private one myself, you can't trust them . . . and with Robert Maxwell, you know you don't know what's happening to it, and whatever happens somebody else is making the interest out of your money.
>
> (Polly; offered occupational scheme but chose to stay in SERPS, in Peggs 1995: 173)

With both state and private pension options perceived as risky, how did the women make a choice? In respect of APPs several had made a choice on the basis of trusting established companies with whom they had dealt for other types of insurance.

> It's extremely hard getting good advice, because everybody wants you to put it with them, don't they but I've always dealt with a particular insurance company for everything so when he came and talked me into it, and I thought it is a good idea, and that's how it started really.
>
> (Petra; not offered occupational scheme, member of APP, in Peggs 1995: 185)

For many of the retired women who completed the questionnaire there was a feeling that the state pension income they received was inadequate for their current needs. There were clear differences in views according to marital status. Among cohabitees there was not a single respondent who felt that the level of state pensions was adequate. One said,

> It is disgusting. I was married and had five children. I worked all my life, domestic, hospital cook, mother's help, foster mum etc. but because my [NI] stamps weren't paid in full I get £51 per week with ex-husband's [deceased] insurance to help. I cannot live on this as my common law husband doesn't keep me. He pays the mortgage, I have four jobs: cleaning.
>
> (Female cohabitee, retired, in PRA/HtA 1997: 18)

Among divorced respondents, 95 per cent said their state pension was inadequate. The clear conclusion, especially among women who had ever married, was that the level of state pensions is inadequate unless supplemented by an additional source of income.

Women's knowledge of pensions

Both the interviews and the questionnaire responses confirmed the limited knowledge of the state pension system, although women with private pensions generally knew something about their pension schemes. Women's lack of knowledge about state pensions was particularly evident in discussion about SERPS, mostly because they had received no information about it.

> I don't know anything about SERPS. I've never been told anything about it.
>
> > (Myra; occupational pension scheme member for two years,
> > > in Peggs 1995: 212)

The questionnaire responses showed there was a good deal of uncertainty among respondents about basic aspects of state pension provision, such as whether their pension was paid to them in their own right or whether they were members of SERPS. Several women who had been members of occupational pension schemes which had subsequently contracted out of SERPS had either not had their pension entitlement explained to them or had not understood how the system works. Some married women had received insufficient advice and information about benefits when they chose the special rate of married women's contribution, thus forfeiting state pensions in their own right.

Married women were asked about their husband's pension provision. Twenty-six per cent did not know what state pension their husband had and 22 per cent did not know about their husband's private pension coverage. Over half did not know what their pension entitlement would be in the event of their husband's death.

Divorce can transform a woman's pension position by removing the possibility of sharing a husband's pension or receiving a pension as a widow. Almost all the women in the questionnaire group were aware of this. However, half of the divorced women thought that their husband's pension was not taken into account in the divorce settlement. Since divorce is often so traumatic, it is difficult for people to take on board details such as pension provision at the time.

> At the time of divorce I was too upset and unwell to think clearly. It would have been better if someone else could have been

alongside me when I saw my solicitor. At that time I only wanted to die!

(PRA/HtA 1997: 31)

Many women divorce without any proper financial settlement in a court.

I had no divorce settlement. He asked me for money.

(PRA/HtA 1997: 31)

The trauma of being widowed is compounded for women by the challenge of grasping their overall financial positions and coping with the bureaucratic maze when trying to settle financial affairs.

All the women felt that information on state and private pensions is very difficult to understand and most expressed a lack of knowledge about SERPS. This means that the decision to opt out of SERPS in to a private pension was made in ignorance of the relative merits of SERPS. SERPS is at least as portable as an APP and more so than occupational schemes, and contracting out of SERPS is unlikely to be beneficial for people aged over 40 or for lower paid employees of all ages (Davies and Ward 1992 and Chapter 4).

Adequacy of information and advice about pensions

In order to gain knowledge about the complex area of pensions we need to have increasing contact with what Anthony Giddens (1991) calls 'expert systems' (Peggs 2000). However, decisions are seldom made straightforward by consultations with experts since they often disagree amongst themselves. Legislation requires private pension providers to issue explanatory material for potential members and information for members in the forms of trustees' reports, scheme accounts, transfer options and values, changes to the scheme, an annual statement covering their own retirement benefits and those of their survivors should they die after retirement, and the minimum payments made by the employer (Lowe 1997). The present Labour government states that 'much of the information that is available is of poor quality. Because of this, many people run the risk of making the wrong pension choices' (DSS 1998a: 27).

Each interviewee was asked to provide details about the information and advice they had sought and received. In addition to written official information, the women sought advice from financial advisers, colleagues, friends and relatives, and some gained information from newspapers. However, advice was hard to obtain.

I had no advice from my parents, employers, bank managers – and it's only been specific salesmen who have talked about life insurance,

Table 6.1 Percentage using each source of advice on financial aspects of retirement, among those who had sought advice*

Role	Retired (%)	Non-retired (%)
Financial adviser	24	47
Husband/partner	25	34
Company pension manager	15	18
Son/daughter	13	16
Solicitor	8	3
Friend	7	24
Personnel/HR manager	5	13
Building society	5	11
Accountant	5	5
Bank manager	4	11
Brother/sister	3	5
Husband's/partner's company adviser	1	0
Total N	103	38

Note: *Some respondents in both groups reported having discussed pension provision with people in more than one category, so percentages add to more than 100
Source: Derived from PRA/HtA 1997: Table 18

and I've always been quite wary of them really. I don't feel I can trust a salesman. If it was a pension I would really go into it and I'd get the financial papers and try to understand what it means. I don't understand a great deal about it now.

(Sarah; no second-tier pension, working part time in the informal economy, in Peggs 1995: 176)

Of the women in the questionnaire group, 63 per cent had discussed financial aspects of retirement, over half of retired women and three-quarters of the non-retired. Overall, nearly half had turned to a family member (see Table 6.1). Some respondents reported having discussed pensions with people in more than one category.

Non-retired respondents were more likely than retired to go for advice to a financial adviser or a bank manager. This may have been because a larger proportion of this group were divorced or separated rather than indicating that younger cohorts relied more than older on professional advice. The findings do not support an optimistic conclusion that women are becoming armed with better quality information. Among younger non-retired women (aged 50–60), under 20 per cent reported that they had taken financial advice and of these, less than 20 per cent felt they had achieved financial independence in terms of being in control of their own finances.

Most of the women interviewed had found the information from employers about occupational pension schemes was extremely difficult to understand. This is summed up in Clare's response.

> The problem is it's all 'double Dutch' to me, but I work in administration, so I'm not stupid.
>> (Clare; offered an occupational scheme, stayed in SERPS,
>> in Peggs 1995: 178)

For the women who were offered an occupational scheme, the decision about joining was occasionally influenced by the information they had received from their current and previous employers. In most cases the women considered the information to be very poor indeed, and all felt frustrated about the shortcomings of the information. The language in which information was given was unfamiliar to the interviewees.

> I've only had written information. I've never actually had any talks or anything . . . I think the way things are written – it isn't straightforward and I think you can't take it in. So I don't know much about what my pension will be, which is terrible . . . I'm not aware of what I'm entitled to.
>> (Jill; occupational scheme member for 11 years)

> . . . loads of jargon that you didn't understand.
>> (Myra; occupational scheme member for two years,
>> in Peggs 2000: 359)

Most of the interviewees who had received information about their employer's pension scheme felt that it was very difficult to understand. The field of pensions is very complicated and without clear information, in written or verbal form, individuals are hampered in their ability to make an informed choice. At least one of the women had made a seemingly bad pension choice because of the lack of information.

> I had the opportunity to join this [occupational] one here and everybody said how good it was, so after my six month trial period I was allowed to join the scheme, which I did, and when I tried to find out what it would be worth when I retired, I was having trouble finding out details, and since I knew I wouldn't be here for the rest of my working life, I felt it better to come out while I could still get some of the money back, and I could put it into another scheme [an APP]. It was a bit of a struggle getting out of that scheme.
>> (Judy; offered occupational scheme, transferred to APP,
>> in Peggs 2000: 359–60)

A few of the women interviewed felt that pension information had improved but was still not easy to find.

I think you do get adequate information, but it's just knowing where to find it, and most people can now find it, because it's advertised more regularly, as well as through banks and financial advisers, and they are becoming more approachable as institutions. The government has made sure there is information around, because they want people to go for a private scheme.

(Tessa; occupational scheme member for two years,
in Peggs 1995: 184)

Only a minority of the women interviewed, those who had gained information from past employers, were able to make an informed choice about pension options. Even where women did have adequate information, they often had limited pension options, as shown earlier.

Discussion and conclusions

Our research suggests that women in Britain are disadvantaged in pension terms in several ways. Their paid working lives are more interrupted and insecure than those of men and many women do not earn enough money for long enough to make adequate private pension arrangements. Women in this situation require an income from the state that provides a decent standard of living. Other women are able to afford to save for their retirement but are hampered in doing so by the lack of a trustworthy and easily understood pension or savings scheme; pensions are too complex, and there is much distrust of the private pension route. This suggests that state pensions need to be reformed so that an uncomplicated system is in place through which women in part time and short-term jobs can save for their retirement.

Women's disadvantage in pension opportunities is made worse by a lack of clear information and of awareness that pension planning needs to start early if an adequate retirement income is to be achieved. For women who have the opportunity to belong to a good occupational pension, take-up could be encouraged by clear jargon-free information and an explanation of the pension arrangements when they begin their job. It would be helpful if the annual pension statement were written in a way that encouraged women to read it rather than put it aside because it looks too complicated and tedious. We are overwhelmed these days by information, so that it is difficult to see which information is useful and which can be thrown away. This is another reason for state pensions to be restored to a central role in preparing for a secure and dignified retirement.

The current pension system seems to assume that women rely on men for their income in retirement. This is not a valid assumption to make.

Pension reforms need to take into account the increased rate of divorce and that fact that many women choose to remain single. In addition, many married women value financial independence. Since pension schemes are based on male patterns of employment, women have fewer pension options because of broken career patterns, part time employment, work in the informal economy, lower earnings and poorer career prospects.

Financial education is now included in the school curriculum, which should enable women in the future to make informed financial plans for their retirement – to be 'financially conscious'. 'Fiscal empowerment', however, may be more elusive. Women need both improved opportunities in the labour market and a pension system designed to take account of their working lives if they are to achieve financial independence in later life.

CHAPTER 7

Between means-testing and social insurance: women's pensions in Ireland

MARY DALY

As is the case almost everywhere else in Europe, pensions are the focus of considerable attention in Ireland. The issue propelling pensions onto the agenda is not, as elsewhere, the age bulge but rather the inadequacy of Irish pension provision in the light of economic and demographic trends. With a flat-rate and relatively meagre state pension and less than half of the workforce currently covered by voluntary private second-tier pensions, there is cause for concern. In the last few years the government has taken some action. It sought to put public pension provision on a more solid financial footing in 1999, for example by setting up a special Social Welfare Pension Reserve Fund. This move was associated with the first ever major policy review of pensions – the National Pensions Policy Initiative – which was launched in 1996 for the purpose of both facilitating national debate on the issue and formulating a strategy for a fully developed national pension system. Among the main policy recommendations made to date have been the consolidation of a strong first tier of pensions founded on social insurance and a major expansion of the second tier of voluntary pensions. Notably there are no plans for statutory second-tier pensions. The main response of the government has been positive and a new pensions bill is awaited. Changes in personal responsibility for pensions and in the form of the state pension system and how it relates to voluntary pensions are expected in this legislation. Whether these will amount to significant reform of the system and how they will affect women remain uncertain.

Gender issues have hardly figured in the Irish debate. The aforementioned National Pensions Policy Initiative devoted only a page of its report to the position of women and made not a single woman-specific recommendation. This neglect of women's issues in pension provision is something of a paradox. It is not as if gender is a new concept in Irish social policy. At different periods in the past the Irish welfare state has been acknowledged as treating women and men unequally. Moreover, moves have been made towards greater gender equality in other parts of the Irish social welfare system, albeit that these have been driven by EU directives. A gender analysis of pensions is, for these and other reasons, overdue.

The approach adopted here is one that is sensitive to interactive effects at a number of levels. Following Ginn and Arber (1992) my point of departure is a recognition of the interaction between public and private (voluntary) provision and, as a consequence, the view that statutory and private pensions must be considered where possible together. This approach also recognizes that an interaction occurs between the existing pension provisions and the employment behaviour of women and men. Hence some analytic attention will be devoted to the question of how the institutional aspects of pension provision affect material outcomes, especially regarding income levels and poverty. Framed in conceptual terms this involves on the one hand registering the differences and on the other establishing the links between the inputs or components of pension provision and their outputs or consequences. This distinction between the content of policy and its outcomes is to some extent a contaminated one but it is helpful for analytic purposes. The gender sensitive features of my approach lie in a consideration of how the life course and family situation of women are each envisioned in and constructed by pension (and where relevant other social policy) provision. The treatment of unpaid care work and of interruptions in employment are especially important in this perspective.

The chapter is divided into four sections. The first section presents the most significant details of pensions in Ireland and demonstrates how Irish pension provision compares internationally. The second section of the chapter sets out to identify the outcomes associated with the pension arrangements in Ireland. It first considers gender differences in access to pensions and then examines inequalities in pension levels and the associated income distribution and risk of poverty for today's generation of older women and men. A third section looks towards the future, considered in terms of labour market, demographic and social developments and their implications for pension provision and women's coverage. This section is also concerned with the approach taken to pension reform in Ireland. A final overview section draws together the different parts of the chapter.

Old-age pension provision in Ireland in comparative context

The origins of public pensions in Ireland reveal the background of the Irish welfare state itself in terms of both the British colonial legacy and the historical dominance of poor relief rather than social insurance. Pensions were first introduced in Ireland in 1908 during British occupation. The first, and for a long time the only, provision for older people took the form of a means-tested, social assistance pension. While the conditions governing eligibility were less rigorous than those used in the administration of the Poor Law, a number of deterrent clauses, pertaining to pauperism, habitual unemployment and alleged deficiencies of character, were applied to determine entitlement (Carney 1983). This pension, albeit with some altered conditions, lives on to the present day in the form of a non-contributory, tax-financed, means-tested, social assistance programme designated specifically for low income elderly people.

The Poor Law legacy took a long time to wane in Ireland and it bequeathed the Irish welfare state an enduring attachment to social assistance. Hence Ireland is unique among welfare states in having a social insurance and social assistance version of practically every welfare programme (e.g. unemployment, sickness, pensions) (Daly and Yeates 1999). In the pensions domain it was 1960 before social insurance-based old age pensions were introduced in Ireland, payable at that time from age 70. This provision, very late in European terms, adhered to a key Beveridge principle in that the pension was flat-rate.

The story of the subsequent development of public pensions in Ireland is of a gradual, but still far from complete, supplanting of means-tested pensions by social insurance pensions. To complete the public pension architecture, widows' and orphans' pensions date from 1935 and a flat rate retirement pension, then payable at 66, was introduced in 1970, mainly to fill the age gap before the old age pension was payable. Nowadays the Retirement Pension and Old Age Pension (OAP) are virtually the same, except that the former is available at age 65, the latter at age 66. Both are financed by social insurance contributions from employees and employers with a contribution from the state. For the sake of clarity they will be treated together throughout this chapter, referred to jointly as OAP.

Ireland's old age pension provision is a two-tier edifice, with a first tier of public flat rate pensions and a second tier of voluntary private pensions which consist of occupational and personal pensions (see Table 7.1).[1] Public pensions are attainable as social insurance rights under certain conditions by most of the employed and self-employed. Some 52 per cent of employed men and women also have private pension coverage, which is especially common in public sector employment (83 per cent covered). However, only 27 per cent of the self-employed are covered. Private pension provision is class specific in Ireland in that only 3 per cent of those in the lowest income decile are covered compared with 90 per cent of those in the top two deciles (Pensions Board 1998: 47). A high level of private pension coverage tends to be common in states

Table 7.1   The Irish pension regime

Public pensions – Contributory Old Age Pension and Retirement Pension (OAP)

Proportion receiving	50–60% of those aged 65+ in 1996 (including widows' pensions)
Eligibility	Age (65 and 66), contribution years, marital status
Financing	Employees, employers and state
Function	Social insurance, income replacement

Social assistance – Non-contributory Pension (NP)

Proportion receiving	A quarter of those aged 65+
Eligibility	Age and low income/assets
Financing	General taxation
Function	Poverty relief, social inclusion

Private pensions – occupational pensions

Proportion receiving	(estimates not available)
Eligibility	Employees in organizations operating a scheme
Financing	Employee/employer contributions + tax subsidy
Function	Income replacement

Private pensions – personal pensions

Proportion receiving	(estimates not available)
Eligibility	All with sufficient surplus earnings
Financing	Employee contributions + tax subsidy
Function	Individual provision for old age

---

with meagre public pensions. Coverage in Ireland is similar to that in the UK (see Chapter 3).

Certain characteristics of pension provision in Ireland merit emphasis. In some cases these derive from the nature of the Irish social security system, while in others they are peculiar to pensions. The first characteristic to note is the flat-rate nature of public pensions. Ireland never went the British way of supplementing the flat-rate pension scheme with an earnings-related second tier of public provision. Second, the means-tested social assistance pension, which functions somewhat like a basic minimum, is far from being residual in that significant sections of Ireland's elderly population are dependent on this form of pension (see Table 7.2). Social assistance is centrally administered and the means-test pertains to family (rather than individual) income. Third, unlike other countries, the difference between the value of social assistance and social insurance pensions is not very large in Ireland. Nominally the level of full social assistance pensions is equivalent to 88 per cent of the full contributory old-age pension which is IR£96 per week for a non-married person from May 2000. However in terms of the average payments made in January 2000, the Non-contributory Pension (NP), at IR£76 a week, is equivalent to only 81 per cent of the contributory old-age pension (averaging IR£93.67). Fourth, by international standards public responsibility for pension provision in Ireland is high yet spending on pensions is low. In the mid-1990s Ireland expended the equivalent of 4.8 per cent of GDP on its public pensions and total spending on public and private pensions was equivalent to 9 per cent of GNP (Pensions Board 1998: 79). A final relevant characteristic of the Irish welfare state is that it provides many benefits in kind for old age pensioners. Such benefits, which include free travel on public transport, free television licence and some free electricity and telephone services, account for about 3 per cent of total social welfare expenditure (Department of Social, Community and Family Affairs 2000: 4). They are estimated to be worth IR£9 a week to the average public pension recipient.

To the extent that pension provision in Ireland pursues a clear aim, it is to prevent poverty in old age. This distances it from both the continental European model which strives to maintain standards of living over the life course and the Scandinavian practice of reducing income inequalities among older people. The Irish pension system does not have any close comparator in Europe. Its pension model was originally closest to that of Britain but the two systems diverge in two important regards. First, Ireland has no earnings-related second tier in its public pensions (as Britain does with the State Earnings Related Pension Scheme). Second, Ireland has a designated means-tested pension for low income older people which sets them apart from, and to some extent gives them priority over other low income groups. It also means that low income older people in Ireland do not have to compete in a general low income programme as happens in Britain with Income Support.

In a wider international comparison, Ireland's public pension system is distinctive not only for its relatively meagre compensation levels but also by virtue of its low coverage of the aged population. Doering *et al.* (1994: 12) characterize Ireland's core old age income security system as being of 'the extensive selectivist' type, in that, like Greece, Italy, Portugal and Spain, it poses relatively few barriers to pension entitlement and operates with a minimum insurance period for qualification. Other research also helps to locate the Irish pension system in an international context. Kangas and Palme (1992), for example, found Ireland's basic pension to be among the meanest in the developed world. On the basis of the prevailing replacement rates, Ireland, offering somewhat less than 30 per cent of the average wage, compares poorly in international comparison. Its closest comparators as regards the generosity of state pensions are the UK, Canada and Australia. However, it should be noted that the flat-rate public pensions in Ireland are considerably more generous than in Britain, where the basic pension replaced only 15 per cent of average earnings in 2000.

The gender dimension of pensions in Ireland

As outlined in Chapter 1, it is useful analytically to differentiate between the process of gaining access to a pension and that focused upon the calculation of pension amounts. Even though they are interrelated, treating them as separate for analytic purposes helps to identify the criteria whereby the Irish and other pension systems can be evaluated as gendered. Following Table 1.1, the universe of factors for a comprehensive examination of the relationship between gender and pensions centres upon the structure and conditions of pensions as they govern access/entitlement and the amount paid. This general framework will be used to consider women's and men's access to pensions and the amount of pension they receive.

Access to public pensions

It is estimated that in Ireland 82 per cent of all those over the age of 66 receive a public pension, either on a social insurance or a social assistance basis (Pensions Board 1998: 4). The vast majority of these receive a pension for themselves alone. It is established practice for the Irish welfare state to pay additions to the main claimant for adults or children considered to be dependent on him or her. While such provisions owe their origins mainly to an anti-poverty orientation, they also have strong connotations of dependency in marriage, an aspect of the gendered nature of the Irish welfare state. In the year in question, an adult supplement was paid in respect of some 25,000 people in this age group. No statistics are available on the gender of the recipients but it can be reliably assumed that the majority of them are women. Table 7.2 shows the gender breakdown of those receiving contributory social insurance pensions and non-contributory social assistance (NP) in their own right in the last decade.

These figures reveal that there is considerable dynamism in the type of public pension received in Ireland. The trend is away from means-tested pensions towards rights-based, social insurance pensions. As can be seen from Table 7.2, the 1990s alone witnessed a substantial drop (in the order of 22 per cent) in the proportion receiving NPs (social assistance). This drop notwithstanding, 38 per cent of all public pensions paid out in Ireland in 1999 were means-tested pensions. Hence a sizeable proportion of the older population has no pension as of right.

The gender differences in pension receipt are very marked. While all the women in Table 7.2 receive pensions in their own right, women's pension arrangements tend to differ to those of men. The majority of women pensioners, almost double the proportion of men, are still dependent on

Table 7.2   Percentage of men and women receiving each type of public pension in Ireland, 1991, 1995 and 1999 (among those with public pension in their own right)

	Men	*Women*	*Total*
1991			
Contributory Old Age/Retirement	63.9	36.3	51.9
Non-contributory (NP)	36.1	63.7	48.1
1995			
Contributory Old Age/Retirement	67.9	41.5	56.7
Non-contributory	32.1	58.5	43.3
1999			
Contributory Old Age/Retirement	72.8	47.6	62.5
Non-contributory	27.2	52.4	37.5

Source: Department of Social, Community and Family Affairs (1992, 1996). Figures for 1999 were kindly made available especially by the Department for this chapter

means-tested pensions. Overall, 48 per cent of female pensioners in 1999 received rights-based pensions compared with 73 per cent of the men. While women too are moving away from means-tested pensions, this movement is slower than it is among men. It is only a slight exaggeration to speak of two pension systems in Ireland – a male, rights-based pension and a female, needs-based one.

While the Irish means-tested pension proves a failsafe for some women, only 42 per cent of older women, compared with 78 per cent of older men, are actually accounted for in the figures presented in Table 7.2. In the light of this it is vitally important to try and identify the income situation of the entire population of those aged 65 and over, including those outside the public pension system. Table 7.3 presents estimates for 1996, the latest year for which national population statistics are available, but the figures should be treated with caution due to lack of full information. What emerges is that a significant number of the older population, and especially the male population, is 'untraceable' in the social security system. A second notable tendency, which confirms some of the findings above, is for older women and men to be located in different parts of the public income support system. Quite sizeable numbers of women do not receive an OAP in their own right, the vast majority receiving survivor benefits derived from their husband's social insurance pension. Derived pensions are similar in value to the husband's pension. Thus derived benefits continue to be of great significance in Ireland, in that over a third of older women rely on this form of provision for their

Table 7.3 An approximation of social security provision for women and men aged 65 years and over in 1996

	Women		Men	
	N	%	N	%
Receiving pension in own right	100,302	42.5	140,348	79.3
(insurance-based OAP)	(44,217)	(18.7)	(97,598)	(55.1)
(means-tested social assistance)	(56,085)	(23.8)	(42,750)	(24.1)
Paid for as an adult dependant in OAP	24,925	10.5	–	–
Receiving survivor's pension	80,122	33.9	2,404	1.4
Receiving other social security provision	3,773	1.6	1,846	1.0
Unaccounted for	27,417	11.5	34,173	18.3
Total	236,539	100.0	178,771	100.0

Source: Department of Social, Community and Family Affairs 1997

income in old age. Notably there seems to be little urgency among policymakers about the desirability of women securing their own pensions in Ireland.

In all, 15 per cent of older people are missing from these social security statistics. Some of the women and men unaccounted for may have occupational or private pensions. However, since these are typically received simultaneously with public pensions, this is unlikely to account fully for those who are missing. A small group of the 'missing Irish elderly' may be those aged exactly 65 (since these are included in the population figures in Table 7.3 but most are unlikely to qualify for their pensions until age 66). It is likely that many of the missing men and women were engaged in agriculture or self-employment during their active years. Since these were for long eligible only for means-tested pensions, they will be missing from these statistics unless they pass the low income rule. They may therefore be providing for themselves or in receipt of only private/voluntary pensions.

Information on the proportion of older people receiving private pensions is unavailable but it is known that there are marked gender differences in coverage of private pensions among the current working population (Hughes and Whelan 1996): nearly 58 per cent of employed men are covered compared with 43 per cent of employed women. The preponderance of male coverage characterizes all employment sectors but is especially strong in the public sector. When one takes account of the gender imbalance in employment participation, in effect only about

15 per cent of all women of working age are covered by private pensions, compared with 45 per cent of men. Given that private pension coverage is less available to women than to men, the recommendation to increase the role of these pensions in the future without women-specific measures is less than friendly to women.

Which factors are likely to account for these gender differences in access to pensions? Following the framework outlined in Chapter 1, one must look first to the nature of pension provision itself. The absence of a citizen's pension, a tried and tested women-friendly measure, is the first factor frustrating Irish women's access to a pension in their own right. Table 7.3 shows that the majority of older women have been unable to secure access to an OAP or NP in their own right. This is because they either have an insufficient employment record or fail the test of means. For entitlement to the social insurance pension, a person must have commenced paying social insurance by age 56 – 10 years prior to the social insurance pension age. They must also have three years of full-rate contributions (or five years if the yearly contribution average is between 10 and 19 contributions). Not only does duration matter therefore but so also does continuity. For the maximum pension, a yearly average of at least 48 full-rate contributions paid or credited since 1979 is required. Effectively then, qualification for a full old-age pension in Ireland in 1999 requires 20 years of unbroken labour market participation. While these are not, in comparison to pension provision elsewhere, draconian standards, the fitful labour market presence of Irish women renders the conditions rather difficult to fulfil (see the following section).

Low employment participation takes its toll on women's access to social insurance and private pensions. Little more than a half of women who receive a social insurance pension receive the maximum amount, compared with 62 per cent of men. There is no hours' threshold for entry to social insurance but an earnings threshold of IR£30 a week does exist. This is, though, a very low threshold by current earnings' standards in Ireland – and only 1.3 per cent of all those registered for social insurance fall into this grouping. However, it is a condition that bears most heavily on women in that three-quarters of those excluded from social insurance coverage in this manner are women, mainly part-timers. Even though there is no formal differentiation for social insurance purposes between part time and full time workers, an informal distinction may therefore operate. Occupational pension schemes militate even more against female membership. Such schemes typically require a minimum length of service of three years and part-timers have been until recently ineligible for membership in most schemes.

The final feature relevant to gender centres on the treatment of unpaid carers. Ireland makes some provision for those who have spent time caring through a system of pension credits. Under the Homemaker's

Scheme (introduced in 1994), a person engaged in homemaking (caring on a full time basis for a child up to age 12 or caring for an incapacitated adult) can have up to 20 years of homemaking activity disregarded for the purpose of calculating the number of qualifying years required for entitlement to full social insurance pensions. Recipients of the Carer's Allowance (similar to the Invalid Care Allowance in Britain, but means-tested) can also benefit from these provisions. In effect then, Ireland resembles the UK in making allowances in social insurance pensions for the time spent in family caring.

Pension amounts and living standards among the elderly

The flat-rate nature of social insurance pensions in Ireland reduces the likelihood of a gender difference in the amounts of those pensions, even though a smaller proportion of older women than men receive the maximum amount. Women are disadvantaged in occupational pensions, however, due to the way the pension is linked to length of service and earnings in the year prior to retirement.

It is difficult to assess the gender effects of the pension system as a whole because no information is publicly available on the value of the public pensions received by women and men in Ireland. To compound this difficulty, a recent report on income, deprivation and well-being among older people in Ireland remarkably presented no information on the incomes of women and men or on those of female and male-headed households (National Council on Ageing and Older People 1999). However, the report did indicate that older female heads of household were two and a half times more likely to fall under the 50 per cent poverty line than working-age multiperson, male-headed, urban households. Analyses of the same data set (the 1997 wave of the Living in Ireland Panel Survey) carried out especially for this chapter augment the available information on older households and individuals.[2]

This analysis indicates significant gender inequalities among Ireland's older people. Comparing the individual incomes of all women and men aged 65 and over in 1997, women's mean equivalized income at IR£114 per week was 87 per cent of men's (IR£131).[3] The gender gap at household level was considerably greater. When household income is the basis for analysis, the mean equivalized income of households headed by an older woman was only 75 per cent of that of older male-headed households. The actual amounts are instructive – IR£96 per week for women's households compared with IR£130 for men's households (and IR£116 for the elderly population as whole). Apart from the scale of the income gap, these results suggest that older women are much more likely to be under income pressure when they head a household themselves than when they live in a household headed by an older man or by someone else. This is a classic feature of a male breadwinner-oriented social security model.

What is the situation with regard to poverty among the older population? Defining poverty as having an income less than half the average, households headed by an older person had in 1994 the lowest risk of poverty of any household type in Ireland, while those headed by a person under 30 years of age had the highest risk (Nolan and Watson 1999: 28–31). The risk of poverty varies with gender, however, to the disadvantage of women's households. With a poverty rate of 15.5 per cent in 1994, older women's households were twice as likely to be poor as those headed by older men (which had a poverty rate of 7.5 per cent). Moreover, while the household poverty rate of older men had declined somewhat from 1987, that of older women had tripled. This increase in women's households was so great that it significantly raised the poverty rate among older households as a whole between the 1980s and the 1990s.

Can people currently of working age expect a different old age?

Development and change

The question of how future cohorts of pensioners will fare depends on economic, social and demographic developments as well as policy reform and change.

Economically and socially, change is a key word in contemporary Ireland. With unprecedented economic growth and prosperity, Ireland appears to have changed as much in the last ten years as it did in the preceding century. The labour market has been a major focus of development. In a situation where employment levels are extraordinarily high – to all intents and purposes full employment exists – women are bound to be affected. However, women's economic activity rate – at 39 per cent in 1997 – is low by European standards. In fact, Ireland has, along with Italy and Greece, the lowest level of women's labour force participation in Europe. This is changing though. While the Irish labour market was in the past relatively resistant to large scale female employment, there are indications that a new labour market regime is underway. Spurred by buoyant economic growth, the rise in female employment between 1991 and 1997 has been spectacular, outpacing that of the previous 20 years. Between 1993 and 1997, for example, the number of women in regular employment grew by 26 per cent (double the male growth rate) and between 1997 and 1998 alone the proportion of women in the labour force grew by 7 per cent. Such growth is mainly due to increases in married women's employment, which rose from 20 per cent in 1983 to 37 per cent in 1997, an increase of almost 87 per cent over the period (Ruane and Sutherland 1999: 26). Were this growth to continue, women of working age today would be likely to have greater financial security in old age as compared with contemporary pensioners. However, continued labour market expansion is far from assured and employment that is part time will bring little increase in private pension income. Moreover, the majority (53 per cent) of Irish women aged between 15 and 64 years are not in the labour force, two-thirds of them being engaged in home duties (Ruane and Sutherland 1999: 29). This naturally varies by age group. Among women aged 15–24, 39 per cent are employed, compared with 61 per cent of women aged 25–44 and 32 per cent of women aged 45–64. The employment rate is high among single women in all age groups, while that of childless married women declines in older age cohorts, from the late 30s. In contrast to Britain, employment among married women with children peaks (at around half) among those aged 25–34, thereafter declining steeply.

There is also the question of part time work, which affects not only the quality of the employment relationship but also access to income in the short and long term. Ireland is not, in European comparison, a large part time economy; only about 11 per cent of those in regular employment in 1997 were in part time jobs. Although less marked than elsewhere, especially Britain, there is a trend in Ireland towards increased part time working. Between 1993 and 1997 the number of regular part time workers in Ireland rose by 42 per cent (Ruane and Sutherland 1999: 34). Women dominate the part time sector but again in a lower volume than for the EU as a whole. Throughout the 1990s women comprised 75 per cent of part time workers, and 23 per cent of all employed women worked on a part time basis (compared with 32 per cent in the EU on average) (Ruane and Sutherland 1999: 47–8). Part time work is primarily a form of employment for married women and single men; half of women employed part time in 1997 were married.

The implications of these trends for women's access to pensions are difficult to identify but occupational pension coverage of part time workers, at around 10 per cent, is extremely low (Hughes and Whelan 1996: 48). If part time work continues to grow and if it becomes the norm for women (re-)entering the labour market, then gender inequalities in private pensions are likely to persist and may even be magnified. Overall, Rake's (1999: 239) observations appear to apply to Ireland as well as Britain; women are far more likely to be employed in sectors of the labour market where there is no occupational pension provision, in part time employment which has frequently been excluded from coverage, and/or in employment for too limited a period of time to qualify for membership of an occupational pension scheme. The women-friendly and women-adverse features of the Irish pension system are summarized in Table 7.4.

Table 7.4   Women-friendly and adverse features of the Irish
pension system

Women-friendly features

Public pensions: Contributory Old Age and Retirement Pensions (OAP)
• Flat-rate basic pension, based on years of contributions or allowances
• Homemaker Scheme (HS) protects years of childcare and eldercare
• Widows receive 93 per cent of deceased husband's pension

Social assistance: Non-contributory Pension (NP)
• Flat-rate income support, a fail-safe for women

Private pensions: Occupational (OP) and personal (PP)
• Early retirement possible

Adverse features

Public pensions: Contributory Old Age and Retirement Pensions (OAP)
• Low basic pension, 28 per cent of national average earnings
• Female dependency is reinforced by husband's ownership of his pension
• Women have no entitlement to husband's pension on separation or divorce
• Recourse to means-tested social assistance is very widespread
• Unit for means-testing is the couple

Private pensions: OP and PP
• Provision of OPs not mandatory
• Pension amount linked to earnings
• OPs and PPs less available to the low paid, part-timers and temporary
  employees
• Minimum three years' service required for eligibility for OP
• Early leavers receive a poorer return on contributions
• Transfer between OPs difficult or impossible
• Only 60 per cent of OPs and PPs pay a survivor pension
• High charges in PPs, especially for the low paid
• No consistent indexation for inflation

It is possible that policies may change in such a way that gender
differences in economic activity will be neutralized for pension purposes.
Welfare is currently an active policy domain in Ireland. The country is
unusual in that the thrust of its welfare state development is towards
consolidation and gradual expansion rather than being under threat.
The basis on which people can make claims on the state's resources, the
reliance they can place on the state for income security and the balance
between the state, family and market in welfare have all remained largely
unaltered. For long tied to developments in Britain, Ireland's economic
and social development, as well as close ties to the European Union, are

leading the country on a very different welfare trajectory to Britain's. While there were some cutbacks in the 1980s, there has been no attempt to radically reform welfare state citizenship in a negative manner. In fact Ireland has even considered a citizen's or basic income, a move towards universalism, while Britain has favoured increasing selectivity. One very visible trend has been towards the expansion of social insurance, considered attractive because it does not penalize thrift or enterprise. In the pensions' domain this kind of ideology has been realized by such measures as the extension of entitlement to state pensions to the self-employed (1988), part time employees (1991) and new civil and public servants (1995).

Judging from the National Pensions Policy Initiative of 1996–98, the expansionist trend is continuing and there are no plans for pension retrenchment. The underlying strategy indicated by this policy document is two-fold: to improve payment rates for the social insurance pensions and to place greater reliance on private or occupational provision. Social insurance is, therefore, considered inadequate only as regarding the level of pensions it provides. A target replacement rate of 50 per cent of the individual's gross pre-retirement income has been suggested. This translates into a general target for a public pension replacement rate of 34 per cent of average industrial earnings (an increase from the current replacement rate of 28.5 per cent). Public pensions will be complemented by private pensions, which are intended to play an even more important role in the future. The report of the Pensions Initiative devotes most of its attention to private pensions and states as its goal that 70 per cent of the total workforce aged over 30 would have such supplementary pension provision. At present 46 per cent of all those employed are known to have this type of pension coverage.

Resistance to change in the gender culture

One of the most striking aspects of the current reform process is that there are no specific measures planned to improve women's access to pensions. Rather than an oversight, this omission is due to the fact that the family, and women's role within it, is one of the most contested issues in contemporary Irish society. One can understand current developments only by taking a broad view. Female and male relations touch very deep roots in Irish society, one of the most conservative in Europe. The traditionally very dominant position of the Catholic church made for a society which was both morally and socially conservative. The implications for gender relations become clearer when the proclivities of Catholicism in Ireland are highlighted (Daly 1999). Irish Catholicism not only held the family dear but favoured a particular kind of family: one embodying the tradition of patriarchal authority. While these norms are now beginning to be challenged, the moral conservativism has made change in gender relations slow and hard fought. Change is resisted not only by the Catholic church. Gender relations connect in a fundamental way with the ethos and value system of the entire society. Associated with the religious changes but also extending beyond them, a contest is taking place between familism, for long the guiding ethos of Irish society, and individualism (in the sense of freedom from traditional family obligations). Women are caught up in this battle, part of their dilemma being expressed by the contradiction whereby Irish society is prepared to grant women liberation but only on condition that the family and family relations remain traditional. This kind of contest is reflected in the fine line which social policy tries to tread between the well-being of families and that of individuals. Policy and policymakers regularly oscillate between proposals giving incentives to women to be employed and those rewarding women who stay at home. For example, in December 1999 the government announced its intention to increase tax allowances of dual-earner families, while less than four months later it was considering measures to allow women to continue their pension contributions while out of employment for family reasons.

While it is important not to read too much into the absence of attention to gender in the deliberations on pension reform, the invisibility of women draws upon deep-seated roots in Irish social policy (indeed in Irish society itself). Given the tendency towards the status quo and the opposition provoked by any attempt to change it, the gender bias in Irish social policy has tended to be altered only under pressure. The equality thrust of the EU regarding social security provision in the late 1970s and 1980s provided the single most important impetus towards more progressive welfare and labour legislation in Ireland. The relative dearth of pressure from this source since the 1980s has left the national policy scenario somewhat stagnant in relation to gender. In addition, Ireland does not share the demographic pressure that is driving pension reform elsewhere. Indeed, of 20 developed countries recently studied, Ireland is the most favourably placed from a demographic perspective in relation to pension provision (Pensions Board 1998: 70). The prediction is that Ireland's dependency ratio will not reach current levels in other European societies until the second decade of the new century.

Concluding themes

All welfare states tend to favour, and indeed disfavour, certain sectors of the population. Although it may not be apparent from the foregoing discussion, Ireland's particularistic and client-oriented welfare state has tended to treat pensioners as one of the most deserving groups. In a welfare state that retains elements of a Poor Law ideology, pensioners are seen as having paid their dues and hence as 'deserving poor'. There has been variation, though, in the priority attributed to pensions by public policymakers over time. In the reforms that followed the most important review of the welfare system ever carried out in Ireland (the Commission on Social Welfare in 1986), a policy was pursued of targeting increases in benefits on those programmes which paid least (that is the unemployed and the minimum income programmes). As a consequence the payment rates in the programmes on which many female-headed households relied lagged behind (Nolan and Watson 1999: 123). Pensioners are currently back in favour. Since 1994 the value of old-age pensions has risen faster than that of payments to any other sector of the benefit claiming population. Pensioners are in fact one of two groups prioritized by the current government (the other being children). Hence pensioners have been granted larger than average benefit increases in each of the last four Budgets. However, targeting pensions for general increases does not of itself do much to improve or overturn gender differences in a system where women's rate of receipt of both public and private pensions is inferior to that of men.

Irish pension provision is not as women-friendly as it might be, mainly because of the lack of a universal pension. The mixture of flat-rate social insurance and means-tested pensions leads to systematic gender differences in pension source and amount. Men primarily receive the more generous insurance pensions while women receive either these or means-tested pensions. Women's difficulties in gaining access to social insurance pensions are not unique to Ireland; pensions and other social benefits which require contributions secured through labour market participation are notorious for their gender inequalities. Despite rapid increases in recent years, Irish women's employment rate continues to lag behind that of European and North American countries. Mitigating provisions such as the Homemaker's Scheme will help more women in the future to obtain a social insurance pension but on the other hand the minimum qualifying years for social insurance will increase to five in 2002 and to ten in 2012. Hence most working-age women in Ireland are likely to share the pension disadvantage of women who are currently pensioners. In the kind of traditional situation that obtains in Ireland, survivor benefits have a major significance for women – but so also do means-tested pensions. Ireland is unusual in a European context in having a large proportion of the elderly dependent on means-tested pensions; almost a quarter of all those aged 65 and over are dependent on these social assistance pensions.

There is little evidence that gender inequalities in pensions have exercised the minds of policymakers in Ireland. The recent pension initiative shows little recognition that serious gender inequalities drive a wedge through pension receipt. While women's access to pensions is sometimes considered separately, the policy recommendations in tying pension access more closely to labour market participation and private provision appear blind to the reality that systems dominated by voluntary private pensions favour men over women in retirement (Hutton and Whiteford 1994: 215). In order to understand the relative neglect of women's issues in pension provision, the wider structures of power and social beliefs obtaining in Ireland must be appreciated. Looked at through a sociological lens, women's lack of independent access to pensions as well as to other benefits touches upon a deep-seated conservatism. This issue cannot be understood outside of the ongoing battle that is taking place in Ireland between familism and individualism.

Notes

1 For the sake of comparability with other chapters these pensions will be designated as private throughout this chapter. Technically they are not strictly private, though, for they consist of public service pension schemes, funded occupational pension schemes and personal pensions arranged by individuals.
2 The author would like to express her thanks to both Richard Layte and Tony Fahey of the Economic and Social Research Institute (ESRI) for providing the additional information. The data source is the 1997 wave of the Living in Ireland Panel Survey (ESRI) Dublin.
3 The incomes are equivalized on the basis of the weighting implicit in the Irish social welfare rules (1 for the first adult, 0.66 for the subsequent adults and 0.33 for children aged less than 14).

CHAPTER 8

Social insecurity? Women and pensions in the US

DEBRA STREET AND JANET WILMOTH

Nowhere in the advanced western democracies is income inequality in old age higher than in the United States (Smeeding *et al.* 1993). The US is the prototypical liberal welfare state, having much less comprehensive social welfare policies than most other developed countries. Working-age individuals in the US have no federal entitlement benefits, such as health insurance, paid maternity leave, or family allowances, which are often taken for granted elsewhere. In fact, the only comprehensive US welfare state programmes – Social Security and Medicare – are targeted mainly toward citizens over the age of 65. In spite of these programmes for older adults, older women are much poorer than older men.

US women's future financial status depends on how their work and family biographies intersect with structural aspects of the pension regime. Growth in the national economy has driven unemployment rates to historic lows and Social Security Trust Fund surpluses to historic highs. More women than at any other time in US history are engaged in paid work. Longer spells in the labour force and higher earnings for current women workers seem likely to translate into wider private pension coverage, higher levels and longer spells of contributions to Social Security, and more opportunities to save for future needs. However, potential pension improvements for some women does not imply all women will experience these gains or that the gains will be sufficient to ensure financial security.

Older US women's financial security may be at greater risk in the future if Social Security is reformed in line with neo-liberal preferences. The programme has been under political attack for two decades, with the most prominent reform options considering privatization or partial privatization (Street 1996). Reforms to date have amounted to little more than tinkering at the margins, in part because of the overwhelming public support for the programme. However, retrenchment efforts have been redoubled in recent years, and well-financed, media-fuelled crisis rhetoric about Social Security has reduced confidence in Social Security's capacity to pay future benefits (Street 1996; Reno and Friedland 1997). Whether this decline in confidence fosters radical reform to Social Security remains to be seen.

In this chapter, we detail the US pension regime, and how women gain access to retirement income as workers, wives and widows. Attention is given to the most vulnerable subgroups – low income and minority women. Finally, we discuss some recent neo-liberal Social Security reform proposals, taking into consideration their implications for retirement income security for future women retirees.

The US pension regime

Taken together, the US pension regime includes the public Social Security (hereafter SS) programme and private pensions that are regulated and tax subsidized by the federal government. Table 8.1 summarizes key features of the US pension regime. The twin legacies of its male breadwinner foundation and liberal orientation are apparent. The regime's public component is SS, with earnings- and family-linked eligibility criteria. For most people, SS alone is insufficient to guarantee adequate income

Table 8.1 The US pension regime

Public pension: Social Security	
Per cent receiving	Over 90% of aged men and women
Eligibility	Age + paid work
	Age + marital status + spouse's paid work
Financing	Employer/employee contributions
Pension function	Social insurance (earnings-link) and welfare (progressivity)
Private pensions	
Per cent receiving	26% of aged women, 46% of aged men
Eligibility	Employees in firms offering pension plans (DB/DC)
	Earners with surplus to save (IRA)
	Age + paid work (DB/DC) + marital status (DB)
Financing	Employee/employer contributions + tax subsidies (DB/DC)
	Individual savings + tax subsidy (IRA)
Pension function	Income replacement (DB), individual provision (DC/IRA)

in retirement. Income adequacy depends heavily on access to private income, consistent with the liberal welfare state's heavy reliance on the market. The private component of the US pension regime, favoured by neo-liberal reformers, consists of occupational pensions (defined benefit, DB, and defined contribution, DC, plans), and personal pensions (IRAs). In the following sections, we consider each of these components in turn, assessing their impact on women's pension prospects.

Social Security

Social Security, implemented in 1935 at the height of the Great Depression, is the cornerstone of retirement income for most older people. While the language of SS has always been race and gender-neutral, to this day it is racialized and gendered in its effects because women's and minority workers' life course experiences involve undervalued paid and unpaid work. From its inception, legislation was based on the 'strong breadwinner' model of paid work/family relations. Traditional women's occupations, such as teachers, librarians, social workers, nurses and hospital employees were initially excluded from coverage (Harrington Meyer *et al.* 1994). Moreover (to gain political support for SS from legislators in the segregationist southern states) domestic and farm jobs, where African-Americans were overrepresented, were also excluded (Quadagno 1988). Subsequent expansions covered more classes of workers, so that now 95 per cent of working-age adults participate in the programme.

SS is a Pay-As-You-Go (PAYG) social insurance programme, funded by payroll taxes on wages (7.65 per cent employer/7.65 per cent employee) up to an annually adjusted ceiling (US$76,200 in 1999).[1] SS pension eligibility is established by earning credits that are based on minimum earnings. In 2000, one credit was allocated for each US$790 earned. Up to four credits can be earned per year and a total of 40 credits (in effect, at least ten years of work) are required to receive SS. At retirement, average earnings over the working life are revalued. The benefit is then based on the 35 'best' years of earnings between ages 21 and 62. Benefit amounts are substantially reduced if workers have no or low earnings in the 35 'best' years.

SS retirement benefits paid in 1996 under SS represented 3.9 per cent of GDP (US House 1996). Average monthly benefits for retired workers that year were US$745, approximately 32 per cent of the average annual wage for all workers (15–64) and 21 per cent of full year, full time average male earnings (18–64) (Census Bureau 1997: Tables 9 and 11). These averages mask gender differences in pay and the value of SS benefits, discussed later in this chapter.

The SS benefit structure balances equity (benefits linked to prior earnings) and adequacy (redistribution to the low paid) within a single programme. Several SS programme features reduce minority workers' and women's likelihood of low income in old age. First, progressive SS benefit calculations ensure a higher replacement rate for the low paid. Thus, SS replaces 57 per cent of average lifetime earnings for the low paid (45 per cent of average wage), 41 per cent for average earners, and 25 per cent for high earners for those retiring at age 65 in 2000 (US House 1998). Second, unlike private pensions and assets, SS is the one source of retirement income automatically indexed for inflation and that beneficiaries cannot outlive.

Women can establish eligibility for SS benefits as paid workers, wives, or widows. Thirty-six per cent of women qualified for retirement benefits in 1998 as workers (SSA 1999a). By 2060 approximately 60 per cent of women will receive benefits determined on their own earnings (NEC 1998). Women's unpaid family work is partially taken into account under SS. First, SS is based on 41 years of paid work (age 21–62) and a 35 'best' years formula effectively ignores the six lowest earning years. This helps women who had relatively few years of zero or low earnings. It gives some leeway for interrupted work arising from family responsibilities, although the drop-out provision is insufficient for most women. For women retiring in 1996, median years in paid work were only 27, compared to 39 for men (NEC 1998). Half of women had at least eight years of zero earnings counted in their Social Security calculation, reducing its value substantially. Even by 2030, it is estimated that 60 per cent of retiring women will have some zero earnings years included in their benefit calculations (Urban Institute 1988).

Second, ever-married women may receive SS benefits as dependent spouses, ex-spouses, or widows. However, benefits derived from family status are not as secure as benefits based on paid work (Harrington-Meyer *et al.* 1994). In 1998, 37 per cent of older women qualified for benefits under these conditions. Almost all spouse beneficiaries are women; only 1.2 per cent are men (SSA 1999a). Spouse's benefits – 50 per cent of the breadwinning spouse's monthly benefit at age 65 (averaging US$384 in 1996) – are paid to married women aged 62 or older. Benefits can be paid to married women under age 62 if disabled or caring for a child under 16. Spouse benefits are permanently reduced if the breadwinning spouse retires prior to age 65. Survivor's monthly benefits averaged US$707 in 1996, ranging between 72 to 94 per cent (for widows between ages 60–64) and 100 per cent (for widows 65 and older) of the deceased spouse's SS retirement benefit. Divorcees who were married for at least ten years can draw on the ex-husband's record, but women married less than ten years are ineligible.

Twenty-seven per cent of women were dually entitled to Social Security benefits in 1998 (SSA 1999a). Dual entitlement occurs when a woman's 50 per cent spousal benefit is greater than the benefit she would receive based on her own working record. This represents the 'working wife's penalty' (Harrington Meyer *et al.* 1994: 62). The dually-entitled wage-earning wife gets the same spousal benefit as a wife who never worked for pay, if both husbands had similar earnings histories. Thus, the dually-entitled wife subsidizes the household with a stay-at-home wife.

Despite an imperfect promise of income security, SS does a better job of meeting the needs of women and minorities than do private pensions, to which we turn next.

Private pension coverage

Occupational pensions

Occupational pensions are voluntary, offered to employees at the discretion of employers or through collective bargaining agreements. Employers and employees receive tax subsidies as incentives to participate. Contributions made to pension plans are tax free (to an upper limit) and earned interest is not taxed. Income taxes are only paid on receipt of benefits in retirement, typically at a lower marginal tax rate than when the pensioner was employed.

Occupational pension plan coverage in the US is skewed in ways similar to Britain and Canada. Coverage is higher in public versus private sector jobs, in large firms versus small, among FT versus PT workers, in manufacturing versus the service sector, and for high versus low income earners. Despite near gender equality of coverage among employees, women's lower rate of employment and wages mean many will receive low pension benefits at retirement. Official statistics overstate women's private pension coverage, since they count all *eligible* employees as covered, but many low income covered workers do not participate in employers' plans because they cannot afford to (Borzi 1995). For example, in 1993, 33 per cent of all FT women workers were recorded as 'covered' under DC plans, but only 20 per cent contributed (Dailey 1998).

Among minority ethnic women, risks of low income multiply. They suffer the additive effects of low coverage and low incomes based both on gender and race differentials in earnings and employment experience (Hardy and Hazelrigg 1995). Although their rates of labour force participation are high, minority women earn lower wages, have fewer full time, full year jobs, and less access to pension plans at work. Lower

Table 8.2 Percentage distribution of pension coverage by race and gender

	No coverage	Occupational pension only	Social Security only	Both
White				
Men	6	4	45	44
Women	6	2	65	27
Black				
Men	12	3	55	30
Women	11	3	69	18

Note: All values are weighted. Includes survivors' benefits provided by occupational pensions and social security. Veterans Administration pensions are not included. Percentages do not total 100% due to rounding.
Source: 1999 Current Population Survey March Supplement (US DOL 1999a)

private pension coverage of ethnic minority men, combined with high rates of divorce and non-marriage leave ethnic minority women with small or no spousal or survivor benefits (see Table 8.2).

Until the mid-1980s, most occupational pensions were defined benefit (DB) plans that provide predictable pensions based on earnings and years of service with the employer. From 1975 onward, growth in defined contribution (DC) plans outpaced DB plans (see Chapter 9). DC plans operate as individual accounts, similar to money purchase schemes in the UK. Employees own their fund (employer/employee contributions and accumulated interest). DC plans are not pensions per se, as there is no predictable, periodic benefit upon retirement specified by the plans. DC funds may be used to buy an annuity on retirement, or minimum annual withdrawals must be made once fund owners reach age 70. If plans are annuitized, women with DC funds identical to men's receive lower monthly benefits because women's longevity is taken into account.

Derived benefits are a critical difference between DB and DC plans. Since the 1980s DB plans (but not DC plans) must offer survivor coverage. Previously, married men could opt for a higher pension that ceased at death. Current law requires that joint and survivor benefits must be paid, unless the wife explicitly rejects the widow's benefit option in writing. In DC plans, funds remaining at death can be bequeathed to a surviving spouse, although there is no requirement to do so, making survivor's pensions less secure in DC plans. For divorced women, all derived occupational pension benefits are insecure, since benefit sharing is not mandatory and is only negotiated during divorce proceedings. As individually-owned accounts, DC plans have some attractive features for women, including portability between jobs and flexibility arising from permitted withdrawals before retirement. It appears unlikely, however, that the benefits of such plans outweigh their disadvantages for women.

Implications of the changing mix of DB and DC plans for women's income inequality are discussed in more detail in Chapter 9, but several points can be made here. The expansion of DC plans has increased women's pension coverage, yet women's future pension income may be more insecure than ever. By individualizing the responsibility to save for retirement and eliminating some women-friendly features of traditional DB plans (e.g. survivor benefits, predictable income and no sex-differentiated contributions or benefits), DC pensions may increase women's risk of financial insecurity in old age.

Individual pensions

Individual Retirement Accounts (IRAs) are personal retirement savings accounts to which earners can make tax-free contributions and which can, under some circumstances, be held in addition to other private pensions. Historically, IRA participation has been lower for women than for men, partly because eligibility was limited until 1997 if one partner (usually the man) in dual-earner couples already had private pension coverage (Harrington Meyer 1990). In 1993, only 19 per cent of working-age Americans owned an IRA and only 7 per cent were making IRA contributions (Lichtenstein and Wu 2000). IRA participation increases with age as workers prepare for retirement and, until tax changes in 1986 limited their contributions, high earners were much more likely to contribute than low earners, mirroring personal pension trends in Canada and Great Britain. However, IRAs are not as widespread in the US as their equivalents in Britain (see Chapter 4) or in Canada (see Chapter 10), mainly because the US tax code has not treated them as generously. Since 1997, tax-free IRA contributions have been limited to US$2000 per annum per individual and US$4000 per couple.

In the future, women should be more likely to receive tax-subsidized private pension income in retirement, whether from occupational pensions or individual accounts, than older women do now. It is unclear, however, whether amounts will be high enough to insure income adequacy. Private pensions will help securely employed, high-income women gain sufficient retirement income (see Chapter 9). However, structural factors and life course experiences constrain most women's chances to take advantage of private pensions.

Tax subsidies: social welfare for the well-to-do

The high-income bias of private pension tax relief places women at a disadvantage. Consider the tax advantages for two hypothetical US tax-payers – a low-income earner whose marginal income tax rate is 20 per cent and a high-income earner at 39 per cent. Assuming each individual contributes US$2000 to an IRA or DC plan in a given year, the government would 'spend' (i.e. forgo revenue of) US$400 for the low earner (20 per cent of US$2000) and US$780 for the high earner (39 per cent of US$2000). The regressive nature of the tax subsidy applies to both current and future income. Estimated after-tax income of future pensioners, stemming from the tax subsidy is substantially higher for groups in which women are underrepresented – high-income workers and married couples (CBO 1987).

Tax subsidies are an integral part of the US pension regime, representing indirect government spending and the largest deduction under the US tax code. In 1998, tax subsidies to private pensions were US$101.4 billion (OMB 1998: 109), equal to a third of direct spending for SS retirement benefits that year at US$334.4 billion (SSA 2000) and 27 times more than the US$3.7 billion for means-tested Supplemental Security Income (SSI) benefits paid to older Americans in dire poverty (SSA 1998a).[2] High earners benefit most from US tax spending, since 81 per cent of FT workers with earnings above US$75,000 are covered by tax subsidized private pensions, compared to just 8 per cent of workers with earnings below US$10,000 and 27 per cent with earnings between US$10,000 and US$15,000 (US DOL 1994). Pension tax subsidies, on average, represent a transfer from the low to the high paid, from women to men, and from the pension poor to the pension rich (Street 1996).

Variation in older people's financial status

Reliance on public and private pensions

Social Security is the main single source of retirement income for older people, but is particularly important for women, who are less likely than older men to have significant income from private pensions or earnings. In 1996, SS benefits provided about one-third of older married couples' income (see Table 8.3). However, non-married older women (widowed, never-married, divorced or separated), who represent 60 per cent of all older women, receive half their income from SS. For 25 per cent of non-married women, SS is their only source of income, compared to just 9 per cent of married couples and 20 per cent of non-married men (NEC 1998).

Table 8.3   Sources of income for persons 65 and older by gender and marital status (percentage of total income) (1998)

Income source	Non-married women (%)	Non-married men (%)	Married couples (%)
Social Security	50	36	33
Private pensions	15	22	20
Assets	19	21	20
Earnings	12	16	25
Public assistance	2	1	–
Other	3	4	2

Notes: Columns do not sum to 100% due to rounding
Source: Census Bureau (2000)

Single older women and minorities are disadvantaged in all aspects of pension income. Although they depend on SS for most of their retirement income, the amounts of SS they receive are much lower than white men's (see Table 8.4). Furthermore, the gap in total income between older men and women increases when private pension income is taken into account (see Table 8.5 and Chapter 9). For 65- to 69-year-olds in 1998, median private pension income (among those receiving any income from that source) was US$3942 per annum for women, compared to US$8559 for men (SSA 2000). Among single women approaching retirement, their total pension wealth is a mere 37 per cent of men's (NEC 1998). Table 8.5 illustrates differences in sources and amounts of retirement income for women and minorities, who have less coverage and receive smaller payments than white men. This results in substantial differences in total pension income.

For older African-Americans, many have worked in unstable jobs with low earnings and few benefits, leading to low levels of private sector pensions and SS benefits (Gibson 1996); this kind of work history likely affects income prospects for Hispanic retirees as well (Select Committee

Table 8.4   Median value (US$) of Social Security benefits by sex, marital status and race/ethnicity, 1998

	White	Black	Hispanic
Married couples	$15,712	$12,701	$12,343
Non-married individuals	$9,029	$7,113	$7,234
Men	$9,729	$8,023	$8,544
Women	$8,824	$6,813	$6,486

Source: SSA 1998b

Table 8.5   Per cent receiving pensions and median pension amount (US$) among persons aged 65 and over in the US by pension source, race and gender, 1999[1]

	Occupational Pensions		Social Security		Total	
	Per cent receiving	*US$ amount[2]*	*Per cent receiving*	*US$ amount[2]*	*Per cent receiving*	*US$ amount[2]*
White						
Men	49	$9,600	89	$10,425	94	$13,377
Women	29	$4,800	91	$7,725	94	$8,037
Black						
Men	33	$6,840	85	$8,925	88	$10,125
Women	21	$6,402	87	$6,525	89	$6,991

Notes:
1 All values are weighted. Includes survivors' benefits provided by occupational pensions and social security. Veterans Administration pensions are not included.
2 Based only on respondents who received income from this source.
Source: 1999 Current Population Survey March Supplement (US DOL 1999a)

on Aging 1992). Minority pensioners are less likely than whites to have any pensions other than SS and women of any minority group are particularly disadvantaged.

Wealth

As the previous discussion indicates, pension income is a critical component of financial security in late life. Another is accumulated wealth. Assets account for approximately 18 per cent of income among older adults and the percentage of older adults with asset income has increased over time. Almost two-thirds of older adults receive income from assets (SSA 1998b). Therefore, it is important to take assets into account when considering financial security among older people in general, and women in particular. While pensions, in particular SS, provide an essential and stable source of income for older adults, assets can provide income as well as a financial buffer against the contingencies of later life including illness, changes in residence, and marital dissolution.

For many older adults, housing equity represents the single largest financial asset. Among adults aged 65 and over, nearly 44 per cent of total net worth (assets minus debts) is due to housing equity. In comparison, interest-earning assets at financial institutions and stocks/mutual fund shares are only 17 per cent and 9 per cent of total net

Table 8.6   Median net worth of assets (US$) by type of household and age of householder, 1993

	Total	Excluding home equity
Married-couple households		
55 to 64 years	$127,752	$43,543
65 years and over	$129,790	$44,410
Male householders		
55 to 64 years	$44,670	$10,905
65 years and over	$60,741	$12,927
Female householders		
55 to 64 years	$44,762	$6,475
65 years and over	$57,679	$9,560

Source: Eller and Fraser 1995

worth respectively (Eller and Fraser 1995). This is not surprising, given cultural values and tax incentives favouring home ownership in the US.

Table 8.6 shows median net worth of assets by type of household, indicating that older married couples have substantially higher total assets than the non-married. In 1993, median net worth among households headed by single older men or women was less than half that of married couple households. Furthermore, a larger proportion of their net worth was due to housing equity, a non-liquid asset. This was particularly true of older households headed by women.

While we know economic and political institutions influence asset accumulation, considerably less is known about the influence of marriage and the family over the life course. We know, for example, there are substantial intergenerational transmissions in wealth via bequests and inter vivos transfers (e.g. income sharing in families) (Holtz-Eakin and Smeeding 1994). However, the impact of marital events (as well as the interaction between family and work) on wealth accumulation is not fully understood.

Recent analyses of the Health and Retirement study (Wilmoth and Koso 2000; Wilmoth 1998) show substantial differences in pre-retirement wealth across marital history groups. Non-married individuals have significantly lower wealth than those who remain continuously married. The difference in wealth is greater for never married, divorced and separated women compared with widows. While remarriage significantly offsets the negative impact of a marital dissolution for men and women, the time spent between marriages is particularly important for divorced women. Later life wealth is reduced by approximately 3 per cent for each year a woman spends between divorce and subsequent remarriage.

Table 8.7   Older women's poverty rates, 1975 and 1998

Marital status	1975	1998	% of older women
Married*	8	5	40
Widowed	23	18	45
Divorced/separated	33	22	7
Never married	22	20	8

Note: *Assumes equal sharing of income in marriage.
Source: SSA (1999a: 3)

Poverty status

Older women are heterogeneous, with some women at particularly high risk of poverty in old age. The official poverty threshold applied to individuals over 65 is nearly 10 per cent lower than for working-age adults (Census Bureau 1999). Consequently, official US poverty rates understate the incidence of very low income among the older population. Women are more than twice as likely to be poor in old age as men. Among non-married older women, one-fifth had incomes below official poverty in 1998. Older women's poverty has declined over the past two decades, although mainly among married women, who are presumed to share equally in a couple's income (see Table 8.7). Without SS, 52 per cent of older women would be in poverty instead of 13 per cent (NEC 1998).

The decline in older women's poverty rates is partly due to substantial increases in the value of SS benefits, rising real wages and labour force participation that facilitated asset acquisition and pension entitlements, and increasing income from occupational pensions.

Gender and being non-married are not the only risk factors for poverty in later life. Race/ethnicity and age are also implicated. Race-based differences in poverty are striking (see Table 8.8). Among older people,

Table 8.8   Poverty rates for individuals aged 65 and older by gender and race/ethnicity, 1995

	Men (%)	Women (%)
All	6	14
Black	15	31
Hispanic	16	29
White	5	12

Source: US Bureau of the Census 1996

black and Hispanic women are more than twice as likely to be poor as white women, and five times as likely to be poor as white men.

Women's advantage in longevity over men – approximately seven years at birth and four years at age 65 – is a mixed blessing, since the risk of impoverishment increases with age. Women over age 85 are twice as likely to be poor as women between ages 65 and 74 (US House 1998: Table A7).

Prospects for future retirement cohorts

Early life events, chances and choices set the stage for later life financial circumstances. Thus, differences in income among older women stem from life course statuses (age, gender, race/ethnicity, patterns of employment and marital status) and the structure of the US pension regime.

Relative to previous cohorts of women, current working-age women have more opportunities to gain access to different sources of income for retirement, primarily because of their increased participation in paid work. However, structural constraints operating in labour markets and families create barriers to pension equality between men and women. Furthermore, pension inequality among women may increase (see Chapter 9), particularly if SS is partially privatized. In the next sections we explore how these issues are likely to shape the pension future for working-age women.

Women's employment and wages

Since the 1960s, women's labour force participation has increased among all age groups, but especially among the youngest (Goldin 1990; Farkas and O'Rand 1998) and among married women (US DOL 1999b). Since 1970, US women have increasingly worked in full time full-year jobs (see Table 8.9). Furthermore, the percentage with FT jobs (defined as

Table 8.9 Employment characteristics of women aged 25–54

	Per cent employed FT (35+ hrs/week)	Per cent employed FT for full year	Average weekly hours at work
1969	na	28	34
1979	66	36	34
1989	73	46	36
1998	70	50	36

Note: na = not available
Source: US DOL 1999b

Table 8.10   Median weekly earnings (US$) of persons 25–54, by gender and race/ethnicity, 1987 and 1997 and percentage of white male earnings

Age 25–54 Years	1987	Per cent of white male earnings	1997	Per cent of white male earnings
White women	$290	68	$299	76
White men	$428	100	$393	100
Hispanic women	$232	54	$212	54
Hispanic men	$296	69	$250	64
Black women	$258	60	$249	63
Black men	$320	75	$292	74

Source: adapted from Castro 1998: Table 4

35 hours per week or more) has increased from 66 per cent to 70 per cent and the average number of hours at work per week has increased almost two hours. However, US women are far more likely to have PT jobs than are men (although less commonly than in the other countries considered in this book).

Increased levels of education have improved women's occupational opportunities and women's wages have increased relative to men's (Farkas and O'Rand 1998). Even so, women's earnings have not caught up, compromising women's potential to gain adequate retirement income.

Wage levels of FT workers are structured by both ethnic origin and gender. Table 8.10 shows trends in median weekly earnings of FT employees, expressed in 1997 terms to permit comparison across time. Minority employees earn significantly less than white workers. Hispanic women in 1997 received just 54 per cent and African-American women only 63 per cent of white men's pay. In each race/ethnic category there is also a gender gap in pay, with women earning less than men.

The gender gap in pay narrowed during the 1980s and 90s. In 1983 women earned, on average, two-thirds as much as men; by 1995, women earned, on average, three-quarters of men's earnings (US DOL 1999b). But 'recent increases in the female-to-male earnings ratio have been due more to declines in the earnings of men than to the increases in the earnings of women' (Census Bureau 1997: ix). In real terms, women's earnings have been stagnant since 1990, while men's have dropped over 3 per cent.

Women's wage gains arise partly due to some movement from traditional 'female' occupations into non-traditional jobs. Yet women still earn less than men in 99 per cent of all occupations for which data are available (BLS 1997). In addition, women have lower median earnings than men at all levels of education, despite women's recent wage gains from education. Women's movement into professional jobs brings them higher wages than in clerical and teaching jobs, but still far less than their male counterparts.

Following a pattern evident in most other countries, the US gender gap in pay is related to age. Women's and men's pay is most similar among workers aged under 25, where women earned 92 per cent of men's weekly earnings, compared to just 74 per cent for women aged 25–54 (Castro 1998). The gender gap emerges at precisely the time that most women make family transitions like marriage and childbearing, and then persists for the rest of their working lives.

Women and families

Only 13 per cent of US families fit the male breadwinner–female home-maker model that served as the basis for SS and traditional DB occupa-tional pensions (BLS 1997). Juggling unpaid family responsibilities with paid work has become the norm, with a larger proportion of US women working the 'second shift' (Hochschild 1989) combining paid work with childcare and eldercare, than in other liberal welfare states. Figure 8.1 shows the dramatic increase in labour force participation among married women, compared to women heading single parent households and women living alone. In 1996, 46 per cent of all employees were women and between 1996–2006, women and men are expected to enter the labour force in equal numbers (US DOL 1999b). As Figure 8.1 indicates, in 1969 slightly more than 40 per cent of wives and 20 per cent of women with children under 3 were in the labour force compared to over 70 per cent and 60 per cent respectively in 1998.

In addition to contributions to household income, women perform the bulk of unpaid household work and family caring (Shelton 1992). Among employed adults, women spent 16 hours more per week, on average, in household labour than did men. Employed husbands did barely half the amount of household work (52 per cent) that employed wives did. Children in the household increased men's hours of unpaid work, but women's increased even more (Shelton 1992).

The US has no national childcare policy, creating problems for mothers in paid work, particularly those with preschool-age children. For high income earners, formal care through licensed daycare centres and in-home nannies are options. Over two-thirds of women, however, depend on informal arrangements for childcare, mainly by fathers, grandparents, or siblings. Twenty-eight per cent of working mothers use other sources of childcare, usually unlicensed providers in private homes (BLS 1992).

Figure 8.1 Labour force participation rates for women age 25–54 years by family type, presence of children, and age of children, March of selected years, 1969–98

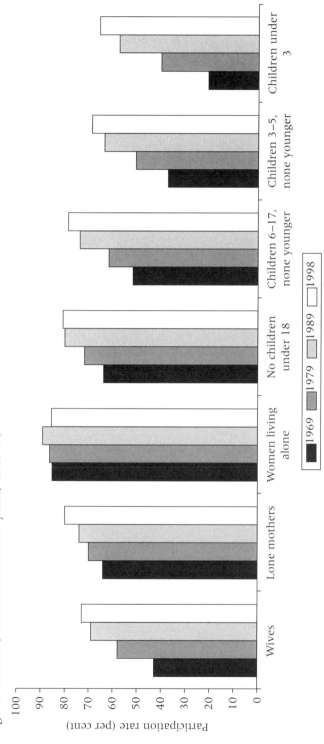

Source: adapted from US DOL 1999b, Charts 3–22 and 3–23

Whether because mothers cannot find affordable quality care for their children, or because they believe they are the single best source of care for young children, many decrease their hours of paid work or leave employment altogether when they have children. As Figure 8.1 shows, female labour force participation rates are systematically related to the presence of children. Women with no children or school-aged children have the highest rates, while women with children under age 6 have the lowest rates. Despite this, over the past 30 years labour force participation rates have increased the most among women with children under the age of 3.

Women are also more likely than men to be caregivers for older adults. Almost three-quarters of all older adult caregivers are wives, daughters, or other female relatives or friends (Stone *et al.* 1987). Approximately 10 per cent of caregiving wives and 44 per cent of caregiving daughters are employed (Stone *et al.* 1987). The strategy of quitting employment to cope with caregiving responsibilities is more likely to occur among women who are older and have lower status jobs (Boyd and Treas 1996). One study finds that mid-life women (aged 53–65) were 75 per cent more likely than men to give two or more hours of care weekly to frail parents. This commitment reduced, on average, mid-life women's paid work by 459 hours each year (worth US$7800 pa), compromising their wages and their ability to earn pension and SS credits (Johnson and Lo Sasso 2000).

As with women in other liberal countries, US women's commitment to unpaid caring and domestic work jeopardizes income security in retirement, given its tight link with paid work. The neo-liberal SS reform agenda could make women's pension outcomes even worse, instituting a regime of social insecurity for older women.

Implementing social insecurity? Proposals for change

Social Security is one of few US social programmes that encompasses collective risk sharing against death of a spouse, disability and low income in old age. Despite reforms that created survivors' benefits, entitlements for divorced spouses and increased the value of benefits, the SS programme has not kept pace with rapid change in US society. Since the male breadwinner model no longer encompasses the life course experiences of most working age adults, some argue that benefits should be more responsive to new family structures, periods of unpaid caring and women's increased employment (Urban Institute 1988; Beedon 1991; Burkhauser and Smeeding 1994; Steuerle and Bakija 1994; Rappaport 1997).

There are other legitimate concerns driving SS reform in another direction. Projections indicate that by 2037, combined payroll taxes and SS

Trust Fund revenues will be insufficient to pay full benefits to retirees (although 75 per cent of benefits could be paid even under the worst economic assumptions). Even moderates agree that the programme should be brought into actuarial balance. But the Advisory Council on Social Security reform, which met from 1994 to 1996, reached no consensus on how best to reform SS; instead it offered three minority positions for reform (see Rix and Williamson 1998 and Advisory Council on Social Security 1997 for more detail). SS supporters advocated maintaining benefits (MB plan) through small increases in payroll contributions or lengthened benefit computation periods, or investing a portion of the SS trust fund (at the agency level) to capture market gains. These steps would preserve the programme's risk-pooling and benefit levels.

Others preferred radical reforms, seizing on SS insolvency 35 years in the future to promote an agenda of public pension cuts in favour of private alternatives. Two partial SS privatization alternatives to the MB plan – Individual Accounts (IAs) and Personal Security Accounts (PSAs) – were consistent with a neo-liberal retrenchment agenda. IAs would divert 1.6 per cent of workers' earnings into individual accounts with limited investment choices and mandatory annuitizing on retirement, raise benefit computation periods to 38 years, and index SS benefits inversely to increases in population longevity. Spousal benefits would be reduced to 33 per cent, and survivor benefits increased modestly (Rix and Williamson 1998). PSAs more radically departed from current SS design. Under PSAs, a flat-rate tier-one benefit, based on 35 years of earnings, would provide about two-thirds of the poverty level income for individuals. A second tier of PSAs would be created by diverting 5 per cent of earnings into individual investment accounts. Spousal benefits would be the highest of their own benefit or half of their retired spouse's in tier one; survivors would receive 75 per cent of the couple benefit and inherit any balance in the PSA (Rix and Williamson 1998).

Since the two partial privatization initiatives pose the biggest potential change for SS, discussion is restricted to these proposals. Diverting SS contributions to market investments may create some pension winners whose return on investment would produce high incomes in retirement. However, changing some or all of SS from a government-guaranteed DB to a privately managed DC plan under IAs or PSAs would greatly reduce collective risk-sharing and undermine predictability of benefits.

Any policy change implies a new set of risks and rewards, but most of those advocating individual accounts ignore effects on women (although see Shirley and Spiegler 1998). Well-educated, financially savvy women employed in high-paid, high-status occupations might do very well under a partially privatized SS programme. Other women might hold their own, breaking even under a new regime. For many women, however, privatization would heighten the risk of financial insecurity in old age for several reasons. This is the same reform agenda, and much the same argument, that the UK followed when SERPS benefits were cut to entice workers to take out personal pensions. As Chapter 4 demonstrates, privatization initiatives create pension losers, especially among women.

- The 'security' in Social Security would disappear, with only a low residual benefit being predictable. Rix and Williamson (1998) note that for low income workers (often women) benefit predictability is a key aspect of retirement planning since assets are low.
- Individual accounts, because there would be no redistribution towards the lower paid, would widen the gender gap in pensions.
- If a percentage of payroll taxes were invested in private accounts for many years, the gender gap between men's and women's benefits would widen, paralleling O'Rand's findings (Chapter 9). This is because women's contribution would be based on lower incomes and more time out of paid work, with less capital for compounding.
- The race gap in pensions would also widen, reflecting the race gap in pay, especially for minority women.
- While SS uses unisex contribution and benefit calculations, reform proposals would not. The conversion of individual savings plans to annuities would mean that for women and men with identical work and savings records, women would receive lower annual benefits due to gender differences in mortality (Rix and Williamson 1998). Gender inequality would be magnified by sex-based annuity rates.
- Under PSAs, plan owners need not purchase annuities and can take a lump sum payment, leaving spouses without any survivor benefits (Rix and Williamson 1998), to the detriment of women.
- Divorced women would be hard hit because sharing would not be required in individual accounts (Williamson 1997).
- Cuts in SS spousal benefits and requirements for more contribution years would penalize women more than men, since most have low or zero contribution periods and because women usually qualify for higher spousal than worker benefits (dually-entitled women) (Baker 1998).
- Women invest more conservatively than do men, so their accumulated fund would be worth less, on average, than men's (Hinz *et al.* 1997) even when contributions were equal.
- Low earners have little capital to spare for high risk investments, and consequently receive poorer returns on average.

SS reform will depend, in part, on the political orientation of a new presidential administration and Congress in 2001, with the Republican platform including SS partial privatization. However, the strong US economy has promoted growth in the SS trust funds, and deficit spending has stopped for the time being, removing the sense of fiscal urgency for reforms. Neo-liberal reformers and their allies in the financial industry have prepared the way for considering SS privatization initatives; however, Democrats are relying on recent swings in the stock market to help persuade the US public that an overreliance on individual investment is not the best path to retirement income security. Few expect the current buoyant market to continue indefinitely (Williamson 1997; Baker 1998).

Conclusion

The interrelationship between low wages, interrupted work histories, and no compensation for women's essential unpaid work means future pension income is likely to be inadequate for many US women. Women and the low paid have the most at stake in maintaining a comprehensive, universal Social Security programme, since SS offers at least partial compensation in every area where they are disadvantaged. As we have discussed in this chapter, different components of the US pension regime have relatively more women-friendly or adverse features. Table 8.11 reviews them. One point that emerges is that private pensions do little to address needs arising from women's typical life course experiences.

No evidence suggests that men and women will soon share equally in the unpaid work that impedes women's choices regarding types and levels of labour force participation. Given this, the women-friendly features of SS could be improved by providing drop-out credits for women who leave work or cut back hours to undertake caring responsibilities; by guaranteeing minimum annual benefits above poverty level; and by mandating SS contribution record sharing when any marriage ends in divorce instead of restricting this to marriages of ten or more years. Improving US women's pension prospects also involves thinking about how private pensions can be improved, since they are realities in liberal welfare states. Women (and all low earners) would benefit if occupational pensions were mandated (as in Australia, see Chapter 11) as private pension coverage would increase. They would be treated more equitably if tax subsidies for private pensions were eliminated (as they were in New Zealand, see Chapter 12) or at least limited to the lowest marginal rate of taxation. Earmarked refundable tax credits, directed to IRAs or DC pension plans, could partially compensate women for years of interrupted or part time work due to caregiving; national childcare and eldercare policies could relieve some of the burden of women's unpaid caring. Meaningful enforcement of equal pay legislation could improve all women's chances of having a surplus to save for retirement.

The narrowing gender gap in pay seems to have plateaued and the gender gap in unpaid work remains. Because private pensions do not

Table 8.11 Women-friendly and adverse features of the US pension regime

Women-friendly features

Social Security
- Nearly universal coverage of workforce
- Fully portable between jobs and across gaps in employment
- 35 'best' years in benefit calculation takes some account of women's interrupted work
- Spousal and survivor benefits ensure lifetime security
- Redistributive benefit formula, benefiting low earners
- Benefits for divorced spouses (married over ten years)
- Indexed against inflation (important given women's longevity)
- Insurance against disability and widowhood early in life

Private Pensions
- DB plans must offer survivor benefit option
- DB plans cannot use sex-differentiated contribution or benefit criteria
- Vested DC plans and IRAs fully portable for job changers

Adverse features

Social Security
- Dually-entitled women gain no benefit from contributions if spousal benefits are higher
- No provision specifically for childcare or eldercare
- No benefit entitlement for divorced individuals married less than ten years

Private Pensions
- Non- or poorly-pensioned women redistribute towards the higher paid through tax subsidies
- Option of early withdrawal from DC plans and IRAs undermines saving for retirement
- No requirement that pensions be split on divorce
- No required indexing against inflation
- Annuitizing DC plans or IRAs creates lower monthly benefits for women
- Survivor benefits insecure under DCs and IRAs

take these realities of women's lives into account, any shift to increased reliance on private pensions, whether through degrading the value of SS benefits or through partial privatization, will intensify the disadvantages many US women face in securing late life income. Such reforms would create better pensions for an elite group of securely employed, high-income women. However, for most working-age women, their income security in later life will continue to depend on a strong public SS programme that recognizes women's undervalued and unpaid contributions to US society. As long as women live longer, earn less, and interrupt their careers more frequently than men, only the political will to redesign pension structures to take account of women's experiences can ensure they will have adequate retirement income.

Notes

1 'Social Security' is the common term for the federal OASDI programme that also includes important social insurance for disability and survivor benefits for working-age spouses and minor children of eligible workers. We restrict our discussion in this chapter to those aspects of the programme affecting older Americans.
2 Supplemental Security Income (SSI) is a federal means-tested programme for aged, blind and permanently disabled people. Most SSI beneficiaries are blind and permanently disabled, hence receive the bulk of SSI funds. SSI information provided in this chapter relates to impoverished individuals aged 65 and older only.

CHAPTER **9**

Perpetuating women's disadvantage: trends in US private pensions, 1976–95

ANGELA M. O'RAND

Cross-national comparisons of wage and income inequality reveal that economic inequality across the life course is highest in the United States and other liberal (occupational) welfare regimes such as the United Kingdom (Smeeding *et al.* 1993; O'Rand and Henretta 1999). The older US population exhibits among the highest levels of economic inequality of all age groups in advanced industrial economies. Moreover, while in most countries inequality among the retired population is less than that among workers, in the US the opposite appears to be true, with mounting evidence that inequality within and between all age groups has increased since the early 1980s (Levy 1998). The US also has among the highest rates of poverty in the general population and among the elderly when compared to other advanced industrialized countries (Smeeding 1997).

Private pensions in the form of employment-based annuities are the primary sources of income and inequality in the retired population. Social Security and employer pension income account for over four-fifths of the median incomes of retired households (Smith 1997), but the shares of retirement income derived from these two sources vary across the income distribution. When moving from the second to ninth decile (each decile represents 10 per cent of the income distribution, with the first decile having the lowest incomes) of retiree household income, Social Security drops from over 80 per cent to 25 per cent of income; meanwhile pensions rise from under 25 per cent at the fourth decile to over 35 per cent in the eighth and ninth deciles. These two primary income sources are derived from employment over the lifetime. Means-tested public welfare for the elderly accounts for over one-third of income in the lowest decile and disappears as an income source above the third decile. Finally, income from other assets and from earnings is restricted to the highest deciles (Clark and Quinn 1999). Publicly-based old age pensions, Medicare, and monetary and in-kind transfers tend to offset inequalities in old age stemming from the workplace, but their levelling effects are modest (Crystal and Shea 1990). Thus, lifetime earnings and related Social Security and private pension benefits create retirement inequality for the majority of an ageing cohort.

Gender is also a major dimension of income inequality in old age and retirement (see Chapter 8). This inequality is reflected in three facts:

- women retire with greater relative dependence on Social Security and means-tested welfare rather than occupational pensions;
- women retiring as dependent spouses (as derived beneficiaries) face the long-term prospect of reduced benefits when their husbands die, since widows and surviving spouses cannot retain couple-level benefits; and
- all older women face relatively higher risks of poverty sometime during old age, especially following the death of a spouse and when reaching the oldest age categories.

The US occupational welfare system provides market-centred income protection in which employment, rather than citizenship, is the basis of access to income and health protection for the general population, contributing to gender stratification. However, workers and their families are not entitled to a universal set of protections. Rather, they have access to an uneven, and unequal, mix of worker benefits, which usually require employee contributions for participation. Depending upon employers' benefit offers, workers can contribute portions of their earnings to different tax sheltered pension plans or pay different premium amounts to participate in health maintenance organizations offering services based on premium levels. The mix of benefits ranges widely for retirement saving and for health insurance, placing considerable responsibility upon individual workers and their families to select plan types and to invest shares of their income (O'Rand 2000).

Since women and men are unevenly distributed across occupations, industries and firms (and across divisions and levels within firms), their access to benefits and their abilities to contribute to them are stratified. Occupational segregation thus influences earnings through the gender wage gap (see Reskin and Hartmann 1986) and through benefits via an employee benefit gap (O'Rand 1986). Even when men and women have access to the same benefits, their unequal capacities to contribute to them based in earnings inequality contribute to a cumulative disadvantage among women over their work careers.

This chapter focuses specifically on two US trends in gender inequality in the level of retirement income derived from non-Social Security sources, that is, from private employee pensions and annuities and from military and governmental employment. First, women's private pension incomes relative to men's have actually declined. Second, women have become more unequal in private pension income among themselves. These patterns might appear to be paradoxical in light of women's increased participation in employment throughout their lives, their generally improved wage and salary ratios relative to men's, and their increased access to pensions in recent years. Yet they are consistent with other long-term trends associated with shifts away from manufacturing and towards service sector employment and changes in the employment relationship reflected in employers' preferences for a flexible, contingent workforce. Since the early 1970s increases in women's labour force participation have coincided with the spread of private pensions in the workplace. However, the change in the mix of pensions has tipped towards more individualized savings and investment accounts (see Chapter 8) at the same time as the long-term employment relationship between workers and employers has declined (Farkas and O'Rand 1998). Individualization and privatization create increased inequality between women and men as well as within these groups (O'Rand and Henretta 1999).

These trends are tracked using original analyses of the US Department of Labor's March Current Population Surveys between 1976 and 1995 that permit comparisons of between- and within-gender private pension income inequalities.

Gender inequality over the life course

While US women have become more integrated in the market economy than ever before, their gains have been modest because the earnings and pension gaps persist (see Chapters 2 and 8). Also by the mid-1990s, working women's participation rates in employee pension plans rose to about half, while men's dropped to this level (Farkas and O'Rand 1998). Yet, two indications of persistent pension inequality remain. First, in 1995 only 26 per cent of women aged 65 and over received income from an occupational pension or annuity, with an average benefit amount of US$6684, while 46 per cent of men in this age group received an average of US$11,460 from a pension or annuity (EBRI 1997); these figures reproduce pre-retirement wage and salary gaps extending over the previous three decades. Second, younger working women participating in pensions did not accumulate pension account levels as high as men's due to lower average lifetime earnings and seemingly more risk-averse pension investments in voluntary, defined contribution or account balance plans offered to them by employers (to be discussed later in this chapter).

Other interdependent changes complicate gender stratification in private pensions even more. First, married women's as opposed to single women's increased labour force rates have been the stronger driving force in the postwar period (Bianchi 1995). We also know that women's employment behaviour is constrained by family roles, especially by variations in gender-specialization among spouses. Traditional gender-specialization following a 'breadwinner model' (see Sainsbury 1996) constrains wives to more part time work with its accompanying lower pay and inferior employee benefits.

Second, according to Francine Blau's (1998) most recent analyses, educational differences between women have produced increased wage inequality among them, especially between those with and without college credentials. The education–wage relationship is mediated by other factors, however, chief among them part time versus full time work (Hakim 1997) and degree of occupational and rank segregation in the jobs women find (Reskin and Hartmann 1986; Bianchi 1995). The more highly educated, full time category of workers has more opportunities to achieve higher relative wage and pension equality along with higher workplace status. On the other hand, part time and less educated workers are constrained to lower quality employment and compensation in sectors where employers prefer shorter work contracts and where few opportunities for promotion or a coherent career are available (Drobnic and Wittig 1997).

Third, educational homogamy – or the tendency for men and women to marry spouses with similar educational credentials and occupational aspirations – exacerbates household inequality in earnings, benefits and wealth (Blau 1998). Married couple households in which both spouses have higher educational attainment have pulled further away from other households with lower educational attainment – a pattern with consequences for inequality in the retirement population where widows and divorcees dominate the poverty categories (Smeeding 1997). In effect, the interweaving of educational, occupational and marital opportunities across women's lives produces a complex set of pathways to late-life inequality with men and with each other.

From wage inequality to pension inequality

Wage inequality translates directly into pension inequality within and between gender groupings. Average pre-retirement earnings and retiree pension benefit ratios between women and men are remarkably similar (O'Rand and Henretta 1999). Differences in earnings over the career produce pension benefit inequality (Lazear and Rosen 1987), but the relative importance of human capital versus structural (labour market) factors is still a matter of some dispute among economists and sociologists. Some studies find that labour market characteristics such as industrial sector and firm size to be as, or more, important than individual-level characteristics in producing pension benefit inequality across gender and race/ethnic groups (see Even and Macpherson 1990 for a review of this issue).

Complicating pension inequality studies is the so-called 'pension mix'. Defined benefit (DB) pensions have dominated major industrial labour markets (manufacturing, finance, and communications) since the mid-twentieth century and still cover most workers who have private pensions, but they are being rapidly replaced in newly expanding sectors by defined contribution (DC) plans. DB plans are collectively organized arrangements that promise a benefit upon retirement defined by earnings levels and years of service. Employers have been the providers of these benefits and liable for them under legislative and regulatory provisions.

DC plans, on the other hand, may or may not include employers' independent contributions to the plans. Instead, they are primarily workers' savings accounts accompanied typically by tax shelters and rules that regulate first, withdrawals prior to retirement age (usually prior to age $59^{1}/_{2}$) and second, short-term loans for specific purposes that must be repaid within a specific time to avoid penalties. These are cash balance accounts that are invested in the bond and equities markets. Many of these new plans are used as supplementary investments by workers already covered by DB plans, but workers in rapidly expanding service and new manufacturing sectors and those newly covered in the past decade are highly likely to have access to DC plans only (Turner and Beller 1992).

An overriding implication of the mix of DB and DC is their stratifying effects on retirement income. Private pensions have always contributed to aged income inequality. DB plans have mainly been offered in jobs that historically excluded women and lower status workers, but now as more workers gain access to DCs, either as supplementary or as primary retirement accounts, the pattern of inequality is changing. Two countervailing trends are emerging. The first is an increase in aged (as well as non-aged) income inequality (Smeeding *et al.* 1993). The continued unequal availability of private pensions and the dependence of DC plan accumulation on individual choice and risk-taking introduce even more variability and increase inequality. The second is the spread of flexible and individualized savings strategies has introduced a potential new source of leveling in retirement income inequality.

In short, pensions readily stratify the worker and retiree populations, permitting the examination of the patterns and implications of pay and pension inequalities for subsequent retirement income distributions. Private pensions (like wages) are direct links between the workplace and retirement economic status.

For these reasons, private pension income is the primary focus of this study. This restriction presents only a partial (and conservative) picture of inequality, since it focuses only on workers retiring with private pension income. Only slightly over half of all workers since the early 1970s have been covered by private pensions. Today about 49 per cent of women and 51 per cent of men in the workforce have private pension coverage – reflecting a 10 per cent increase for women and a 7 per cent decrease for men since 1980. Many of these workers are likely to retire early as a result of pension eligibility schedules (in the DB case) and higher pension wealth (in both the DB and DC cases), but the dynamics of heterogeneity and inequality within pension recipient groups deserves study in its own right.

The persistent gender pension gap

This chapter tracks inequality among those aged 50 to 64 who were receiving private pension income, by analysing data from matched Current Population Surveys from 1976 to 1995. In each year, income information was available for over 50,000 individuals. This period was riven by economic cycles, economic restructuring and changing labour participation patterns (see Chapter 2). Studying this age-range of retirees purposely restricts this analysis of inequality by omitting the oldest age groups to gain a view of the so-called 'early retirement' populations of the past two decades. Men and women have been retiring early – that is, prior to institutionalized ages of full-benefit social retirement (65) – over this period, although some downturn in this trend in the mid-1990s has been observed for both groups (O'Rand and Henretta 1999). The income resources with which they enter retirement condition their subsequent trajectories in old age.

Figure 9.1 displays median private pension income by gender between 1976 and 1994 and shows a steady widening of gender inequality. In the earlier period (early to mid-1970s), when a smaller segment of the population between these ages (men and women alike) received private pension income (less than 20 per cent overall), there appears to be more equality among pension recipients. We know from past research that in the 1970s these early-retiring women came overwhelmingly from traditional female professions such as teaching, government employment (especially social work and public administration), and health (especially nursing), where earnings were not as high as men's but where benefit packages were available (and better than for women in other sectors).

When this distribution is weighted by age (see Figure 9.2) women's median private pension income was about 72 per cent of men's in 1976,

Figure 9.1 Median private pension income by sex and year among 50–64-year-olds

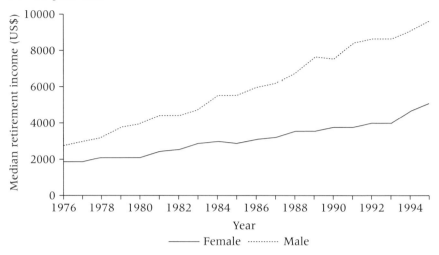

Notes: Lines represent the means of age-group-specific median retirement income. Means are weighted by age-group sizes. Data come from the March Current Population Surveys of the US Bureau of the Census and are based on respondents' reports of income from their own employment-based pensions from private and/or government employment excluding Social Security.
Source: US March Current Population Survey Data

Figure 9.2 Ratio of female to male median private pension income across time among 50–64-year-olds

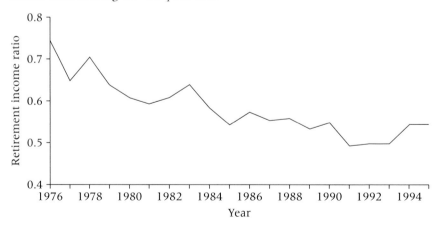

Notes: Line represents the mean of age-group specific median retirement incomes. Means are weighted by age-group size.
Source: US March Current Population Surveys as described in Figure 9.1

declining to just 55 per cent of men's in 1997. In effect, there has been a 24 per cent decline in income equality among women and men receiving private pensions in the age range 50–64. In short, the private pension gender gap in the 50–64 age group, when measured as age-weighted median female/male pension income ratios, has increased rather than decreased among early retirees.

Pension inequality among women: above and below the median

The next question that presents itself is whether this gap is consistent across income classes of women and men. To explore this issue, the annual age-weighted income distributions of women and men across income deciles are compared. Figure 9.3 reports ratios of female to male private pension incomes by income decile cutpoints (the dollar amounts that demarcate succeeding deciles) for selected years between 1976 and 1995 for the 50–64 age range. Weekly wage distributions of women and men are also compared at the decile cutpoint levels for full time and part time workers.

The solid lines represent the wage-cutpoint ratio distributions over time for men and women aged 50 to 64 receiving salaries and wages. A rising and flattening pattern is revealed between 1976 and 1995. By 1995 for this age group the gender wage ratio is relatively constant across deciles at 0.5. Trends are, first of all, persistent average wage inequality between women and men across the distribution and second, greater relative increases in gender equality at the lower deciles than at the upper deciles.

The changes in the pension income are somewhat more complex. In 1976, pension income across the distribution when compared to wages was relatively more equal, but with higher relative equality above the median (fifth decile). Between 1976 and 1995, pension parity maintains a median of approximately 0.4, but patterns above and below the median diverge. The highest two deciles achieve a female/male ratio of 0.6 between 1981 and 1986 and increase slightly more in 1995. Below the median, inequality increases after 1986, falling to 0.3 or below for the second, third and fourth deciles in 1995.

Overall, uneven patterns of levelling, constant inequality, and divergence in inequality between men and women are apparent. A *levelling process* is observable in the rising and flattening wage ratio and in the higher pension income deciles where female to male pension ratios increase. The persistent median wage inequality reveals *status maintenance* as the dominant between-gender pattern in wages (a pattern for this age group found repeatedly across studies; e.g. Blau 1998), but, among women at

Figure 9.3 Ratios of female to male weekly wage and retirement pension incomes (excluding Social Security) by income deciles, 1976–95 (ages 50–64)

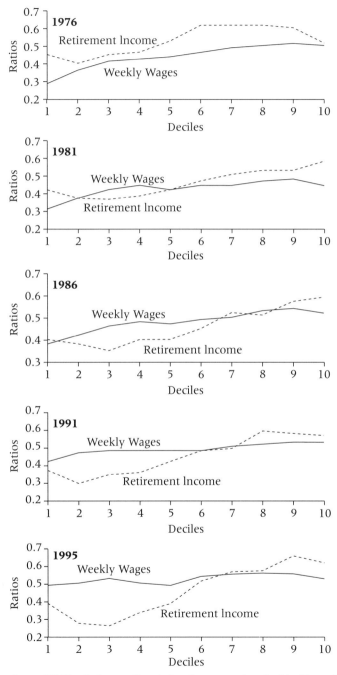

Source: US March Current Population Surveys as described in Figure 9.1

and below the median pension income ratio (decile 5) relative to their higher income counterparts, a *divergence* in fortunes is evident.

It is important to note that the women in this analysis were relatively privileged, in that they were currently collecting income from their own private pension accounts. The conditions under which women gained private pensions cannot be determined by this analysis. Nevertheless, we can assume that this category of women is very diverse. Some are career women from more privileged labour market sectors. Some are lifetime workers, but with mixed careers encompassing part time and full time work and interruptions of labour supply. Some are women with access to and participation in pensions arriving late in their careers or restricted to only a portion of their total careers. These and other possibilities define the basis of heterogeneity among women's private pension incomes.

The increased gender inequality between the upper and lower deciles is remarkable. The highest deciles may be the easiest to classify – they are career women in labour markets with strong earnings-benefits packages that include the public sector and the rapidly growing non-manufacturing sectors (excluding low-end services) that reward higher levels of education and sustained tenure. At the lowest deciles are women in occupationally segregated jobs in smaller firms and in low-end service sectors. Also in this group are women with limited participation in plans due to some mix of labour market segmentation, discrimination, and interrupted or truncated lifetime labour participation. In short, inequality is highest at the lower margins of private pension income.

Growing inequality among women

The apparent variability in women's private pension incomes over the distribution invites an analysis of the differences in the dispersions of pension incomes between men and women and among women over time. These analyses use the Theil index, summarized in the Appendix to this chapter, which measures income dispersion and permits decomposition and between- and within-group comparisons. Table 9.1 and Figure 9.4 report global Theil coefficients by gender between 1976 and 1995. The average coefficients for women are always higher than those for men, and they increase steadily relative to men's across the period. Until about 1984, men's and women's patterns of private pension income dispersion appear to be influenced similarly by cyclical changes. However, after 1986, women's within-group inequality increases and diverges from earlier patterns.

Table 9.1 reports the decomposition of the Theil coefficients that indexes relative within- and between-group inequalities. The results reveal the overwhelming importance of within-group dispersion over the period

Table 9.1   Decomposition of annual private pension inequality among US women and men aged 50–64, 1976–95

Year	Male Theil	Female Theil	All Theil	Between M and F	Within M and F
76	0.321	0.377	0.358	0.025	0.332
77	0.315	0.391	0.353	0.022	0.331
78	0.31	0.378	0.351	0.026	0.324
79	0.351	0.442	0.409	0.043	0.366
80	0.326	0.491	0.4	0.042	0.359
81	0.301	0.404	0.355	0.035	0.321
82	0.368	0.471	0.42	0.034	0.387
83	0.356	0.432	0.4	0.028	0.372
84	0.308	0.412	0.369	0.04	0.329
85	0.319	0.456	0.391	0.043	0.347
86	0.316	0.431	0.381	0.04	0.341
87	0.311	0.45	0.374	0.031	0.343
88	0.332	0.465	0.395	0.034	0.36
89	0.307	0.464	0.366	0.033	0.333
90	0.312	0.459	0.369	0.031	0.338
91	0.296	0.412	0.351	0.033	0.318
92	0.272	0.419	0.326	0.028	0.298
93	0.3	0.41	0.351	0.032	0.319
94	0.298	0.45	0.351	0.023	0.328
95	0.281	0.478	0.347	0.028	0.319

Source: US March Current Population Surveys as described in Figure 9.1

that remains relatively stable (refer to columns 3–5 in the table). When Theils that are calculated separately for women and men are compared (in columns 1 and 2) interesting differences are clear. First, while men's average dispersion decreases over the period by 12 per cent (from 0.321 in 1976 to 0.281 in 1995), women's increases by 27 per cent (from 0.377 to 0.478). Accordingly, greater relative inequality among women is substantiated by the decomposition. Also, the overwhelming share of inequality across the board is accounted for by women's inequality that is growing while men's is decreasing.

Possible compositional and structural sources of these trends

Why is pension inequality growing? It appears paradoxical that after five decades of increasing labour participation among women and more

Figure 9.4   Theil coefficients of private pension income by gender,
1976–95

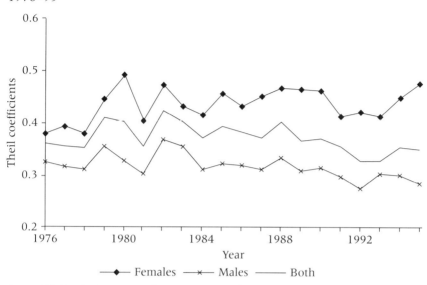

Year

━◆━ Females   ━×━ Males   ━━━ Both

Source: US March Current Population Surveys as described in Figure 9.1

recent trends towards increased wage equality for women across the age
span that private pension inequality should increase. Age-specific trends
in wage inequality provide part of the answer. The highest relative wage
increases have favoured the youngest workers in the past two decades
(see Blau 1998). The wage ratios of women on average have reached
about 0.74, with the highest ratios among youngest workers above 0.9
and those of women aged 50 and at around 0.5. To the extent that
wages and pension benefits are positively correlated, the resilience or
growth in pension inequality may be cohort-based. Younger women
who start at higher relative wages and remain in the labour force throughout their careers may, in fact, retire with more equal private pension
incomes in the coming decades.

However, another explanation presents itself. The mix of pension types
and their differential availability to men and women probably produces
inequality in private pension income. Lower pension income can result from the unavailability or inconsistent availability of plans to some
workers *or* from highly varying levels of pension saving based on income, worker choice and risk-taking. In the latter case, private pension
income is strongly influenced by the *type* of pension offered. As mentioned earlier in this chapter, two types of plans are available: defined
benefit (DB) and defined contribution (DC) plans, the latter shifting
responsibility from employer to worker.

Figure 9.5 Distributions of defined benefit and defined contribution pension plans, 1975–94

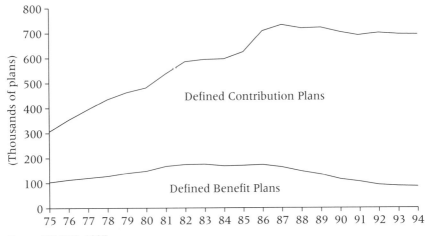

Source: US DOL 1997

These new DC plans have come to dominate the private pension landscape over the past 15 years. Figure 9.5 shows the relative growth of these plans from 1975 (following the passage of Employee Retirement Income Security Act which stimulated their development) until 1994. The ratio of DC to DB plans has grown from 2:1 in 1975 to over 6:1 in 1993. In addition, DC plans are relatively more dominant in female-concentrated industries (see O'Rand and Henretta 1999). Nearly half of all DC plans today are offered in the service industry sectors where women are highly concentrated.

Those sectors with lower proportions of DC plans – mining, manu-facturing, communications and utilities – have lower concentrations of women (O'Rand and Henretta 1999). Yet sectors offering higher propor-tions of the DC plans have relatively lower rates of female participation in them. Actual participation rates reveal that women are often disin-clined to accept these offers. In the services sector – where 48 per cent of all DC plans are available – less than one-third of workers (including women) have access and less than one-fifth actually participate. In nearly all sectors, there are large gaps between availablity and participation rates. Lower wage workers are far less likely to take these opportunities.

In addition, when women do participate in a DC plan, they contribute less and avoid high risk (stock versus bond) accounts (Gordon *et al.* 1997). The risk-aversion factor is now the subject of much research in the US, especially given the dramatic market environment of the 1990s (O'Rand 2000). We know very little about investment behaviour – the distinction between gambling and rational choice in investments is blurred at best. The gender component may be critical, since women's and men's traditional roles and obligations from childhood on have separated their experiences and delimited their aspirations and expectations about the future. The move towards increasingly privatized and individualized pension savings promises to be amplified by differences in gender experiences in the labour market, with certainty in the short run that women are relatively more focused on family security and less advantaged as primary breadwinners. However, in the long run, it remains unclear whether gender differences will be superseded by class differences, since men are also being affected by a changing global economy that has torn down the protective institutions such as labour unions and internal labour markets that once afforded men some confidence in predicting career options. For the time being, however, women's dispersed market experiences yield more uneven and unequal private pension saving then men's.

Conclusions

Gender inequality over the life course in the US is influenced by the employment participation patterns of women and men that have consequences for economic status in retirement. Labour force participation, earnings trajectories, pension participation patterns, and pension type all contribute to gender inequality in retirement. Recent increases in private pension income inequality may be only temporary products of women's more recent sustained attachments to the workplace and access to pensions, but structural transformation in employment relationships, evident in changing pension types, suggest otherwise. Long-term labour market changes raise questions about the future of income security in retirement for the twenty-first century in liberal welfare states dominated by market institutions.

The new defined contribution (DC) pensions available to workers require less of employers and more of workers. These individualized plans are even more dependent on current wages than the traditional defined benefit plans. The latter were components of an 'employment contract' in the workplace predicated on a long-term relationship between worker and employer in which the worker received retirement benefits heavily determined by tenure. Defined benefit (DB) plans base benefits on the highest earnings years weighted by service to the employer. DC plans, which are more portable than DB plans and permit greater mobility across employers, are based primarily on workers' voluntary salary reductions and portfolio choices.

The individualization of pension saving through these new plans is probably captured in women's experiences today. In the near future however, 'baby boom' cohorts – including women and men alike – may reflect stronger differences among population groups than gender alone can represent. Individualized and voluntary pension saving presents challenges to all workers with stagnating or declining wages in globalized economies (Levy 1998).

The changing employment contract is affecting men and women alike. Economic restructuring reflected in downsizing and the growth of 'nonstandard' employment (including part time, contingent and contract work) has led to worker displacement across all occupational groups – including the college educated and the older worker. Still, persistent gender stratification that influences wage inequality bears upon the long-term prospects for pension inequality – especially in the face of increased day-to-day responsibility by workers themselves to save for their retirements. Since women earn less and live longer than men, their prospects for lower pension income and higher risks of poverty in old age – particularly old-old age – promise to persist into the twenty-first century.

Now the privatized pension options represented by DC plans are being proposed as models for public pension reform in the United States and elsewhere. Serious proposals to convert some or all of the US Social Security system into cash balance accounts following the DC model are matters of regular discussion. Since the Social Security system can be fairly characterized today as a safety-net and residual system of public transfer, its status in a new era of semi-privatized public transfers forecasts significant disadvantage among marginal workers and their families that cross gender lines. Women's current patterns of pension inequality may be harbingers of stronger forces of inequality in future ageing populations.

Appendix

The data for these analyses are from the US Department of Labor's matched March Current Population Surveys (CPS) from 1976 to 1995. In each CPS data set, there are approximately 50,000–100,000 individuals. From these we excluded persons who were not age 50–64. Further, we only included persons who were collecting private pension income based on their own employment (and excluding Social Security). We aggregated these private pension recipients over several levels of observations across years of observation:

- yearly by gender of recipient to calculate indices of inequality and plot general between- and within-group trends in inequality; and
- yearly by income deciles within gender groups to calculate gender-decile income ratios.

The dependent variable (private pension income) is drawn from the Current Population Survey's measure of income from retirement funds from a previous employer or union, defined specifically as any money from private pensions or annuities, military retirement, and other federal, state or local government employee pensions other than Social Security.

Aggregate inequality of private pension income is indexed with the Theil coefficient, which is a measure of dispersion divided by the mean (Wolfson 1997). The coefficient can be decomposed into a between-groups and a within-group component. The first component is the value of the Theil obtained if everyone in each group received the mean income of the group. The second component is a weighted average of within-group Theil values. Other measures of inequality (e.g. the Gini coefficient) are not as conveniently decomposed as the Theil (Wolfson 1997).

Private pension inequality is also measured as female/male income ratios at two levels: first median annual female/male pension income ratios are calculated and then the retirement income distributions of these two groups are compared by taking the female/male decile cutpoint ratios. The latter approach is taken to capture variations in inequality across the income distribution (or across income classes).

CHAPTER **10**

Creeping selectivity in Canadian women's pensions

DEBRA STREET AND INGRID CONNIDIS

By comparison with many other countries, the Canadian public pension system is a success (Myles 2000). The proportion of Canadian seniors with incomes less than 50 per cent of the median is among the lowest in the OECD (Hauser 1997). This is an unusual outcome for a liberal welfare state which seeks to balance the rights of citizenship with the principle of equity (i.e., return on earnings-linked contributions). The maturation of Canada's old age security system has reduced the number of older Canadians living on low incomes dramatically, and with relatively low levels of public expenditure by international standards (OECD 1997). Even taking Canada's rapidly ageing population into account, future levels of public expenditure are expected to remain modest (Myles 2000). Few public pension systems can claim to be both relatively cheap and comparatively effective at providing income security for older citizens.

Not all Canadian seniors, however, share equally in the Canadian pension system's success and recent changes may undermine the momentum of this success. Thirty-four per cent of Canadians aged 65 and older in 1980 had incomes below the Statistics Canada low-income cut off (LICO, 56 per cent of median income); by 1996 only 21 per cent did (Myles 2000). Poverty was highly concentrated, however, among 'unattached' – never married, divorced, widowed – older women, 53 per cent of whom had incomes below the LICO level (Statistics Canada 1999a). Low rates of labour force participation among the current generation of older Canadian women mean that few of them have private pension income in old age, a key to retirement income adequacy in a liberal welfare state. Women's roles in Canadian society have changed profoundly since the 1950s, when today's youngest retired women were young adults. Canadian working-age women are now more likely than ever to be engaged in paid work. Will these women also be less likely than current older women to experience poverty in old age?

Canada's contemporary mixed-welfare pension regime is a complicated system of public and private sector pensions, with eligibility rules and beneficiaries differing across its components. Modest pension retrenchment over the past two decades has undermined the universality of Canadian public pension benefits and enhanced private ones (Street 1996). In this chapter, we detail how this complex pension regime structures current pensioners' retirement income. We focus on the ways women's changing labour force experiences, unpaid domestic work, and the pension regime interact to condition their future pension prospects. Finally, we consider how recent pension reforms are likely to affect contemporary working women's pension acquisition.

Canada's pension regime

Canada's three-tiered system (Battle 1997) is outlined in Table 10.1. The first tier includes federal and provincial benefits, primarily Old Age Security (OAS), Guaranteed Income Supplement (GIS), and Spouse's Allowance (SA, for low income spouses aged 60–64 of retirees). Entitlement is based on age (OAS), or a combination of age and need (GIS and SA). The second tier Canada/Quebec Pension Plan (C/QPP) social insurance programme is based on earnings and contribution years, covering all paid workers and their dependants. Pay-As-You-Go (PAYG) financing dominates Canadian public pensions, although C/QPP reserves will increase from two to five years under the new C/QPP contribution schedule (discussed below). The third tier is private, based on registered pension plans (RPPs) and individual Registered Retirement Savings Plans (RRSPs).

The public component of the Canadian pension regime reflects tensions between the values of individualism with entitlements based on contributions (often termed equity) versus collective social provision and the rights of citizenship (emphasizing equality) (Myles 1989; Clark 1993). On one hand, C/QPP emphasizes individualism in providing benefits based on earnings-linked contributions. On the other, a collective orientation is embedded in general welfare entitlement (OAS, GIS, SA) to adequate income in old age. Current regulations governing the public programmes are gender neutral in principle; however, in practice, women's and men's different life course experiences contribute to gendered outcomes in public pensions. Indeed, one might argue that this was an intended consequence of legislation initially enacted at a time when men so clearly dominated the labour force and politics (for a related example, see Snell 1993).

In common with other liberal welfare states, income adequacy among older Canadians depends on receiving private pension income. Canada's

Table 10.1 Canadian pension regime

Public Pensions: OAS, GIS, C/QPP	
Per cent receiving	Nearly universal (OAS), 47% of women and 34% of men (GIS), 64% of women and 86% of men (C/QPP)
Eligibility	Age + residence (OAS)
	Age + low income (GIS/SA)
	Age + contributions (C/QPP)
Financing	General revenues (OAS/GIS/SA)
	Employer/employee contributions(C/QPP)
Pension function	Social inclusion (OAS/GIS/SA)
	Earnings replacement (C/QPP)
Private Pensions: RPP, RRSP	
Per cent receiving	28% of women and 53% of men (RPP), less than 50% (RRSP)
Eligibility	Employees in firms with plans (RPP)
	Surplus earnings to save (RRSP)
Financing	Contributions and tax subsidies
Pension function	Earnings replacement (RPP), individual provision (RRSP)

expensive, tax-subsidized private pensions (RPP, RRSP) reflect the principles of individualism, best serving the securely-employed and high-income earners. Predictably, the criteria that produce generous private pension incomes are more likely to be met by men because they are based on male employment patterns from which women's life course experiences deviate. Each component of the pension regime has implications for the income security of older Canadian women.

Public pension programmes

Old Age Security
Old Age Security (OAS) is the cornerstone of retirement income security for Canadians. Implemented in 1951, OAS started as a universal citizen's pension, delivering flat-rate benefits to (legal) Canadian residents aged 65 and older, independent of labour force participation or contributions. Eligibility is based on residence for at least ten years, with a one-fortieth benefit reduction for each year in Canada less than 40 after the age of 18. OAS is a taxable pension paid out of general revenues. Since implementation, some OAS reforms have enhanced benefits by lowering the age of eligibility from 70 to 65 (1965) and indexing fully against inflation (1972).

More recent reforms, however, have retrenched the OAS pension. In 1989, a special surtax clawed back OAS benefits from Canadian seniors with individual annual incomes over C$50,000 with the entire benefit taxed back from individuals with incomes over C$76,333 (Battle 1997). Initially, the appearance of OAS universality was maintained by sending monthly cheques to *all* eligible Canadians. By 1996, the pretence of universality was abandoned when a 'clawforward' tactic used the previous year's taxable income as the basis to eliminate the pro forma delivery of OAS pensions to high-income earners (Battle 1997). Because the ceiling for full OAS benefits is not fully adjusted for inflation, projections for 2000 were that 'the clawback will have lowered its bite to pensioners with incomes above an estimated C$41,400 [1989 dollars] and those with incomes above C$61,886 will receive no OAS' (Battle 1997: 532). Between 1981 and 1993, the proportion of all OAS benefits that were partial increased from 0.8 to 5 per cent (CCSD 1996; NCW 1999).

Still, the vast majority of older Canadians receive the now 'nearly universal' OAS citizen's pension, which has been particularly important for older Canadian women's income security. Because OAS is paid to each individual, independent of family status or work history, it tends to level the gender playing field. For a woman whose dominant activity has been homemaking or caring and/or whose labour force participation was insufficient to establish meaningful earnings-related pensions, OAS represents a secure claim to income for most women in their own right. However, OAS (at C$97 per week) is insufficient on its own to prevent poverty.

Guaranteed Income Supplement (GIS) and Spouse's Allowance (SA)
The GIS was established in 1967, with episodic improvements to the value of the benefit since. Intended as a stop-gap anti-poverty measure, policymakers expected to phase GIS out once C/QPP matured and most working Canadians qualified for benefits under that programme. GIS is an income-tested programme for low-income senior Canadians, with non-taxable benefits based on total income for non-married individuals and combined income for married couples. No assets test is involved. Except for individuals with residence-reduced OAS, all Canadian residents 65 and older are entitled to public pensions that at least equal full OAS plus maximum GIS. This, in effect, is a guaranteed minimum income from the combined OAS/GIS (Myles 2000), worth C$212 per week in 1999 for a non-married older person.

Maturation of C/QPP (see next section) has reduced the average level of GIS benefits (since more individuals now receive higher C/QPP benefits based on longer contribution periods), but has not eliminated the need for it. In 1999, 37 per cent of all Canadians over age 65 had incomes from other sources so low that they received at least partial GIS benefits. The highest monthly GIS benefit for single persons was C$492 in 1999, compared with C$320 for each spouse in couples. Individual

GIS benefits are reduced by $1 for each $2 in monthly income, and for couples by $1 for every $4 combined income, over the OAS/GIS threshold.

Spouse's Allowance (SA) benefits, established in 1985, are paid to low-income 60–64-year-old spouses (married or common-law) of an old age pensioner who qualifies for GIS, or to widow(er)s whose incomes fall below the threshold. Same-sex unions are excluded. Because single and divorced individuals and those married to someone under 65 are not entitled to the SA, it was challenged under the equality clauses of the *Canadian Charter of Rights and Freedoms* (Townson 1995). The Court ruled that, in principle, this discriminates against some women, but only the legislature could extend benefits to them because of the cost involved (*Globe and Mail* 1999).

In 1993, 47 per cent of women and 34 per cent of men aged 65 and over received GIS. Two-thirds of GIS recipients were women; 48 per cent were non-married and 17 per cent were married women (CCSD 1996). The SA benefit is also received overwhelmingly by women.

Canada/Quebec Pension Plan (C/QPP)
Implemented in 1967, earnings-linked C/QPP (together with GIS) was the government response to concern about high poverty levels among Canadian retirees and the realization that occupational pensions were unlikely to cover more than a small fraction of Canadian workers. The C/QPP programme has been amended several times since, with the last round of reforms occurring in 1998. Those reforms were mainly concerned with containing costs; no benefit improvements were enacted and contribution rates were substantially increased (NCW 1999).

C/QPP pensions cover all employed Canadians over 18 with contributions made on earnings between C$3500 (the year's basic exemption, formerly set at 10 per cent of the average wage, but fixed in 1998) and C$36,900 (indexed annually to be equivalent with the average wage). The upper earnings limit for C/QPP contributions means that a larger proportion of women's than men's earnings are deducted because women's earnings are lower. Contributions are shared equally between employer and employee, rising from 5.85 per cent in 1997 to a 'steady-state' 9.9 per cent in 2004. This is meant to forestall larger contribution rate increases in the future and to expand C/QPP reserves from two to five years in preparation for baby boom retirements, starting around 2013. The extra reserves will be invested in financial markets (NCW 1999).

C/QPP retirement benefits replace approximately 25 per cent of an individual's adjusted lifetime earnings. Benefit calculation is complicated, based on credited lifetime earnings between age 18 and 70, with adjustments made on the last five years of pensionable earnings to align the benefit with previous earnings. Individuals can exclude up to 15 per cent (approximately seven years) of lowest earnings (because of unemployment, further education, or below average earnings) as well as periods spent caring for children under 7 from C/QPP benefit calculation. These exclusions help women preserve future pension benefits when they undertake family responsibilities or seek further education. Complete C/QPP portability and immediate vesting are also important to women, given their typically interrupted work histories.

Other C/QPP features help women maintain financial independence. Inflation-indexed pension benefits at age 65 (available earlier with reduced benefits, or later with increased amounts) preserve purchasing power for Canadian women, who live on average nearly six years longer than men. Almost 80 per cent of survivor's benefits (60 per cent of the deceased partner's pension if the survivor is 65 or older) are claimed by women. The combination of a survivor benefit and worker benefit (for women with earnings periods) cannot exceed the maximum C/QPP benefit (C\$763 in 2000), but can continue after remarriage. A one-time death benefit also goes mainly to women. The death benefit, now capped at a maximum of C\$2500 compared to \$3580 until 1998, is a recent benefit cut that hurts widowed women (Zimmerman 1998).

Since 1987, C/QPP credit sharing is required in the event of divorce (unless superseded by provincial law). Common-law spouses (male–female couples in conjugal relationships for at least 12 months) whose relationships end also split C/QPP credits, if application is made within four years of separation. All C/QPP credits acquired during the relationship are added and split equally between the former partners, since CPP recognizes that 'both spouses contributed equally to the well-being of the family, even if one of the spouses was not in the paid labour force' (HRDC 1999).

Spouses in continuing marriages or common-law relationships may share C/QPP pensions when they retire. If both partners are over age 60 (minimum age to receive C/QPP pensions), the C/QPP pension or pensions both have earned can be added together, then shared equally. In couples who choose this option, women gain C/QPP pensions equivalent to their husband's, receiving income in their own name, even if they had no or low pay prior to retirement (Townson 1995).

A number of C/QPP programme features help women maintain a claim to autonomous income in old age, modifying the earnings link. Few such features are included in private pension arrangements.

Private pensions

Occupational Pensions (RPPs)
Some Canadians participate in occupationally-based Registered Pension Plans (RPPs). Most are defined benefit (DB) plans based on final or

average wages and length of service. Contributions from employers and employees represent a deferred wage and employers are responsible for paying pensions. RPP contributions and earnings accumulate tax-free, attracting generous tax subsidies, although pensions are taxed when received.

RPP coverage is connected with high earnings, long job tenure, union-ized workplaces, large organizations and full-year, full time (FYFT) employment, all more common among men than women (Frenken and Maser 1992; OECD 1995). However, Canadian working-age women are now nearly as likely as men to be covered by RPPs, but overall coverage has declined from 48 per cent of all paid workers in 1978 to 41 per cent in 1997. By the 1990s, the traditional gender gap between employed men's and women's RPP coverage rates had closed substantially, more due to declining men's coverage than by striking increases in women's coverage. Between 1978 and 1997, employed women's coverage increased from 38 to 40 per cent, while men's declined from 54 to 42 per cent (Statistics Canada 1999b, 1999c).

Women's movement into higher-paying jobs over the past 15 years has improved their RPP coverage, although more among prime-aged (35–54) than young (25–34) women (Morissette and Drolet 1999). RPP coverage for prime-aged men remained steady, but young men's declined substantially. This decline occurred at the same time as young men's real earnings also declined (Morissette 1997). These trends may spell bad news for young men, to the extent that their retirement income is affected, and good news for midlife women, if their transition into better-paid occupations is permanent (Morissette and Drolet 1999).

Canadian RPP coverage varies systematically by income and job type. Data from the Survey of Ageing and Independence (1991) show that just 24 per cent of 45–64-year-olds with annual incomes under C$20,000 were covered by RPPs, compared to 81 per cent with incomes between C$40,000 and C$59,999 (Crompton 1993). RPPs are twice as likely to be offered in manufacturing jobs as in consumer service jobs (Morissette and Drolet 1999) where low-skill, low-pay jobs predominate. Thus, women's low earnings and predominance in service sector jobs reduce their pension coverage.

Regulations enacted in the 1980s and 1990s attempted to improve RPPs by addressing problems of coverage, portability and vesting. Coverage was mandated for regular part time (PT) workers, with potentially beneficial effects for women. However, some employers may have abandoned existing plans to avoid covering PT workers (NCW 1989: 42). Vesting (the time that must elapse before a covered worker is eligible to receive benefits) was changed from employers' discretion (often ten years) to from two to five years. Improving portability (transferring vested RPPs to a new firm upon job change) has proved difficult because of the structure of most Canadian RPPs. Just as these modest improvements were made to workers' rights to RPPs, however, coverage patterns changed.

Overall, RPP coverage peaked by the early 1980s (OECD 1995) and has declined since, mainly due to structural changes in the economy (Morissette and Drolet 1999). Decreased levels of unionization in Canada, shifts in job growth from manufacturing to service sector jobs, increased employment in small firms, as well as legislation making RPPs more complicated and expensive for employers, contributed to the decline. At the same time, maximum tax-free contribution limits for individual retirement savings were quadrupled, making them much more attractive.

Registered Retirement Savings Plans (RRSPs)
RRSPs are Canada's version of individual retirement savings accounts. When offered by employers, RRSPs are defined contribution (DC) plans to which employers and employees contribute a percentage of the workers' wages. Individuals (those without RPPs, or with annual RPP contributions under maximum allowable amounts) and the self-employed can also shelter current earnings from income taxation by contributing to an RRSP.

RRSPs expand workers' pension choices and overcome vesting and portability problems built into RPPs, although at the cost of individualizing risk. Stemming as they do from contributions into individual accounts, RRSPs offer immediately vested, fully portable pension savings, theoretically available to all wage-earning Canadians. In 1997, for the first time, contributions to RRSPs outstripped – in both number of contributors and value of annual contributions – those for RPPs (Statistics Canada 1999d). Approximately 36 per cent of eligible Canadians contributed in 1997.

RRSP participation has risen since they were introduced in 1957, with marked increases coinciding with periodic increases in contribution ceilings. RRSP contribution limits were raised substantially in 1991, to encourage greater participation and decrease future reliance on public pensions (Street 1996). Individuals can make tax-free RRSP contributions up to a ceiling (C$13,500 in 1997) or 18 per cent of earned income, whichever is lower. Withdrawals at any time are taxed, although presumably at a lower rate after retirement than individuals would experience were they still employed. Between 1991 and 1997, 25 per cent of taxfilers (individuals with income high enough to require filing a tax return) aged 25 to 64 made annual contributions to RRSPs, while 40 per cent made no contributions at all (Statistics Canada 1999d; Akyeampong 2000).

Like RPP coverage, participation in RRSPs varies in systematic ways. Men's RRSP contribution rates have consistently exceeded women's (Weitz 1992; Akyeampong 2000). For example, in 1997, two-fifths of

Table 10.2 Average annual RRSP contribution (C$) by gender and income, 1997

		Average annual contribution
Gender	Men	4515
	Women	3196
Income	Less than $10,000	1101
	$10,000–19,999	1758
	$20,000–29,999	2366
	$30,000–39,999	3164
	$40,000–59,999	4255
	$60,000–79,999	5906
	$80,000 or more	9572
Average	all taxfilers	3936

Source: adapted from Akyeampong 2000: 5

eligible men compared to one-third of eligible women contributed. Further, the value of men's contributions is 30 per cent higher than women's, in line with their higher average earnings (Akyeampong 2000). RRSP participation rates and contribution value increase with income (see Table 10.2) and until age 55. This reflects early labour market exit, shortening time horizons for retirement planning and higher average incomes among mid-life workers (Akyeampong 2000).

More high-income than low-income Canadians contribute to RRSPs. In 1997, only one in 20 with annual incomes under C$10,000 contributed to RRSPs, while 18 out of 20 with incomes over C$80,000 did. When high-income earners make contributions, the amounts are substantially higher (Weitz 1992; Akyeampong 2000; see also Table 10.2). The tax expenditures that subsidize private sector pensions have distributional implications, since tax allowances against income or capital can only benefit individuals with sufficient income or capital to invest in RPPs or RRSPs in the first place (Myles and Street 1995). The distributional consequences of various components of the Canadian pension regime condition women's retirement incomes.

Canadian women and pensions

The state's role in the Canadian pension regime creates a paradox in terms of women's income inequality in later life. The first tier of public pensions (OAS/GIS) reduces income inequality between older men and women, but through earnings-related C/QPP and the subsidization of private pensions, the state exacerbates retirement income inequality. Despite the success of the Canadian pension regime in decreasing rates of low income among the senior population in general, poverty in old age is linked systematically to gender, age, and marital status, with older women much more likely than men to be poor.

Canada has one of the most rapidly ageing populations in the world. While only 10 per cent of the population were over age 65 in 1995, by 2037, nearly 23 per cent will be 65 or older (CCSD 1996). Women represent the majority of pensioners in Canada, comprising 58 per cent of all seniors and 70 per cent of those aged 85 in 1997.

Pensions are gendered in many ways, and women are systematically disadvantaged whenever pensions are linked to prior wages and contributions. Because women are much more likely than men to have low earnings, delayed, interrupted, or PT work histories, and to have taken on caregiving commitments within families (see Chapter 2 and later this chapter), women's pension benefits are predicated on smaller incomes and fewer years of 'service' than are men's. The interrelationship between low wages and interrupted work histories means that women are penalized by strictly earnings-linked pensions.

For Canadians, the cumulative effects of life course experiences in paid and unpaid work are reflected in amounts and sources of their retirement income, shown in Table 10.3. Different pension regime components interact to produce gendered income inequality. Women actually receive higher dollar amounts and a larger proportion of their income than men from the OAS/GIS, the first tier, reflecting their heavier reliance on the income-tested GIS benefit. The gender balance of earnings-related

Table 10.3   Income sources for men and women aged 65 and over (C$)

Source	Women		Men	
	Per cent receiving	*Average amount pa**	*Per cent receiving*	*Average amount pa**
OAS/GIS/SA	97	6,090	98	5,500
C/QPP	64	3,680	86	5,260
Pensions and annuities	28	6,780	53	11,520
Investments	51	5,930	57	5,910

Note: *for those with income from this source
Source: Statistics Canada Survey of Consumer Finances Microdata 1993 (adapted from CCSD 1996: 2, Table 2)

C/QPP is reversed, providing higher payments and a larger proportion of pension income for men. The greatest source of variation in old age income occurs between Canadians with and without access to private pension incomes, because private pension contributions can be based on high income ceilings. Men are twice as likely as women to receive private pensions and among those with this source of income, men receive nearly twice the average amount of income compared to women (see Table 10.3).

Public pensions make an important contribution to the income of most Canadian retirees; however, Canadian women rely on them much more heavily than do men. As Figure 10.1 shows, gendered income stratification is least in first tier (OAS/GIS) public pensions, with men and women receiving similar amounts. Through its link to earnings, C/QPP partially reproduces women's disadvantages in the labour market. Although welfare state researchers have emphasized the stratification inherent in public pension systems in liberal democracies, the combination of C/QPP with OAS/GIS generates *relatively* compressed income distributions among Canadian pensioners (Myles 2000) as shown in Figure 10.1 under total public pensions. Private sources of retirement income reproduce gender stratification in the labour market most starkly, intensifying gender inequality in retirement income.

Canadian women's pension disadvantages are even more evident when household composition is taken into account. Thirty-eight per cent of all women 65 and older and 53 per cent of women aged 85 and older in 1991 lived alone. While never married women tend to have stable retirement incomes due to their long, continuous work careers, most 'unattached' (in Statistics Canada terminology) Canadian senior women are widowed, divorced, or separated, many of them plunged into poverty when marriage ends through death or dissolution (McDonald 1997). For these women, the level of public sources of income, particularly OAS/GIS, is critical since 42 per cent of them are poor, compared to 27 per cent of unattached men and just 7 per cent of married couples (NCW 1999). As Table 10.4 shows, unattached poor women are less likely to receive any income from C/QPP, occupational pensions, investments, or RRSPs than individuals in non-poor households.

Gender differences in private pension tax subsidies

Contributions to RPPs and RRSPs receive large tax subsidies. Unlike payroll taxes, tax subsidies for private pensions go, not to the elderly for pensions, but to segments of the working-age population to subsidize their savings for old age. Thus, overall income tax rates are higher than would otherwise be necessary if the tax system were neutral toward

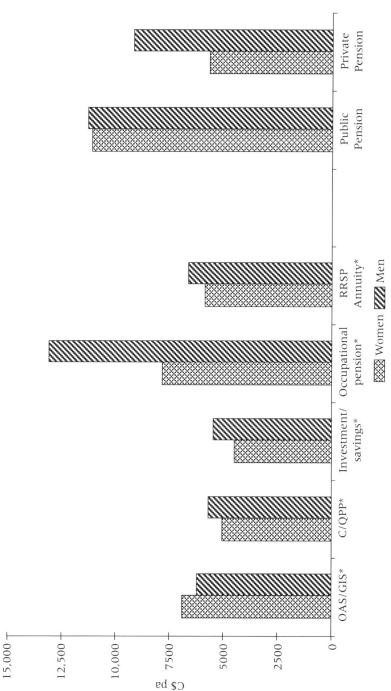

Figure 10.1 Average annual incomes (C$) for non-married individuals over 65, by gender (1997)

Note: *average for those with any income from that source
Source: NCW 1999, author's calculations

Table 10.4 Sources of income for Canadians 65 and older by household type and poverty status

	Poor unattached women	Poor unattached men	Poor married couples	Non-poor unattached women	Non-poor unattached men	Non-poor married couples
Per cent receiving income from source						
Public						
OAS/GIS	98	96	91	99	99	100
C/QPP	72	81	84	93	94	97
Private						
Occupational Pension	15	14	24	48	59	65
RRSP Annuities	3	*	6	22	18	29
Earnings	*	8	11	4	14	23
Investment/Savings	29	*	27	62	55	66
Average annual income (C$)						
Annual Public Transfers	$11,808	$11,784	$16,324	$12,370	$12,694	$18,181
Total Annual Income	$12,818	$12,661	$17,864	$22,441	$28,705	$41,722
Percentage of income from public sources	92	93	91	55	44	45

Note: *sample too small
Source: Adapted from Tables 13, 14, 15 (NCW 1999)

retirement savings as in New Zealand (see Chapter 12). Since middle-aged workers are most likely to belong to RPPs, and because planning for imminent retirement means that RRSP take-up is high if their income allows, they reap the largest benefit from tax-subsidized pensions (Myles and Street 1995).

Although the gap between women's and men's RPP coverage has been shrinking, 60 per cent of employed women are not covered. Tax subsidies for RPPs have actually become more selective (and less progressive) than previously, as fewer workers are covered. RPP coverage of employed men and women is almost equal while RRSP participation is theoretically possible for any Canadian with earnings. However, only those with a surplus to save can take advantage of RRSPs. Women's relative disadvantage is apparent. Tax subsidies for private pensions – and high private pension incomes in the future – are most likely to go to high-income, middle-aged men. This represents a net transfer to them from younger workers, pensioners, the low paid, and women, through Canada's distorted tax system.

Selective benefits, like the GIS, are usually conceived as public benefits directed toward the poor. However, in the case of tax subsidies, the selection criteria are 'upside down' (Sinfield 1993) as they are targeted mainly to securely-employed individuals with high wages and surplus income to save. The structure of Canadian tax provisions means that tax deferments for high-income taxpayers are more valuable than for low and middle-income taxpayers since first, tax rates for upper income taxpayers are higher and second, tax deferred benefits are typically greater for upper income taxpayers (Myles and Street 1995). Schellenberg's (1994) study of Canada's 'semi-public' tax-subsidized private pensions contrasted contribution rates and the value of tax savings for low and high-income contributors. Fourteen per cent of Canadians earning between C$10,001 and C$20,000 made RRSP contributions, averaging C$1429, yielding a tax saving of 25 per cent ($358) in 1991. In contrast, 70 per cent earning above C$100,000 made RRSP contributions averaging C$7805, saving 46 per cent ($3592) of the value of their contributions in taxes (Schellenberg 1994). Clearly, the selective benefit of tax subsidies is skewed heavily towards the highest income earners in both incidence and amount.

In sum, tax subsidies provide tax-savings for some segments of the working-age population at the expense of those who cannot afford private pension contributions. Public spending on pensions for all Canadians in 1999 was C$42.5 billion ($C19.6 billion for C/QPP, C$4.9 billion for GIS, C$18 billion for OAS), while tax expenditures for private pensions were estimated at C$14.7 billion (C$8.5 billion RRSP, C$6.2 billion RPP) (NCW 1999). Tax expenditures reduce revenues, limiting the state's capacity to accomplish other social policy goals. These could include increased public pensions for current pensioners (particularly older women) or improved public pension promises for currently disadvantaged workers. Alternatively, reduced income taxes for the young and/or low paid would free up resources for current needs or savings. Childcare could be subsidized to help working parents acquire the jobs they need to maintain financial independence. It is to working-age women that we next turn our attention.

Women's paid work

Labour force participation

Canadian women's labour force participation has changed profoundly since 1961, increasing from just 29 per cent of women in paid employment to nearly 60 per cent in 1996 (Gunderson 1998: 24–6). Contemporary Canadian women are more likely than in the past to have FYFT employment, but they are still significantly more likely than men to work in part time jobs. Historically, many women worked for pay until they married and had children, and then exited the labour force until children reached school age. More recent cohorts of women are less likely to leave paid work upon the birth of a child, although they often work part time rather than full time when children are very young (Gunderson 1998).

Differences in men's and women's employment patterns are conditioned by the social and cultural norms underlying the gender contract. Canadian women who are married or are mothers experience conflict between their family commitments and their careers. Among working women giving birth in 1993 or 1994, nine out of ten went back to work within a year, taking an average of 6.4 months off work (Statistics Canada 1999e). Many women are torn between meeting their family responsibilities and maintaining full time (FT) paid work – and many struggle to do both. The gender contract means that women, but not men, are expected to adapt their patterns of paid work to caring for children or frail relatives. One common strategy for women is to substitute PT for FT paid employment when family circumstances require high levels of unpaid work. According to Morris and her colleagues, this is because women are confronted with choices men do not have to make: 'Men are not expected to choose between their paid job and their children. Nor are they expected to quit their jobs in order to care for elderly or incapacitated relatives' (Morris *et al.* 1999: 15). Nearly 25 per cent of all women work part time, compared to only 9 per cent of men. Just over two-thirds of Canadian PT workers are women (Statistics Canada 1995).

The gender gap in pay

Canadian women, like their counterparts in the other countries discussed in this book, consistently receive lower incomes from paid work than men do. Data from the Survey of Consumer Finances (Drolet 1999) show that in 1997, FYFT working women earned just 72.5 per cent of FYFT men's annual earnings (see Table 10.5). Among all earners, women's annual earnings are not quite two-thirds of men's.

Drolet (1999) also assessed the gender gap in hourly wages versus the more conventional annual earnings. She found that among the youngest, single, never married men and women, women earn 96 per cent of men's hourly wages, despite apparent similarities in household responsibilities and commitment to work. At this point in a worker's life course, the effects of 'career interruptions, job advancement and differentiated household responsibilities have not yet taken place' (Drolet 1999: 22). The hourly wage gap is higher among working-age married women and men, with married women earning 77 per cent of men's average hourly wages (Drolet 1999: 22). Women's higher levels of education and increased labour force attachment have contributed to closing the gap (Gunderson 1998; Drolet 1999), but women's and men's work experiences and pay still differ considerably.

Even rapid return to employment after childbirth is not enough to protect many women's earning potential. The presence of children does not harm men's incomes, but causes a substantial decline in both single and married women's incomes, a gap that is never closed. When

Table 10.5 Women's to men's annual earnings ratios, 1997

Characteristics		Full time, full year Earnings ratio (per cent)	All earners Earnings ratio (per cent)
Overall		72.5	63.8
Age	15–24	80.8	na
	25–34	76.3	68.7
	35–44	73.4	63.4
	45–54	69.8	61.0
	55–64	63.7	54.7
Marital	Single	91.8	82.7
status	Married	67.5	56.7
	Other	80.3	74.6

Note: na = not available
Source: Adapted from Drolet (1999) based on Survey of Consumer Finances 1997

combined with women's substantially higher rates of unpaid housework and caregiving, this suggests that the presence of children and women's caregiving responsibilities are a major contributing factor to the gender gap. Among married women, 15 per cent of all hours worked are PT, compared to just 2 per cent for married men (Drolet 1999).

Canadian women in Drolet's (1999) study spent 75 per cent of their potential years of work experience in FYFT work, compared to 94 per cent for men. As women's age increases, so does the pay gap. The later the life course state, the more likely women are to have experienced interruptions or withdrawals from work, and, consequently, the shorter their job tenure, all factors that influence wages and future pensions.

Women's family work

Canadian women perform more unpaid domestic work than men do. In 1996, 51 per cent of FT working wives did more than 15 hours of unpaid housework per week, compared to only 23 per cent of husbands. Seventy per cent of non-employed wives did at least 15 hours of unpaid work per week, compared to only 36 per cent of non-employed husbands (Statistics Canada 1998).

Family caring is also carried out disproportionately by women, who pay social, financial, physical and emotional costs for their efforts. Women perform most childcare, both in intact marriages and as heads of lone-parent families. Increasing rates of birth among the single and divorce among all women have increased levels of lone parenthood. Four-fifths of lone parents in Canada are women, and three-fifths of lone-parent households headed by women have low incomes (Statistics Canada 1995). Shortages of subsidized licensed childcare (Cleveland and Krashinsky 1998) limit opportunities for women to gain skills and well-paid jobs. Right-leaning provincial governments have cut income assistance to lone parents, mimicking US efforts to compel lone mothers of young children into the labour market. Inadequate childcare puts these women at high risk of taking low-wage, low-skill jobs. Such jobs undermine opportunities to gain access to RPPs, or to have a surplus to invest in RRSPs.

Most caregiving to older people by those of working age is done by women – wives, daughters, and daughters-in-law (Kaden and McDaniel 1990; Vezina and Roy 1996). One study found that, among married caregivers, women contributed three-quarters of caregiving compared to about one-quarter from men; of all care provided by adult children, 87 per cent is provided by daughters, compared to 13 per cent from sons (Kaden and McDaniel 1990). Family eldercare significantly interferes with paid work for women, but not for men. The highest proportion of any age and gender group providing more than 10 hours of eldercare per week is women aged 45–64 (Gignac *et al.* 1996). Increased longevity has increased the likelihood that mid-life women have living parents and parents-in-law. Canada's rapidly ageing population suggests that this will be even more likely in the future. Mature women workers may be called upon to assume unpaid caring burdens at precisely the time when they have the greatest need to prepare for their own retirement (see Martin Matthews and Rosenthal 1993).

Women bear multiple risks as unpaid family carers and underpaid employees. The two groups of Canadian adults most vulnerable to low income are single mothers and 'unattached' older women. Among today's seniors, this group is predominantly widowed and comprises women who have generally spent a lifetime doing what was expected of them: staying home and caring for children and a spouse. Recognition of this fact is the basis for treating widowed women as a special category of unattached women, entitling them to benefits to which divorced and single women cannot lay claim. The growing number of poor single mothers are at particularly high risk of becoming poor old women, given the barriers they face in gaining adequate pension benefits. Women's reproductive work within families is a societal necessity that goes largely unrewarded (see Chapter 2). In summary, the gendered nature of paid labour and of family care combine to jeopardize women's capacity to accumulate independent capital or pension entitlements when compared with men. Women are, first of all, less likely to be FYFT labour force participants, second, earn less then men, and third, engage in more unpaid family work. Clearly, the market does not compensate Canadian women for these disadvantages, but the government can.

Recent trends in Canadian pension reforms

Mixed-welfare pension regimes like Canada's may ameliorate or reproduce systems of gender (and other) stratification. The impact of each type of pension varies, depending on the presence of women-friendly adaptations (see Table 10.6). Taken as a whole, Canadian public pensions (OAS+GIS+C/QPP) only partially reproduce systems of stratification originating in market wage labour relations because some pension reforms have created women-friendly benefit structures. In contrast, the government's role in private pensions (RPP + RRSP) *intensifies* stratification, because few women-friendly features address the disadvantages that women accumulate over a lifetime.

The Canadian pension system has been amended over the years, including important women-friendly reforms that enhanced the pension promise for Canadian women. Indeed, during the 1980s, the 'Great Pension Debate' sought to address the retirement income system's failure

Table 10.6 Women-friendly and adverse aspects of the Canadian pension regime

Women-friendly features

Public Pensions
- Flat-rate (nearly) universal pension (OAS)
- No stigma in claiming (GIS/SA)
- No contribution requirements (OAS/GIS/SA)
- Minimum guaranteed income (OAS/GIS)
- Immediate vesting/portability (C/QPP)
- Childrearing and low earnings dropouts (C/QPP)
- Credit sharing on divorce (C/QPP)
- Inflation-proofed, predictable, lifetime benefits

Private Pensions
- Mandatory coverage of PT employees (RPP)
- Mandatory survivor's benefits (RPP)
- Immediate vesting, portable, permit investment choices (RRSP)

Adverse features

Public Pensions
- Low level of earnings replacement (C/QPP)
- No eldercare dropout provision (C/QPP)
- OAS surtax deprives some women of citizen's pension

Private Pensions
- Tax subsidies are expensive and regressive
- Over 60 per cent of employed women lack coverage
- No inflation indexation requirement (RPP)
- Only available to earners with surplus to save (RRSP)

to meets its two primary goals of ensuring 'an adequate basic income for all seniors (the anti-poverty objective) and an adequate standard of living in retirement . . . (the earnings-replacement objective)'(Battle 1997: 521). However, the balance between the two goals has shifted since the mid-1980s when the last women-friendly reforms were enacted. Since then, there has been a tightening of the earnings link and declining attention to ensuring an adequate basic income for all seniors. Retrenchment of public pensions reversed earlier expansive trends, and has intensified the adverse effects of women's caring commitments.

Under neo-liberal Progressive Conservative governments in the 1980s and early 90s, private pension tax relief expanded and a surtax transformed OAS into an income-tested benefit. While the surtax did make

OAS more progressive, the intent of the reform was to cut public spending. There is no compelling reason to tax OAS at higher than regular rates, although some have suggested that universal OAS benefits going to 'the wealthy banker's wife' are too expensive for Canadians (see McQuaig 1993). If cost is the overriding concern, however, it might be cheaper to remove her (and her banker husband's) working-age private pension tax subsidy and pay their taxable OAS benefits in retirement instead. This suggests that OAS universality was undermined to satisfy neo-liberal ideological preferences for market provision.

Canadian pension retrenchment was not reversed when the Liberal party came to power. In 1996, the Liberals announced that a new Senior Benefit would replace OAS and GIS, strictly income-tested to target seniors with the lowest incomes. The Senior Benefit would be withdrawn at modest income levels, so even Canadians with average incomes would no longer receive a citizen's pension, transforming first-tier public pensions into an entirely selective benefit. Because the income-test was based on a couple's income, many married women would have lost entitlement to pensions in their own right. Although the government quietly abandoned the Senior Benefit in 1998, it was because Canada's financial industry was afraid it would undermine retirement saving (and their profits), and not because they were worried about the potential effect on women (McDonald 2000). Since C/QPP contribution rates were raised in 1998, the pension front in Canada has been relatively quiet. Although Canadian retrenchment has not been as deep as in Britain (see Chapter 4), universality has been replaced by creeping selectivity in public benefits and increased reliance on private pensions (see Street 1996).

Conclusions and policy options

Social and cultural norms arising from the gendered division of labour mean that women, even when they engage in paid work, undertake more unpaid domestic labour than men (see Chapter 2). For women, paid work is simply not a legitimate excuse from family responsibilities in the way it is for men (Finch 1989). Consequently, women devise strategies that enable them to juggle the competing demands on their time. Many labour market adjustments that Canadian women make to accommodate their paid and unpaid work have both short-term and long-term consequences. Low wages and PT work to undertake caring responsibilities place an immediate constraint on disposable income. In the longer term, they limit women's capacity to gain employment-based pensions and benefits or to save meaningful sums of money for their retirement.

For some future women retirees, increased labour force participation will yield better private pensions and higher C/QPP benefits. Still, their retirement income will not likely equal men's. Some women will remain outside the work force for most of their lives, although that number is declining. Others will work part time or episodically, undermining their capacity to accumulate sufficient pension entitlements. Thus many women will not gain better pension incomes in the future, widening the pension gap among women.

As inflation erodes the level at which OAS pensions are clawed back, more women at lower levels of income will lose some or all of their citizen's pension. Whether political support will endure as OAS is withdrawn from more Canadians over time is uncertain. Because OAS and GIS are not indexed to wages, gains in the Canadian standard of living will outpace benefit improvement. Consequently, older women living with low income relative to the working-aged population may increase if present trends continue. Periodic increases in line with productivity gains would enhance first-tier benefits, greatly benefiting women.

C/QPP helps women gain income adequacy in old age through benefit structures that address some realities of Canadian women's changing work and family lives. Continued adaptations of C/QPP could incorporate eldercare dropout provisions and end discrimination against same-sex partners and individuals of different marital statuses. Replacing a higher percentage of previous earnings for low-paid workers, similar to the progressive benefit formula under US Social Security (see Chapter 8) would help women most (Townson 1995).

Unless private pensions are mandated (as in Australia, see Chapter 11) so that minimum standards and universal coverage can be required, little can be done to improve them (Townson 1995). The combined effects of Canadian private pension initiatives are mixed. At great expense, some Canadians will have high private pension incomes in the future, but the overall security of private benefits has eroded. Since few women benefit much from private pensions, a more equitable approach would remove tax subsidies for private pensions and invest the savings in enhanced public pensions.

Canada's unique mix of income-tested and earnings-linked public pensions has contributed to a decline in old age poverty and reduced levels of income inequality among seniors. These payoffs of the public pension system may have reached their apex, since few more 'maturation' gains are available. What has not 'matured' is the private pension component of Canada's pension regime. When that happens, retirement income inequality will likely increase again (Myles 2000). Too many Canadian women spend their last years in poverty. Since only a minority have significant access to tax-subsidized private pensions, many women will have low incomes in the future as well. It is clear that public pension reforms made with women's needs in mind are the best way to insure their dignified access to adequate income in old age.

CHAPTER 11

Pension reform in Australia: problematic gender equality

SHEILA SHAVER

The Australian retirement income system has changed dramatically during the 1990s. Long oriented almost wholly to the alleviation of poverty in old age, its concerns have been widened to include support for the retirement living standards of middle- and upper-income groups. Structurally, the system has been transformed by the addition to its twin pillars of public social assistance and private retirement saving of a new third pillar of publicly mandated but privately provided occupational pensions, called superannuation in Australia.

Coinciding with significant growth in women's labour force participation, these changes have greatly extended women's stake in the retirement income system, particularly in its (ostensibly) private sectors. In principle, they offer women the opportunity to enjoy benefits previously limited mainly to men. So far, however, gains in gender equity have been slow to materialize. Looking to the longer term, at least some women's groups foresee a widening of the gender gap in economic well-being in later life.

This chapter examines the treatment of men and women in the public and private sectors of Australia's emerging retirement income system, and locates the prospects for women's incomes in retirement in the gendered relations between these sectors.

The public Age Pension

The Age Pension (AP) was established in 1909, in the first years after the federation of the Australian colonies as a single nation. It was a flat-rate, means-tested payment funded from general revenue, and although it was not universal it nevertheless acquired an ethos of citizenship entitlement

(Shaver 1991). Although other pension models have been debated from time to time thereafter, development has continued to build on this original social assistance foundation. During and immediately after World War II, a comprehensive social security system was enacted on the same basis.

Australian income security is internationally unusual in its central reliance on targeted benefits. The system provides payments, without time limits, to claimants in circumstances such as old age, disability, sickness, unemployment, parental responsibility, education, and the need to care for people with severe disabilities. Virtually all benefits are subject to a test of means. Compared with those in use in other advanced industrial nations, these tests are unusually generous, and are designed less with the aim of identifying those who would otherwise be destitute than with excluding those who have significant economic capacities. Assets tests disregard most owner-occupied housing and personal effects. Benefits are flat-rate, and payments may be reduced through the operation of the means test. Because the primary emphasis is on need and poverty alleviation, benefit levels are low by international standards, leaving substantial scope for private provision. Income disregards and tapered rates of benefit withdrawal enable beneficiaries with private resources to claim partial benefits.

The AP is the clearest, and in some respects the least problematic, instance of the selective Australian model. The system's advocates claim that its targeted basis makes Australian provision of income security to older people very efficient in meeting need at minimal cost, while at the same time avoiding the problems of stigma and take-up usually associated with means-tested provision. Australia devotes a comparatively low share of national resources to APs – in 1995 aged cash benefits represented 3.1 per cent of GDP (OECD 1998b) – and there is little evidence of failure to claim among those with more than marginal entitlements. The weak points in Australian income security are lower levels of benefit than provided in many other countries, and disincentives to economic activity caused by the high effective marginal tax rates resulting from the interaction of benefit tapering and income tax rates. Australian social security provides protection from severe poverty at low levels of social expenditure, but is less effective in securing its citizens against more marginal need (Mitchell 1991; Saunders 1994: 14–50).

Women have an important stake in Australia's AP arrangements (O'Connor *et al.* 1999: 109–56). They are the majority claimants of income security provisions for elderly people, as well as of benefits for sole parents, parental responsibility, and care for people with severe disabilities in earlier life (Commonwealth Department of Family and Community Services (FaCS) 1998). Women also have a stake in the targeting of these payments. Unlike the social insurance arrangements used in many other countries, claims for the Australian AP do not depend upon a history of past contributions made by oneself or an employed spouse. This gives Australian women independent access to a safety-net income conditional only upon present need. At the same time, not all women have an interest in the very basic level of social protection this system affords. Moreover, because means tests are applied to the joint resources of the couple, married women's access to the pension is indirectly linked to their husbands' earnings history and savings. That this may have effects on women's economic independence is discussed below.

In principle, all persons of the requisite age and who have resided in Australia for at least ten years are eligible to receive a pension. The age of eligibility is currently 65 for males. Historically set at 60, women's age of eligibility is being raised, and will reach parity with men at 65 in 2012. It was 62 in 2000. There is also a service pension payable to men and women with eligible war service, on much the same basis as the standard AP but available five years earlier. In addition, there are pensions paid in respect of injury or widowhood related to war service. Some of these are more generous than the basic age or service provision, and are not subject to a test of means. These are not discussed further here.

At 30 June 1998 the standard rate (for non-married persons, or those unable to live with their spouse) of the pension was A$354.60 per fortnight (A$2.59/£1 in 1999). The rate applying to each of the members of a couple was A$295.80, about 80 per cent of the standard rate; their benefits are individual, each receiving half of their joint entitlement. Pensioners living in private rental accommodation are also eligible for rent assistance. Some 10 per cent of age pensioners receive this supplement. While the pension is subject to income tax, thresholds are set so that pensioners without significant non-pension income are not liable for this tax. The availability of a number of fringe benefits increases the value of the pension. These include exemption from contributions to the national health insurance system, free general practitioner care from participating doctors, an allowance to assist with the costs of pharmaceuticals, and discounts on telephone rental, public transport and local government taxes.

In addition to age and residence, applicants must qualify for the pension under separate means tests of income and assets. These tests apply to the combined income and assets of husbands and wives (de jure or de facto). Under the income test, benefits are withdrawn at a rate of 50 per cent above an income test-free amount (25 per cent for each partner of a couple). This withdrawal rate was reduced to 40 per cent from 1 July 2000, as part of the measures associated with the introduction of a goods and service tax. Under the assets test, payments are reduced by A$3.00 per fortnight for every A$1,000 in assets over the permitted limit (non-married person or both members of a couple). Pensions are adjusted

Table 11.1   Rates and income and assets means test limits for Age Pension, 30 June 1998

	Non-married person (A$)	Couple (total for both members) (A$)
Full rate of pension (per fortnight)	354.60	591.60
Maximum income allowable for full pension and income at which entitlement to part pension ends (fortnight)	100–820.00	176–1,370.00
Maximum assets allowable for full pension and limit at which entitlement to part pension ends (home owner)	125,750–245,750.00	178,500–377,500.00
Maximum assets allowable for full pension and limit at which entitlement to part pension ends (not home owner)	215,750–335,750.00	268,500–467,500.00

Source: FaCS 1998: 93

twice yearly in line with the consumer price index. Pension rates and the means-test limits for full and part pension applying at 30 June 1998, are set out in Table 11.1.

In conferring AP entitlement, these means-test limits are far more generous than apply to social assistance in most other countries, and by far the majority – 82 per cent – of age-eligible Australians receive income from the AP or other closely related payments (FaCS 1999). Such a high proportion is evidence that a means-tested pension is acceptable to today's generation of older Australians. Access to the accompanying fringe benefits gives a further incentive to apply even for small pension entitlements. The limits applying to receipt of the pension at full rate are also relatively generous: just over two-thirds of AP recipients are paid at the maximum rate.

With its social assistance foundations, Australia's public AP has clear advantages for significant groups of women. These foundations make women eligible for income security on much the same terms as men, and in particular shelter them from the effects that discontinuities in employment history associated with marriage, childrearing and the provision of care for their parents and partners have on contributory provision for income in later life. At the same time, the social assistance foundations of the AP treat married women as having the same access to the non-pension resources of the couple as do their husbands. In actuality husbands have larger non-pension incomes than wives; King *et al.* (1999: 37) estimate the average male share of retired couples' combined incomes as 56 per cent. Married women may thus have their pension income reduced on account of income practically unavailable to them. The effects of this may be severe. Olsberg (1997: 143) quotes a woman in this circumstance:

> I can't get the pension because Jim got very good superannuation. But he begrudges giving me any money nowadays. He says it's his super and he's going to spend it himself. He goes out a lot, plays golf and has lunch with his friends. He's cut my housekeeping money right back, and I don't even have money to buy myself a lipstick any more.

There are not great differences in the social characteristics of men and women receiving AP income, shown in Table 11.2. Women's ages span

Table 11.2   Characteristics of Age Pension recipients by gender, 30 June 1998

	Men		Women	
	No	*%*	*No*	*%*
Aged 61–4	–	–	187,256	17.5
Aged 65–74	416,603	67.0	451,755	42.2
Aged 75–84	151,098	24.6	304,073	28.5
Aged 85 or older	45,886	7.5	125,947	11.8
Born in Australia	364,991	59.5	710,949	66.5
Born in UK/Ireland	72,160	11.8	120,397	11.3
Born in Italy	47,602	7.8	47,980	4.5
Born in Greece	15,676	2.6	21,895	2.0
Born in other country	113,158	18.5	167,810	15.7
Non-married person	174,675	28.5	625,751	58.5
Member of couple	348,912	71.5	443,280	41.5
Maximum rate	397,094	64.7	746,017	69.8
Reduced rate	216,493	35.3	323,014	30.2
Home owner	444,699	72.5	697,937	65.3
Not home owner	168,888	27.5	371,094	34.7
Receives rent assistance	56,634	9.2	110,438	10.3

Source: FaCS 1998: 5, 85

a wider range than men's, a consequence of their earlier access to the pension and their greater longevity. The larger proportion of men than women born outside Australia reflects postwar immigration patterns in a period in which males predominated. Because their life expectancy is 15 to 20 years less than other Australians, Aborigines and Torres Strait Islanders form a very small proportion of older Australians. In 1996, persons aged 65 or older comprised 2.6 per cent of all indigenous per sons, compared to 12 per cent of the total population. There are more women than men in this age group (ABS 1996: 2).

The most significant gender difference is in marital status. By far the majority of men but a minority of women live with a spouse. Differences in the economic circumstances of male and female age pensioners are intertwined with marital status, and thus partly obscured in the aggregation of men and women in the public statistics.

About 80 per cent of both men and women in the eligible age group receive some AP but taken as individuals, proportionately more women than men receive the pension at the maximum rate. This is because, as a group, women have fewer economic resources. Proportionately fewer women than men are homeowners. Australia has a high rate of owner-occupied housing, which is politically invulnerable and extensively subsidized. Home ownership makes a significant difference to the living standard afforded by the AP and women more often than men have to pay for housing from their pensions. Marginally more women than men receive rent assistance payments (FaCS 1998: 5, 85).

The economic circumstances of non-married (including never married, widowed, separated and divorced) and married people compare slightly differently. Non-married men slightly more often than non-married women have no resources other than their pension, but much more commonly than non-married women have income in the upper ranges where only a part pension is received. Partnered men and women, whose incomes are treated as half of the combined resources of the couple, much less often depend completely on their APs, but are also less often found in the upper ranges and receiving pensions at reduced rates (FaCS 1998: 5). The application of the means test to the joint incomes and assets of the couple works in the same way as tax splitting; it enables couples to spread their income or assets across the larger disregard allowed for two people.

Unlike European and American pension systems, the Australian AP is not intended to maintain pre-retirement differentials in social status and living standards in later life. Historically, it has always been understood as ensuring older Australians a basic flat-rate level of economic support without undermining incentives for individuals to save for retirement on their own account. The level of the pension is accordingly low. Recent governments of both parties have upheld a political commitment to maintain the standard (non-married) pension at 25 per cent of average male weekly earnings. Because pensioners without other income do not have to pay income tax, the after-tax parity of the pension with average weekly earnings is rather higher at 33 per cent. Comparative measures show the level of the Australian AP as not greatly dissimilar to minimum income security provisions in Canada, the United States, and the United Kingdom, but markedly lower than in Europe and Scandinavia (Coder et al. 1990; Palme 1990: 51; Shaver 1997: 70).

For those who depend on it most heavily, the AP furnishes an income that is not far from the poverty line. The measurement of poverty rates is sensitive to the assumptions and methods used, and there is a good deal of variation in the absolute values of the rates that have been reported. The pattern in these rates, as estimated in both Australian and comparative international studies, is nonetheless consistent. In Australia the Henderson Poverty line is widely but not universally accepted as the authoritative measure of poverty rates. This is a headcount measure in which the poverty line is equivalent to the living standard of a family of four dependent on a single minimum wage plus child benefit payments for two children. It defines poverty standards for income both before and after payment of housing costs. King (1998) estimates that 38 per cent of aged non-married men, 32 per cent of aged non-married women, but only 4 per cent of aged couples are below the poverty line when measured on the basis of income before housing costs. The possession of owner-occupied housing makes a substantial difference to living standards on the AP. Because the majority of AP recipients own their homes, it is most appropriate to measure poverty among the aged after housing costs. On this basis, 9.3 per cent of non-married aged men, 4.1 per cent of aged non-married women, and 3.3 per cent of aged couples are in poverty (King 1998). While comparable estimates are not available, other evidence indicates higher rates of poverty among older immigrants, especially those from countries where English is not the first language (Williams and Batrouney 1998: 272–3).

King's study was designed to replicate the measurement of poverty by the Australian Commission of Inquiry into Poverty in the early 1970s (Commission of Inquiry into Poverty 1975). The higher levels of poverty among non-married men than non-married women in these estimates are methodological artefacts of the equivalence scale used in this early work, which assumed higher costs for men than women. As will be shown below, the incomes of older non-married women are actually lower than those of non-married men, and there is no evidence that men are more likely than women to be poor.

Because small sample numbers affect the reliability of estimates for non-married men alone, measures of poverty are rarely presented separately for older men and women. Unpublished calculations by the author using

Luxembourg Income Study data for the mid-1980s show very similar poverty levels among older non-married men and women at that time. The AP benefit level is close to the poverty line, and the incomes of AP recipients tend to cluster at this level. Headcount poverty estimates of this kind are very sensitive to the exact point at which the line is drawn. Given this sensitivity, it is likely that these figures overstate the difference in poverty levels between non-married aged persons and couples. Similar and high levels of poverty were found among aged people in the early 1990s in Australia, the UK and the USA, but lower levels in Canada (Smeeding *et al.* 1993; Bradshaw and Chen 1996: 6; Shaver 1997: 51–9).

The AP incomes men and women receive are very similar, but for both represent safety net provisions intended only to ensure a basic minimum to all. The main source of retirement income above this minimum is occupational pension provision, called superannuation in Australia. As the quotation above suggests, gender differentials in this income are far greater.

Occupational superannuation and the reform of retirement income

A second pillar of voluntary provisions, mainly employer-provided superannuation, developed in the postwar period. By the 1980s it had become an established and tax-supported fringe benefit of employment for certain groups of employees, mainly those in highly paid, professional and/or public sector employment. At the same time other groups, particularly in blue-collar occupations in the private sector, remained excluded from these benefits.

In the private sector, most Australian superannuation funds were company based until the mid-1980s, when the development of superannuation as a condition of pay awards (see below) gave rise to the establishment of large industry-based funds. Most private sector employees belong to defined contribution (DC) pension schemes, also called accumulation funds. Members carry the investment risk, and their funds receive contributions and interest, less costs of fund administration. There are separate public sector superannuation funds. Most public sector workers are in defined benefit (DB) pension schemes at the present time; these pay a guaranteed benefit based on salary level and length of service, with the employer bearing the investment risk. Not surprisingly, there is a trend towards DC schemes in the public sector also. The tax system provides extensive support for occupational superannuation. Employer contributions are tax deductible, and there are tax concessions for personal contributions by low wage employees, self-employed people, and employees without employer support for superannuation. The income of the funds themselves is taxed at concessional rates, though these concessions are reduced for high-income earners. Benefits themselves are also taxed at concessional rates, though the criteria determining these are complex.

Australia is unusual in allowing superannuation benefits to be taken as *lump sums*. These are taxed at concessional rates only when taken at age 55 or older. Both defined contribution and defined benefit funds typically allow benefits to be taken as a lump sum; some defined benefit funds also allow some or all benefits to be taken as an indexed pension. Lump sum benefits are the predominant choice of retirees (Gunasekera and Powlay 1987; Olsberg 1997: 64–6; King *et al.* 1999). At the present time most lump sums are small. In 1995, more than half of those taken by persons aged 45 to 74 were sums of A\$20,000 or less (A\$2.59/£1). Men received larger sums than women; while 62 per cent of men had received lump sums of A\$60,000 or more, 69 per cent of women had received less than A\$20,000 (King *et al.* 1999: 26). Lump sum benefits are at the centre of the problem of 'double dipping', i.e. the scope within existing arrangements enabling people to enjoy both tax-assisted private pensions and the means-tested public pension. Estimates suggest that double dipping is not widespread at the present time, at least on a scale with significant impact on public expenditure (Bacon and Gallagher 1995), but it continues to be viewed as encouraging both early labour force withdrawal and dissipation of private retirement saving. Only those who have accrued generous private pension entitlements have significant capacity for double dipping. In the present generation, this is mainly men. There may be more women in this position in the next decade.

Significant reform of Australian retirement income has been undertaken since the mid-1980s. The system has been changed to extend and support private saving. Most significantly for the longer term, a third pillar of mandated superannuation covering almost all workers has been introduced.

Impetus to reform has come from several sources. One is concern about demographic ageing and increasing claims on the AP. Australia's population, although young in comparison with those of the UK and Europe, is now ageing. The proportion of the population aged 65 or more is projected to increase from 12 per cent in 1999 to 20 per cent in 2031. Immigration, having long kept population ageing at bay, has begun to contribute to it as postwar cohorts of immigrants reach retirement age; fully one-fifth of Australian residents aged 65 or older have immigrated to Australia from a non-English-speaking country (Rosenman 1997: 18). The political significance of population ageing is enhanced by the vocal expectations of the baby boom generation, and their capacity for cultural innovation in lifestyles after leaving the paid workforce. There has also been a recognition that this generation will demand higher retirement incomes than afforded by the AP alone (Olsberg 1997: 1–2). The argument about double dipping has been a second source of impetus.

The first steps in reform came, however, as a bargain struck in the Arbitration Commission, the judicial body at the centre of the Australian system of centralized wage fixation at that time. In the late 1970s the union movement began to demand the extension of superannuation coverage, previously limited mainly to professional, managerial and public sector employees, to all workers. In 1986 the Commission awarded workers a 3 per cent productivity payment in the form of employer-contributed occupational pensions for all workers covered under industry pay awards. Coming as a trade-off of wage restraint for improvement in the social wage under the Accord between the unions and the Labor Government, the payment was granted in lieu of a pay rise and had to be secured in the negotiation of an industrial award. By 1990, 79 per cent of all full time employees were covered, but the same was not true of many part time and casual workers; it was also obvious that the initial 3 per cent level would not generate an adequate retirement income.

When the Commission declined a further trade-off of pay rises for superannuation the government undertook to legislate for mandatory superannuation coverage. The Superannuation Guarantee Charge (SGC), which took effect in July 1992, requires all employers to make minimum levels of superannuation contributions to a complying superannuation fund, or to pay an alternate charge to the government. These contributions are mandatory for all employees earning more than A$450 per month (about 15 per cent of male average weekly earnings); the required minimum level of contributions, currently 7 per cent, is to increase to 9 per cent in 2002–03. A contributions ceiling of about 2.5 times average weekly earnings applies, requiring employers to pay contributions only on earnings below this level. Employees are not required to contribute, but many do so on a voluntary basis. Employees can arrange for part of their salary to be paid in the form of employee contributions to superannuation, securing a tax advantage (Sharp 1995; Olsberg 1997: 38, 74–97; King *et al.* 1999: 14–16).

One of the most important effects of the introduction of the SGC was to extend superannuation coverage, at a very basic level, to large numbers of workers to whom it had previously been unavailable. The decade from 1984 to 1994 saw a dramatic increase in coverage of both women and part time workers. Coverage of male full time employees grew from 51 to 93 per cent, and of female full time employees from 35 to 94 per cent. In 1984 only 12 per cent of male and 6 per cent of female part time workers had superannuation coverage; by 1994 coverage rates had increased to 44 and 68 per cent respectively (King *et al.* 1999: 17).

The result is a complex amalgam of mandated and voluntary arrangements in which some employees receive only the required minimum

Table 11.3 Contributory basis of superannuation coverage, 1995 –
employees aged 15–74 with superannuation (SGC and non-mandated
schemes)

Contributory basis	Men (%)	Women (%)
Personal and employer contributions	48.6	36.3
Personal contributions only	2.8	1.9
Employer contributions only	48.6	61.8
Total	100.0	100.0

Source: ABS (1995)

and others multiple layers of provision. Levels of superannuation
coverage depend on contributions, the make-up of which is shown in
Table 11.3. Employers contribute on behalf of almost all employees who
have superannuation; this includes those who have only the low-level
coverage afforded by the SGC. About half of those with coverage also
make personal contributions. These are most commonly in the range of
5–10 per cent of earnings, but in more than one-third of cases are less
than 5 per cent (King *et al.* 1999: 18–19). As Table 11.3 shows, a much
larger proportion of men than women make personal superannuation
contributions. The level of men's and women's contributions is much
more similar. Self-employed people are required to make superannuation contributions, with both compulsory and additional voluntary contributions supported by generous tax concessions (Olsberg 1997: 38–40).

The overall pattern of superannuation coverage among employed men
and women is shown in Table 11.4. Rates of coverage are higher in the
public than the private sector, and higher among trade union members
than among non-members. Coverage rates increase with age, reach their
highest level in middle age, and decline somewhat thereafter. The decline in coverage at age 55 reflects the fact that assets withdrawn before
this age forgo valuable tax concessions on superannuation contributions
and benefits unless they are paid into 'rollover funds' where they are
preserved until age 55. The availability of benefits as a lump sum creates
incentives for workers to take early retirement and/or for employers to
shed employees in this age group. To reduce scope for double dipping
the preservation age is being slowly increased, and will reach 60 by 2025.

Women's incomes in retirement show the effects of the disadvantages
they face in accumulating superannuation entitlements. On average,
older non-married women have lower incomes than older non-married
men or the combined incomes of couples. In 1995–96, among those old
enough to receive the AP, older non-married women received an average after-tax income of A$209 per week, compared to an average of

Table 11.4   Superannuation coverage (SGC and non-mandated schemes), 1995, employees aged 15–74

	Men (%)	Women (%)
All	82.0	79.5
Aged 15–19	73.8	66.0
Aged 20–4	86.4	84.9
Aged 24–34	92.9	89.7
Aged 35–44	93.9	88.5
Aged 45–54	94.5	91.3
Aged 55–64	90.3	84.9
Aged 65–74	52.9	50.9
Born in Australia*	82.5	79.6
Born in other English-speaking countries	80.2	82.0
Born in other countries	78.1	78.2
Public sector worker	95.8	93.2
Private sector worker	89.5	85.0
Trade union member	97.4	97.5
Not trade union member	87.2	82.6
Permanent employee	97.3	96.8
Casual employee	65.1	65.2
Worked <10 hours last week	76.3	65.2
Worked 10–19 hours last week	62.7	76.0
Worked 20–9 hours last week	84.1	87.2
Worked 30–4 hours last week	91.1	92.5
Worked 35 hours or more last week	94.2	94.7

Note: *Figures for birthplace refer to employed persons, including employees, employers and own-account workers.
Source: ABS (1995)

A\$223 per week among older non-married men and A\$387 among older couples. Non-married older women depend more heavily on the AP than do either non-married men or men and women in couples. In 1995–96, income transfers, primarily the AP, represented almost 70 per cent of the incomes of such women, 55 per cent of the incomes of non-married men, and just over 55 per cent of the combined incomes of couples. Because superannuation benefits are often taken as lump sums and invested privately, the role of private saving in retirement incomes is best presented as the total of private pension and investment income. Together, income from these sources comprised 24 per cent of the incomes of non-married older women, compared to almost 35 per cent of

Table 11.5   Australian pension regime summary

Public pension: Age Pension (AP)
Proportion receiving	82% of those in eligible age group
Eligibility	Age, residence and low/moderate income
Financing	Tax-funded
Function	Poverty prevention, income security

Mandatory private pensions: SGC
Proportion receiving	Separate data not available
Eligibility	All employed earning over A$104/wk (£40)
Financing	Employer contributions + tax subsidy
Function	Income maintenance

Voluntary private pensions
Proportion receiving*	<20% men; <10% women (incl. SGC pensions)
Eligibility	All employees and self-employed
Financing	Employer and employee contributions + tax subsidy
Function	Income maintenance

Note: *Does not include those opting to take benefits as lump sums. Most superannuation benefits are paid in this form and are mainly for small sums

the incomes of non-married men and couples. Private savings were much more important in higher than lower incomes. Only in the fourth and fifth deciles of equivalent income did the AP make up less than 80 per cent of total income (King *et al.* 1999: 35–7, 40–1). Table 11.5 summarizes the Australian pension regime.

Working-age women's superannuation coverage and employment

The spread of superannuation has gone in tandem with the growth of women's labour force participation, and so has given coverage to a larger population of women than is evident from coverage rates alone. In 1988 only 23.4 per cent of all women aged 45 to 54 were covered by superannuation; by 1995 this had risen to 55.5 per cent. Coverage among men in the same age group increased from 63.9 to 71.3 per cent. At all ages, rates of coverage among women nevertheless remain lower than those among men. In 1995 two-thirds of all men aged 15 to 65 were covered by superannuation, but only half of all women of the same ages.

The quality of superannuation coverage, and the security of retirement income it is likely to confer in the future, will be contoured by women's position in the labour market. There are a number of features of women's employment and earnings that suggest that the expansion of superannuation will not serve women as well as it does men. First, women get no pay at all for much of the work they do. One of the main reasons for this is women's role providing care for children and elderly relatives. As Table 11.6 shows, women's rates of labour force participation are lower than those of men, but this gap is smaller among younger than older women. Clare (1994: 7) estimates that on average women spend 17 years in the paid labour force compared to men's 39 years, but that women currently entering the labour force can be expected to work for pay for about 28 years. Until the mid-1980s, immigrant women and especially married immigrant women had higher rates of labour force

Table 11.6   Labour force participation and employment by gender, 1998 – civilian labour force

	Men (%)	*Women (%)*
Labour force participation rates		
All	72.8	54.1
Aged 15–19	55.8	55.7
Aged 20–4	86.7	77.9
Aged 25–34	92.2	69.7
Aged 35–44	92.3	70.8
Aged 45–54	87.2	69.3
Aged 55–9	75.0	43.6
Aged 60–4	45.9	20.5
Aged 65 or older	10.0	3.0
Born in Australia	75.8	57.5
Born in other English speaking countries	74.6	56.0
Born in other countries	64.8	45.2
*Employed persons**		
Employed full time	87.5	55.9
Employed part time	12.5	54.9
Worked <16 hours last week	11.3	25.4
Worked 16–29 hours last week	8.1	20.4
Worked 30–4 hours last week	11.1	13.3
Worked 35–9 hours last week	14.3	14.2
Worked 40+ hours last week	55.2	26.8
Part time, prefers not to work more hours than at present	63.3	79.0

Note: *Figures for full and part time employment and hours of work refer to employed persons, including employees, employers and own-account workers. Part time refers to workers employed for less than 35 hours per week
Source: ABS 1998

participation than those born in Australia. This pattern has since reversed, with labour force participation growing more slowly among immigrant than Australian-born women and growth slowest among women from countries where English is not the primary language. Home duties and childrearing were the reasons given for not being in the labour force (ABS, Social Statistics Branch 1992: 21–4). A still smaller share of Aboriginal and Torres Strait Islander women – 42.6 per cent in 1996 – are labour force participants (ABS 1996: 34). Although the younger age structures, higher fertility and rural locations of indigenous groups explain some of this difference, the fact remains that lower participation rates and higher levels of unemployment among indigenous people diminish their capacity to save for retirement.

While AP provision for married couples is based on this unit, Australian superannuation is based on the employed individual. There is only limited provision for the extension of superannuation coverage to persons not in the labour force. Funds may accept contributions on behalf of employees for up to two years after leaving employment, subject to certain conditions. This is intended to enable employees to maintain continuity of superannuation coverage and retirement savings during temporary interruptions of employment such as those associated with having children. Women's lobbies have differed on whether the two-year limit on this provision should be increased or removed; analysts agree that its primary beneficiaries are households in upper income groups (Cox 1994; Larkin 1994). Reflecting its support for the single-income family, the present Liberal-National Party coalition government first elected in 1996 has introduced a tax rebate for superannuation contributions made on behalf of a non-income-earning or low-income-earning spouse. The provisions also allow superannuation contributions to be split between husband and wife, enabling contributions to be continued during periods when either one is out of the workforce. High income households are the main beneficiaries of this arrangement.

Increasingly, Australian women juggle paid and unpaid work. Except for the peak childbearing years, married women's participation rates differ little from those of women generally. The most significant difference between men and women is the far greater percentage of women working less than full time (less than 35 hours per week). Two employed women out of five work part time, as compared to only one man in twelve. One-quarter of employed women work less than half time (normal full time employment in Australia is 35–8 hours), and a further fifth work longer part time hours. (The ground for concern about widening inequality in work hours can be seen in the fact that more than half of all men and one-quarter of women worked more than 40 hours per week). The take-up of part time work has occurred mainly among Australian-born women and immigrants from English speaking countries. If they are employed, immigrant women from countries where English is not the main language are more likely than others to work full time (ABS, Social Statistics Branch 1992: 41–7). The small numbers of indigenous people in the population and differences associated with urban and rural location make detailed analysis of employment patterns difficult. One study shows that while rural Aboriginal women in employment were less likely than other rural women to work full time, urban Aboriginal women were more likely to do so (Daly 1991).

A number of factors contribute to women's concentration in part time employment, the most basic of which is the social expectation that they will be the primary carers of children. Social policy factors include little availability of maternity and parental leave and the cost of childcare. Women's preferences also clearly play a part in their employment choices; relatively few women in part time jobs say they would like to work longer hours than they do. Whatever their source, factors having adverse effects on women's employment weaken their stakes in retirement income. Access to parental leave and employment flexibility, for example, help to explain the relative gender equality in superannuation coverage among public sector employees as compared to private sector workers. Superannuation coverage is weakest among those working very short hours. Superannuation coverage is higher among women born in Australia and immigrants from English speaking countries than among immigrants from other countries. Lower coverage among this last group may reflect their greater involvement in family businesses. Over the longer term, the loss of earnings flowing from sustained part time employment has significant impact on the value of superannuation entitlements. Women (and men) with a history of part time work lose out on both employer contributions and the income returns from fund investment. In addition to hours of work, the superannuation entitlements of immigrants are constrained by their having fewer years of employment in Australia.

Women also do less well out of superannuation than men because they earn less than men. Gender parities in earnings are comparatively high in Australia, including in fields where pay is low. However, the occupational structure is highly segregated into fields of predominantly male and predominantly female employment. Women's employment is strongly concentrated in clerical and sales jobs, where much of the work is poorly paid (Clare 1994: 7–9; O'Connor et al. 1999: 94–105). These are also fields in which superannuation coverage is thin, and employer contributions limited. Present differentials in pay and conditions translate directly into differentials in retirement income in the future.

Casual workers, mainly young people and women, have gained least from the extension of occupational superannuation. As noted above, employers are not required to pay superannuation contributions for employees earning less than A$450 per month from a single employer. Since 1 July 1998, the contributions in respect of employees earning up to $A900 per month may be paid to them as wages in lieu of super- annuation (Costello 1997: 5). In practice this money is vulnerable to erosion in the competition for jobs. Casual and part time workers earn- ing above the threshold acquire numerous small accounts; recent legisla- tion has simplified the system, limited the erosion of small accounts by administrative charges, and given scope for some workers to integrate their contributions in a single account. Casual and part time workers earning less than the threshold amount, or less in each of a number of jobs, miss out on the benefits of compulsory superannuation. There is an opinion that given the means-tested AP, low-wage workers stand to gain little from compulsory superannuation. It is argued that workers need this money as present salary, and that young workers especially may get better value from investment in home ownership than pension savings (Cox 1994).

Women's pension prospects

Women's present superannuation entitlements are far below those of men – over most age ranges, less than half those of men of the same age (Brown 1994, cited in Clare 1994: 9). Given a gender division of labour in which women bear the long-term costs of fragmented and part time employment histories, wives have an interest in the larger entitlements of their husbands. The division of superannuation assets at divorce re- mains an unresolved issue for policy. While these generally are taken into account in property settlements in some way, no clear formula applies and outcomes vary from case to case. Court practices have in- cluded deferring orders until superannuation becomes payable, adjourn- ing hearings until superannuation has been paid and may be included in a property settlement, or treating superannuation assets at a discounted present value. Commonly, these assets are traded off against the family home, typically the other principal asset of the marriage (Clare 1994: 22–3).

Superannuation represents a new source of income in retirement for many women. Modelling income generated by superannuation on the basis of a female life course pattern, Knox (1994) estimates that she will receive, on average, superannuation pension income of 2 per cent of her final salary for each 1 per cent of salary contributed. Although men's gains will undoubtedly be greater, it is nonetheless essential to recognize the importance of this additional income for women's well- being in later life. Table 11.7 summarizes gender-relevant features of the pension system.

Table 11.7 Women-friendly and adverse features of the Australian pension regime

---

Women-friendly features

Public pension: Age Pension (AP)
• Flat-rate pension, payable equally to each person in a couple
• Benefits not conditional upon marital status, employment or contributions
• Benefits indexed to cost of living
• Generously income and asset tested, alleviating poverty with minimal stigma

Mandated private pensions: SGC
• Provides income supplementing public Age Pension
• Ensures coverage for all employees, including part time and casual workers
• Contributions paid by employers, no employee contributions

Voluntary private pensions
• Improved coverage for employed women, especially in well-paid, professional and public sector employment
• Retirement income independent of spouse
• Tax rebate supports contributions on behalf of non-earning or low-earning spouse

Adverse features

Public pension: AP
• Low benefit levels
• Income and assets tests based on joint resources of couples.

Mandated private pensions: SGC
• Very low pension levels
• Benefits reflect gender inequalities in employment and earnings
• Women not in labour force and those with low levels of employment excluded

Voluntary private pensions
• Benefits reflect gender inequalities in employment and earnings
• Limited provision for coverage to be extended to spouses not in labour force advantages mainly high income couples
• No clear policy specifying division of superannuation resources upon divorce
• Women underrepresented in fund management and control

Because Australian superannuation coverage has expanded only recently, it will be some 30 years before full benefits will be realized. For the foreseeable future, the pension prospects of most women will be shaped in the interaction between the public AP and private retirement saving. Moreover, retired people whose superannuation coverage is limited to the SGC will depend on the AP for the majority of their income for an indefinite future, and women will depend on it more heavily than men. Bateman and Piggott (1998: 558) estimate that a male worker who has received average male weekly earnings for 40 years and whose employer has paid superannuation contributions of 9 per cent would retire at age 65 with a total income equivalent to 79 per cent of his pre-retirement (after-tax) income. A female worker receiving average female weekly earnings and an identical employment history would retire with 75 per cent of her (lower) pre-retirement income. Both would look to the AP for a significant share – 36 per cent for the male and 41 per cent for the female – of this income. Workers with shorter and/or broken employment histories would depend much more heavily on the AP.

Retirement income reform has sought to rewrite the social compact for the provision of income in retirement, assigning a greater share of responsibility to the individual and a greater role in the delivery of support to the private sector. Savings in the cost of the AP to the public purse figure importantly in this goal. Advocates of women's interests fear that with the growth of superannuation those groups having greatest stakes in the public AP, most particularly women, will become a residual minority. Without the legitimacy and visibility of a large constituency, the AP may be allowed to decline in value. While these fears are by no means groundless, the receipt of AP income by only a minority of older Australians appears far off. Projections indicate that even by 2051 some 75 per cent of those aged 65 or more will be eligible for at least a part pension (Clare 1994: 13). This does not take account of the reduction of the benefit withdrawal rate in respect of private income from 50 to 40 per cent in July 2000, increasing the income range over which there is entitlement to a part pension. For these reasons, it is to be expected that at least the same share of the population will continue to receive an AP for the foreseeable future, with budget savings achieved through a reducing proportion receiving the full pension. The sustainability of the social safety net nevertheless remains a continuing theme in the government's policy evaluation framework.

Many women have little knowledge and understanding of the retirement income system and their prospects within it. Olsberg (1997: 151–6) finds it is common for women not to understand the nature of superannuation funds and how their resources are invested, and not to know the balance of their account or whether they have spouse entitlements through their husbands' funds. Many have very unrealistic expectations of the income they will need in retirement, the amount of money they can expect, and the importance of time to cumulate an adequate entitlement.

Women make up around 40 per cent of superannuation fund membership, but only 10 per cent of the trustees of superannuation fund boards. It has been suggested that women's underrepresentation may be even greater in the large industry-based funds (Clare 1994: 23–5). The gender disproportion in fund trusteeship follows directly from gender patterns in the industries, unions and financial institutions from which they are drawn. Olsberg (1997: 158) argues that only with greater representation from women will superannuation develop in ways sympathetic to women's special needs and interests. Whether trustees should be responsible for this is a subject for debate. Legal judgements and customary approaches to the management of private capital resources enjoin trustees not to pursue social goals, but rather to secure the best (and most secure) return on investment for their members. Social goals are said to be the responsibility of public social provision.

Conclusion

Gender forms a key dimension in the public and private sectors of Australia's retirement income system. Women have a greater stake than men in the public AP at its foundation. Centrepiece of the welfare safety net, this pension is at best reasonably secure. Men have a greater stake than women in the second tier of private, wage-related superannuation. Women's achievement of greater equality in retirement income will depend primarily on the pursuit of equality in employment and the labour force with respect to the adequacy of their retirement incomes. Women's gains in labour force participation, although sustained over a long period, have been concentrated in part time employment, while the weakening of central wage fixation has begun to undermine earlier gains in pay parity with men. Though men's involvement is slowly increasing, women continue to be the main carers of children and older people, especially in middle age. Women are building a stake in the growing private retirement income sector, and will be economically better off in later life than older women at present. Men are building an even greater stake. There is little prospect that these developments will represent more than a narrowing of the gender gap in retirement income.

CHAPTER 12

The world's social laboratory: women-friendly aspects of New Zealand pensions

SUSAN ST JOHN AND BRIAN GRAN

Introduction

The New Zealand retirement-income system is highly unusual compared to other countries. The public component provides an individual married pensioner with a flat-rate, taxable pension that must lie between 32.5 per cent to 36.25 per cent of the net average wage. A single pensioner is entitled to 120 per cent of the married person rate, increased to 130 per cent if living alone.[1] Individuals are encouraged to supplement this pension by voluntary savings but there are no tax incentives for such provision. Only a small minority of the workforce have employer-subsidized occupational plans. This system has been equitable in its outcomes for women whose major contributions to society have often been in the form of unpaid childcaring and domestic work. As continuous well-paid, full time work for working-age men becomes less common, men too have the advantage of basic income protection in retirement. Indeed, the public pension may be seen as the harbinger of income security provided through a basic income for the general population.

New Zealand is uniquely placed and has often enjoyed a reputation as 'the world's social laboratory' because of its policy innovations. In 1893, NZ was the world's first self-governing nation where women won the right to vote.[2] In 1898, NZ introduced one of the first public old age pension programmes. Wide-ranging welfare state arrangements implemented under the 1938 Social Security Act, including a universal public pension, earned NZ the reputation of looking after its citizens from 'cradle to grave'. In a second wave of social policy initiatives in the 1970s, a remarkably generous state pension was introduced for everyone from age 60.

The New Zealand retirement income system, comprising a basic state pension and voluntary unsubsidized saving, has the potential to do more than merely relieve poverty. It can also reduce the inequality in retirement income between men and women that arises from unequal earning experiences. The potential for moderating inequality critically depends on the adequacy of the basic pension. If it provides a sufficient income, the basic pension can both mitigate inequality and prevent poverty, compared to a minimal, means-tested, safety net payment that only prevents poverty. The tensions over whether the state pension is a welfare benefit, or whether it delivers a degree of real income security reflecting taxes and other unpaid contributions made in the past, have been played out many times in policy developments in the last two decades.

New Zealand's pension regime

In 2000, the NZ system for retirement income provision remained unique in the OECD. It was remarkably simple, based on the provision of a non-contributory, flat-rate pension for individuals who qualified by virtue of age and residency, and voluntary savings. Thus there were no compulsory saving schemes and no tax incentives for private saving for retirement. Both of these are of less advantage to women who typically earn less than men and have shorter careers in the formal workforce. Eligibility for the state pension, now called New Zealand Superannuation (NZS), is based on meeting the qualifying age (65 by 2001) and simple residency requirements, ten years since age 20 and five years since age 50.

Women who have the means to save can supplement NZS in a variety of ways, including repaying the mortgage on their own home or investing in their future earning capacity by undertaking education. There are no signals from the state that any one way is better than any other. While this system has the advantage of maximum flexibility, on average women are less well placed than men to make significant savings.

Table 12.1 New Zealand pension regime

Public pension	
Coverage	Universal
Eligibility	Age + residence (NZS)
Method of financing	General revenues (NZS)
Pension function	Social inclusion, basic earnings replacement (NZS)
Private pensions	
Coverage	Very low, mostly men
Eligibility	Employees in firms with plans
Method of financing	Employer and employee contributions
Pension function	Earnings replacement

Table 12.2   Average NZ pensioner private income, by gender and age group, 1996

Age	60–4	65–9	70–4	75+
Men				
Per cent with private income	67	29.2	20.7	24.2
Average income (NZ$)	25,063	9,345	6,453	11,571
Women				
Per cent with private income	52	13.7	10.5	9.6
Average income (NZ$)	8,814	5,252	4,381	3,833

Source: Cook 1997: 18

Table 12.2 confirms that in retirement, women are far less likely than men to receive private income, and they receive much smaller amounts when they do. About 75 per cent of women over 65 receive three-quarters or more of their income from the universal pension, compared to 54 per cent of men (Statistics NZ 1997: 30).

Overall, average disposable personal income of women over 15 is only 58 per cent that of men (Statistics NZ 1998a: 47). Women obtain only 77 per cent of their income from private sources compared to 92 per cent for men, and of those who do have private income, women in paid work receive under half of that received by males (see Table 12.3).[3] In part, this reflects differences in hours worked and different occupations. Yet figures for earnings from full time employment, standardized for hours worked, age, highest qualification, ethnicity and occupation, still show women earn only 85 per cent of men's gross weekly earnings (Statistics NZ 1998b: 123). Attention to reasons for the earning gap and other labour market factors that disadvantage women may be needed if the NZ retirement-income system is to fulfil its potential of further equalizing men and women's incomes in retirement.

Table 12.3   Average personal private income (NZ$)*, by gender, 1996

	Earners	Population Aged 15+	Per cent of population with private income	Per cent of gross income from private sources
Men	30,600	27,900	91	92
Women	14,900	12,600	84	77
Total	22,600	19,800	88	87

Note: *gross private income from all sources
Source: Statistics NZ 1998a

Evolution of New Zealand's unique system

The old age pension

New Zealand's public pension system was first introduced in 1898, less than 10 years after Germany's implementation of the world's first public pension programme. The Preamble to the New Zealand Old Age Pension Act declared:

> Whereas, it is equitable that deserving persons who, during the term of life, have helped to bear the public burden of the Commonwealth by the payment of taxes, and by opening up its resources by their labor and skill, should receive from the colony pensions in their old age.
>
> (quoted in Johnsen 1922: 276)

Rather than benefits based on an individual's history of paid work as in Germany, New Zealand's old age pension was funded by general tax revenue and paid to eligible individuals age 65 and older. The legislation's designers viewed the old age pension as a reward for citizens' state-building contributions (Lusk 1913: 102). Nevertheless, it was far from generous. Eligibility conditions were strict, requiring income and asset tests, 25 years residency, 'good moral character' and excluding Asiatics (Thomson 1998: 162). The language surrounding the old age pension was consistently masculine, although women were equally entitled to establish a claim, and on the same basis as men. Few men or women actually benefited from the old age pension due to the stringent means test and good character requirements. Over the first three decades of the 1900s, fewer than 30 per cent of New Zealanders over pension age received the pension, and benefits barely kept pace with prices or wages (Thomson 1998: 162). While the pension recognized insecurities of working life and moved away from charitable aid towards a sense of rights and long-term support, by the 1930s it was clear that benefits were meagre and insufficient (McClure 1998: 23).

The Social Security Act 1938

Problems intensified during the Great Depression. NZ was severely affected, exposing the inadequacies of the social safety net for the population at large and highlighting the need for pension reform. The Social Security Act of 1938 was a broad social programme based on the new Labour government's vision of the needs and rights of citizenship. It consisted of two pensions for the aged. The major form of support was the Age Benefit at age 60, which like its predecessor, was income and character tested (Thomson 1998: 165). The other was a universal flat-rate benefit (Universal Superannuation) for all over the age of 65. Universal Superannuation initially was minimal, but was gradually increased so that by 1960 the two pensions were at parity. At age 65, those receiving the income-tested Age Benefit could continue to receive it, or elect to take taxable Universal Superannuation instead. Benefit increases were typically made near elections and were not specifically related to increases in inflation. However, between 1939 and 1970, benefit levels rose by considerably more than increases in the consumer price index (RCSS 1972: 124).

Labour's earnings-related scheme

Both the Labour Party (drawing political support from workers and unions) and the National Party (employers and farmers) accepted the necessary role of the state in the development of a small, isolated economy. Yet, until 1972, social insurance schemes for pensions, or compulsory saving schemes (common in other western democracies), had not been implemented. The lack of enthusiasm for these ideas had reinforced the NZ tradition of non-contributory, flat-rate pensions for all citizens. By the early 1970s, however, concerns arose because only a minority had access to additional pensions from employment-based private plans, which were largely the preserve of those who worked for government or large companies. Existing schemes had problems of vesting and portability among other deficiencies. Many believed that a state-run, earnings-related pension scheme could provide some continuity of income in retirement through wide coverage, full vesting, and inflation proofing of final pensions.

Following a protracted period of debate, in 1975 the Labour government implemented a fully-funded, state-run, earnings-based, contributory scheme, New Zealand Superannuation, under the New Zealand Superannuation Act (1974). Once NZ Superannuation had matured (after 40 years) New Zealanders would have had a two-tier system, consisting of Universal Superannuation supplemented by an inflation-adjusted annuity purchased from their individual account balances at age 65. While the fund was state controlled, the government limited its fiscal role to the cost-of-living adjustment of the annuity payment. Contributions were to be 4 per cent of wages each for employee and employer once the scheme was fully implemented, replicating differences arising from experiences in the paid labour market. The benefit formula was to be purely actuarial in contrast to social insurance schemes abroad such as US Social Security (see Chapter 8). Few individuals could determine their future benefits under the earnings-related pension, since it was tied to individual contributions and the earnings of the fund, not easily predicted over a working life. The scheme's design reflected an expectation that the breadwinner would use his pension to provide for both himself and his wife who would, more often than not, be financially dependent.

Low-income earners and/or those without conventional 40-year, full time working histories could not expect a generous supplement to the first-tier Universal Superannuation. In 1975, only 31 per cent of New Zealand's paid labour force were women (OECD 1981) and eligible to participate in the earnings-related pension. If a woman temporarily left paid work to raise children, she would inevitably receive an annuity with a lower wage replacement compared to the average man (Treasury 1973). Differences in life expectancy would also make a woman's annuity smaller than a man's, when both had saved the same capital sum in the fund.

Criticism of the scheme quickly emerged in the political environment of the 1975 election year. Some were deeply concerned at the prospect of state control over a vast pool of investment capital. Women opposed the Labour scheme for several reasons. Women were upset that, on average, they would receive lower annuities than men. Lower annuities would increase their reliance on Universal Superannuation, which over time was likely to diminish in relative value. Survivor benefits, important because of women's greater likelihood of outliving her spouse, were not generous, and ceased on remarriage. Little redistribution was possible because actuarial equity rather than social adequacy was the goal (St John and Ashton 1993). The National Party also pointed out that spouses of contributors to the new New Zealand Superannuation had no legal right to the pension (Castles 1985: 40).

The National Opposition attacked Labour's new pension system based on these criticisms, but its strongest attack was the promise of a simpler, more generous pension that was particularly attractive to women. Nine months after its introduction, a new National government dismantled the contributory public pension and refunded contributions.

National Superannuation

Having scrapped the earnings-related pension, in 1977 the National government replaced the remaining income-tested Age Pension and Universal Superannuation with a single, more generous, state pension called National Superannuation (NS). The scheme was Pay-As-You-Go (PAYG), funded from general taxation without a dedicated contributory basis or separate fund. NS was set at 80 per cent of the gross average weekly wage for a married couple and 48 per cent for single pensioners.

It was an individual taxable entitlement, payable at age 60 if residential requirements were met. Many features, including the individual basis of the pension whereby a married person received one half the gross married rate, taxed in his or her own name, were hailed as 'good for women'. While there was no income test, by 1982 a high top marginal tax rate (increased from 60 per cent to 66 per cent), substantially reduced the net NS value for the better off.

The National Party scheme addressed many criticisms of Labour's earnings-related scheme (see comments above). Contributions were earnings-related (to the extent that income taxes paid mirrored wages earned) but the final pension benefit was flat-rate and taxable, yielding a progressive benefit structure that helped women and the low paid. This change substantially increased payments to all those over 60 by the time NS was fully implemented in 1978. In contrast to Labour's scheme, the retired immediately benefited, and problems of poverty among the aged virtually disappeared. One of the significant features was the generosity, not only to women and those who had not been in the paid labour force, but to those aged 60 and older who had not yet retired, as there was no earnings test. When it was implemented, NS probably provided the most generous state pension in the world. It was not limited to previous paid labour force participants, but available to every older resident, simple to understand and people could easily predict the pension they would receive.

The decline of National Superannuation

The NZ economy suffered from the oil shocks as a small and exposed trading nation and by the late 1970s, confidence that postwar affluence would continue was abating. It was clear that some of the largesse of NS was unsupportable and would increasingly become so. The first change to NS was a decrease in 1979, when the net married couple rate of NS became 80 per cent of the average net wage.

Labour returned to government in 1984, with a wide-ranging reform agenda stressing the role of market forces. The government's finance wing advocated 'a state system that reflected the goals, management structure and ethics of the private sector' (Castles and Shirley 1996: 98). The next decade brought dramatic neo-liberal economic reforms and social transformations, possibly unequalled in scale anywhere else in the OECD.

The Labour Party promised prior to the 1984 election that it would not further diminish the universal pension scheme. However this promise appeared forgotten once the election was over. By 1985, the Labour government had imposed a surcharge on NS pensioners of 25 per cent on all other private income over an exempt amount. The effect of this surcharge was to claw back the value of state pension for those with significant private incomes. Thus NS was no longer universal (although it had been taxable as income) but was essentially income-tested, albeit the test allowed a high-income exemption. Reactions to the surcharge were strong, not only because Labour blatantly broke a campaign promise (St John 1992: 129; Castles and Shirley 1996: 96), but also because the universal pension was no longer intended to be universal.

Only 10 per cent of pensioners effectively paid back all of their NS through the surcharge and three-quarters of pensioners were not affected at all (St John and Ashton 1993: 17). Reflecting their low likelihood of having a high private income, few women were directly affected by the surcharge. Because the surcharge was based on individual not joint income, married women could still receive the pension in their own right, even when their husband's income was high. The exemption amount also was on an individual basis, although a married couple could amalgamate their exemptions. Consequently, when one partner's low income meant she did not fully use her exemption, the other partner could use the remainder. This surcharge feature provided married couples with an advantage compared to single people, maybe balancing the married person's disadvantage of having a lower NS rate and exemption.

Tax developments in the 1980s

In the 1980s, the Treasury was determined to reform the tax system by flattening the tax scale and removing special tax privileges. Between 1987 and 1990, the Labour government abolished all tax incentives for retirement savings so that saving for retirement in superannuation plans was treated no differently, for tax purposes, from putting money in the bank. The intent of the reform was not focused on overall retirement incomes policies and the need to ensure adequacy of provision through combined public and private sources. Rather, the reforms were based on efficiency arguments and a desire to remove distortions so that investment money would flow to where it had the highest economic benefit. Elimination of tax incentives also had important equity implications. The benefits of tax incentives went mainly to white men with high incomes in long-term careers with the same firm. Funding for tax incentives came from general tax revenues, so everyone paid for them. Consequently, the abolition of tax incentives had the potential, on average, to reduce the tax burden for women, minorities, and the low paid. The reintroduction of tax incentives to encourage private savings has never been seriously argued since.

In 1988, the various options for the state pension, such as compulsory saving and social insurance, were canvassed. The Labour government, in

1989, decided that the existing arrangements were the most suitable, but that the age of eligibility for NS, now to be called the Guaranteed Retirement Income (GRI), should rise over 20 years to age 65. A dedicated tax of about 8 per cent of the personal income tax base was to be earmarked to meet the payments expected for the PAYG state pension.

The role of the surcharge

As noted above, in 1985 a controversial surcharge on pensioners' other incomes over an exempt amount was introduced (see Table 12.4). When the top income tax rate was reduced from 66 per cent to 48 per cent, and then to 33 per cent in 1986 and 1988 respectively, the effect of the surcharge was to restore some tax progressivity for those over 60 with significant other income (St John and Ashton 1993: 17). The initial rationale was, however, purely cost saving. Regardless of the justification, the surcharge became a political hot potato, eventually damaging to both main political parties.

Table 12.4   Surcharge assessments and parameters since 1985

Income ending March	Amount of surcharge assessed (NZ$ million)	Per cent subject to surcharge	Exemption threshold singe person (NZ$ per annum)	Exemption threshold couples (NZ$ per annum)	Rate of surcharge (%)
1985/86	167	21.9	6,240	10,400	25.0
1986/87	175	22.4	7,202	12,012	24.5
1988/89	237	30.5	7,800	13,000	19.0
1989/90	314	34.5	7,202	12,012	20.0
1990/91	306	26.7	7,202	12,012	20.0
1991/92	287	25.0	7,202	12,012	20.0
1992/93	347	31.1	4,160	6,240	25.0
1993/94	311	27.9	4,160	6,240	25.0
1994/95	289	28.5	4,160	6,240	25.0
Estimates and forecasts					
1995/96	320	31.5	4,160	6,240	25.0
1996/97	324	32.0	4,550	6,825	25.0
1997/98	22	16.1	10,296	15,444	25.0
1998/99	0	0	Surcharge abolished		

Source: PRG 1997a: 48

After promising in the 1990 election campaign to protect the retired and to eliminate the surcharge, the National Party returned to power with a different agenda. The National Party's promise to remove the surcharge implied a return to universal public pensions. Post-election, however, the National government announced it would replace the unpopular surcharge with an even more unpopular income test, transforming the GRI into an income-tested benefit similar to social assistance benefits. Under this joint income test, whether a married couple or a single individual, only NZ$4160 per year was permitted as exempt income. After this, the combination of income tax and clawback of the pension meant that an extra dollar earned over NZ$80 a week was subject to an effective marginal tax rate of 93 per cent. Thus, for a married couple, other income between NZ$4160 and NZ$23,700 (when the couple's pension finally disappeared) would be hardly worth having as only 7 cents in each extra dollar could be retained over this range. The policy was softened a little for those over 70, who could retain one half of the pension as a universal entitlement regardless of income, mainly benefiting the wealthiest who formerly had lost their entire pension with the surcharge. The phased age of eligibility increase was accelerated from 20 years to ten years. At this point it looked as if NZ, alone among the OECD countries, would have no special policies for the provision of retirement income over and above a subsistence, tightly-targeted safety net for the poor (St John 1999: 283). It was a remarkable turnabout from one of the most generous, comprehensive pension systems to one of the least.

Retired New Zealanders were outraged. Many faced the unpleasant prospect of a substantially reduced retirement income.[4] Some married women found that they would no longer be entitled to a pension in their own right without regard to their partner's earnings. Older men, married to younger wage-earning women, also faced the loss of their independent income. Under the new income test for the GRI, divorce would improve some women's incomes. After intense lobbying, these changes were reversed in an embarrassing U-turn for the government.

The government announced in late 1991 that the state pension, with its original name of National Superannuation restored, would remain as before, although the eligibility age would continue to be quickly raised, to reach 65 by 2001. Additionally, a much tighter version of the surcharge would be in place by April 1992. As Table 12.4 shows, the proportion of pensioners subject to the surcharge rose to over 30 per cent. The aborted 1991 changes had heightened public awareness of the impact of targeting so that the scramble to find avoidance schemes with the new surcharge continued. This in turn contributed to the loss of integrity of the surcharge system and allowed its critics ample ammunition to discredit it. As detailed below it was eventually abolished in 1998.

Unstable stability

The events of the late 1980s and early 1990s left many in NZ aware of pension policy instability and pensioners' vulnerability to ad hoc and politically motivated changes to the state pension arrangements. In 1991, the National government appointed the Task Force on Private Provision for Retirement 'to report on policy options to encourage greater self-reliance of retired people' (Task Force 1991: 30). Although the Task Force asked, 'What is the best contribution from each source (public and private), and how can the best mix be found and maintained?' (1991: 43), its primary responsibility was to promote 'private provision' of retirement income, implicitly reducing state involvement in retirement income provision.

The National government asked the Task Force to follow 'broad principles' in considering policies 'in the area of private provision for retirement'. They were:

- encouragement of greater financial self-reliance of retired people;
- promotion of intergenerational equity;
- promotion of economic efficiency in resource allocation; and
- promotion of fiscal sustainability.

The Task Force suggested the evaluation of three options for future retirement-income provision: voluntary provision, compulsion, and tax incentives. In the end, the Task Force recommended the voluntary provision approach over the compulsory and tax incentive approaches. The voluntary option consisted of four parts:

- an improved voluntary regime for private provision for retirement;
- integration of public and private retirement provision policy;
- six-yearly reviews of the operation of this integrated retirement policy commencing in 1997;
- a well-informed public and political consensus on all of the above.

(Task Force 1992: 65)

The Task Force had in mind that New Zealanders, on their own initiative, would set aside funds to provide a supplementary source of income to the state pension, but would not be required (the compulsory option) or provided incentives (the tax incentive option) to do so. The Task Force found the 'voluntary' option attractive because it offered flexibility for individuals to decide whether and how much to contribute to their retirement savings. A voluntary approach would promote competition among suppliers of savings vehicles, and, compared to the 'compulsory' option, would allow for gradual economic change (1992: 17). Since the surcharge on NS was a form of income testing, there was some inherent disincentive to save since individuals could consume their 'retirement savings' during their pre-retirement years to avoid the surcharge. However, as discussed above, the surcharge was a very mild income test, only applied to income above a generous exemption.

Noting previous indecision and broken promises made by governments, an important suggestion the Task Force made was to reduce the uncertainty about policies surrounding the public pension system (Task Force 1992: 27–31) by taking the retirement-income system out of the political arena. In 1993, an Accord between the three major political parties (Labour, National and the Alliance) locked into place New Zealand's unique system of a basic state pension, now to be called New Zealand Superannuation (NZS) and voluntary unsubsidized private saving. The Accord cemented in the voluntary tax neutral arrangements for private saving, a flat-rate NZ taxable pension net of between 65 to 72.5 per cent of the net average wage for couples, and a surcharge for higher income retirees. Under a wage band formula, NZS would only be price adjusted each year, unless the net pension fell below the floor (65 per cent) or rose above the ceiling (72.5 per cent). At this point wage indexation would restore the relativity to wages.

Between 1993 to 1996 the Accord gave retired people protection against ill-considered changes, and those coming up to retirement could plan with a reasonable degree of certainty. This framework was endorsed after a comprehensive review as required by the Retirement Income Act 1993 (PRG 1997a). This review also found that net expenditure on the NZS had significantly fallen as the age of eligibility began to rise. NZS cost approximately 4 per cent of GDP in 1996/97, and would rise to only around 9 per cent of GDP over the next 50 years under the 1997 settings (PRG 1997a: 103). In comparing this cost with other countries it must be remembered that NZ has no hidden tax expenditures for retirement income provision, and a very low cost regulatory regime for private schemes. The PRG concluded that the current pension, with the rise in the qualifying age to 65 by 2001 and the wage band formula for indexation described above was adequate, efficient, and sustainable. From 2015, some well-signalled, moderate modifications could be introduced to curb the cost if required.

Formation of the new coalition government in 1996 began to undermine the Accord. While agreement had been reached on the surcharge for 1997/98, the surcharge itself was abolished from 1998 as part of the coalition agreement. This was the kind of decision that the Accord was to have removed from the disruptive influences of election-year politics. More damaging still to stability in retirement-income planning, in September 1998 the government announced that the wage band floor would now be lowered over time to 60 per cent from 65 per cent. By 1999, the Accord was fairly judged as over, although the legislation endorsing its provisions remained.

The Labour government, elected in 1999, reversed the change to the wage band floor, which had caused a married person's pension to drop to 31.4 per cent of the net average wage. From April 2000 the net pension of a married person was raised to 33.7 per cent of the net average wage, restoring confidence that NZS would be tied to movements in the average wage as before. While the Labour government also raised the top marginal tax rate from 33 per cent to 39 per cent, there was no suggestion of a return to any kind of income testing such as reinstating the surcharge. In 2000, talks between the parties on the left were examining the prospect of partial pre-funding for the state pension as a shift from pure PAYG arrangements.

Current situation

Since the late 1970s, the net couple benefit has fallen relative to the average wage. Nevertheless, until the late 1990s, the pension benefit level was high enough so that even for those with few private resources, few additional means-tested supplements have been necessary to prevent poverty, especially for retirees owning their own homes. In 1999 there was some evidence that the elderly were increasing their use of food banks and use of special welfare supplements. While there is no official poverty line in NZ, a recent study using 60 per cent of median income reported a rise in poverty incidence among the elderly in 1998 due to the slippage in the relative level of NZS (Stephens *et al.* 2000: 29). Concerns were voiced that had the wage band floor of 60 per cent remained, New Zealand could expect the re-emergence of significant poverty among the older age group.

The age for the state pension has been the same for men and women since 1938, and reaching 65 by 2001. A Transitional Retirement Benefit, to be phased out by 2004, is available to those people whose plans have been disrupted by higher age of eligibility for the state pension. As the age of eligibility is being raised for the public pension, workforce participation of older men and women has markedly increased.

Nevertheless, well-paid, full time employment remains elusive for many. Social change such as separation, divorce, and widowhood contributes to a picture of many older women facing retirement without adequate private arrangements. An Invalid's Benefit or a minimal unemployment benefit called the 55+ Benefit maintain those who are not in the paid workforce and who need income assistance during their late 50s and early 60s. The tight income test and low level of these benefits suggest that if women rely on these benefits for prolonged periods, they are likely to reach the age of entitlement for NZS considerably impoverished.

Table 12.5   Proportion of people over 65 receiving occupational pension income as a proportion of total income

	Men	Women
Occupational pension provides:		
Less than 25% of income	11.3	7.4
25–50% of income	9.2	9.5
50–74% of income	10.2	1.8
Over 75% of income	*	*
Proportion over 65 receiving occupational pension	21.4%	9.7%

Notes: Table excludes those with no regular occupational pension income
* sample size too small to give accurate estimate
Source: Statistics NZ 1997

The various tax changes detailed in this chapter are responsible for a general movement away from occupational superannuation plans since the late 1980s. Private pensions now cover a relatively small fraction of the working age population, with access to generous employer-subsidized schemes remaining highly biased towards men. Only about 15 per cent of New Zealanders over 65 had any private pension income and as Table 12.5 shows, older women had much less than men.

Intergenerational equity concerns

David Thomson (1991) first raised the issue that the NZ welfare state favoured some generations more than others. With the approaching retirement of the baby boom generation, the debate over intergenerational equity has intensified. The neo-liberal reforms of the last decade have resulted in tightly targeted social assistance for the beneficiary population under retirement age, more user charges in education and health care, and student loans with onerous interest rates and repayment regimes. The contrast between the treatment of the young and those who have generous universal retirement pensions (even if they are still working or are wealthy) is stark. An increasing emigration of the skilled and highly-trained youth who have incurred considerable debt poses dangers for the future provision of income security for the aged. Promoting private pension provision, however, far from solves the problem. There is a danger that intergenerational inequity will be addressed by hurting those in most need of the state pension through reducing the benefit level, altering the indexation provisions, de-emphasizing the link to wages, or further raising the age of eligibility. The challenge for NZ will be to find acceptable ways of reducing the ever-widening gaps between the rich and the poor, in retirement as well as among the population more generally.

Different groups of women

Statistics NZ (1998b: 108) has demonstrated an overall drop in real median total gross incomes for all New Zealand adults of 13.4 per cent over the past decade. It is clear that declining incomes will exacerbate the problem of providing adequate supplementary retirement savings for many women.

Table 12.6 shows the disparity between men and women's incomes and reinforces the conclusion that women face significant disadvantages in preparing for retirement. Among those aged 65, women have an average life expectancy which is 3.7 years longer than men's. NZ women's median total personal incomes are lower than men's in every ethnic group, although European women have median incomes higher than Asian men's. These differences suggest that non-European women especially will encounter greater difficulties in accumulating private retirement savings. Consequently, the universal pension will continue to be and may become an even greater proportion of retirement income for women and minority New Zealanders.

Table 12.6   Median personal incomes by gender and ethnicity, 1996

Gender and ethnic group	Median annual income (NZ$)	Percentage of European men's incomes
European women	13,100	55
European men	23,900	100
Maori women	11,200	47
Maori men	16,100	67
Pacific Islands women	10,800	45
Pacific Islands men	15,300	64
Asian women	7,100	30
Asian men	12,100	51
Total women	12,600	53
Total men	22,000	92
Total adults	15,600	65

Note: Percentages have been rounded
Source: Derived from Statistics New Zealand 1998b

Discussion

As a social laboratory, New Zealand's approach to providing income security to women through its public pension system may prove useful to other societies undergoing changes in their labour markets and other social domains. The role of private pensions for the retirement-income system has remained small; tax incentives designed to encourage private pensions are not used, removing a typical source of retirement income inequality from the NZ pension regime (see Chapters 4, 8 and 10). Consequently, the combination of the universal pension and voluntary private savings offers flexibility in how people prepare for their retirement years with the state's role as one of reducing income inequality in old age.

Despite the numerous policy wobbles, and neo-liberal reforms in other areas of public policy, New Zealand has maintained a remarkably successful public pension system from the perspective of women since the mid-1970s. Since the first public pension was introduced, NZ has implicitly recognized contributions to the country that are not traditionally measured in money terms. Table 12.7 identifies many attributes of the NZ system benefiting women.

The universal pension has historically been the subject of political debate, as noted above. Past reforms suggest that the NZ retirement-income system is not settled. For example, within six years the Accord on Retirement Income Policies was all but broken. Without the security of the Accord, the future adequacy of NZS may be in doubt. Nevertheless, in contrast to the residualistic approaches to the state pension in other countries where private provision has been encouraged, the recent Labour government has been proactive in reversing the cuts made to the pension level by its predecessor. It has also taken steps to learn more about the living standards of the retired to assess the adequacy of NZS. Overall, however, there seems to be a limited understanding among the public of the importance of maintaining a wages link for pension benefits. Should the value of NZS be allowed to fall as a fraction of the average wage, more older persons, especially women, will require additional assistance. If this assistance is means-tested, stigmatizing, complex to access, and ungenerous, the simplicity and income-equalizing advantages of the traditional NZ approach will quickly be undermined.

As the age of eligibility has increased (effectively lowering the number of individuals eligible for the universal pension) different sociocultural groups have been differently affected, especially Maori males who have lower life expectancies. Consequently, although the universal pension provides a model for retirement-income provision, its future remains uncertain. It is to be hoped that New Zealand will remain a social laboratory, experimenting to maintain and improve its retirement-income

Table 12.7 Women-friendly and adverse features of the NZ pension regime

Women-friendly features
- Generous pension for individuals living alone
- Adequate benefits, particularly for those owning their own homes
- Individual basis for pension
- Few problems arising from divorce, separation and death of a spouse found in most public pension systems in other countries and with private pensions
- Eligibility not based on contributions, earnings, or working career
- Public pension financed from general tax revenue, which is progressive in overall incidence
- Relative living standards protected through link to average wages
- No expensive tax incentives, freeing funds for public pensions and lowering income tax rates
- Flexibility allows a variety of saving approaches suited to the various lifecycle stages of women

Adverse features
- Adequacy has not been maintained for everyone as housing, healthcare and other costs have risen while the pension for a couple has fallen toward the floor of 65 per cent of the net average wage
- Few women have access to employer-subsidized schemes and fewer still will receive a supplementary private pension in retirement
- Lack of political stability of the pension regime, particularly the vulnerability of the universal pension to attack by groups who want to convert it into a welfare benefit that only relieves poverty
- Sociocultural groups do not enjoy equal life expectancies, suggesting inequities will arise from increasing the age of eligibility for the universal pension
- Increased age of eligibility when few women in their 60s have well-paid full time jobs creates many unresolved problems. Women dominate the caring professions such as nursing and teaching, where continued work creates physical demands that become increasingly challenging as they age.

system in ways that not only protect its women, but also promote the well being of all its older citizens.

Note

1 In 2000 the actual married, single and living alone rates were 33.7 per cent, 40.5 per cent, and 43.8 per cent of the net average wage, respectively.
2 In 2000 both the NZ prime minister (Helen Clark) and the leader of the opposition (Jenny Shipley) were female.
3 Private income is gross income from all sources excluding governmental benefits.
4 Some married couples, with incomes from other sources of around $24,000 for example found to their horror that the income test would leave them as much as $10,000 worse off.

CHAPTER **13**

Women's pension outlook: variations among liberal welfare states

JAY GINN, DEBRA STREET AND SARA ARBER

In this chapter, we summarize the pension system structures of the six countries and compare them in terms of a gender sensitive framework, focusing on the extent to which women's patterns of paid and unpaid work over the life course are accommodated. Outcomes in terms of gender inequality of later life income are compared and the likely pension prospects for working-age women considered, given pension reform trends. Finally we outline policy options to improve women's pension prospects.

Pension structures in six liberal welfare states

Table 13.1 summarizes national pension structures in terms of three tiers of pension provision. These are a) statutory provision including pensions and social assistance; b) mandatory earnings-related pensions (public or private); and c) voluntary pensions, which are also related to earnings.

State flat-rate pensions

In the first pension tier, four countries provide flat-rate basic pensions (see Table 13.1a). This is contributory social insurance in Britain and Ireland and tax-funded residence-based pensions in New Zealand and Canada, income tested in the latter case. Although needs-tested social assistance is not strictly part of pension provision, it is included here because Ireland, Canada and Australia have programmes specifically designed for older people, widely used, easy to claim, non-stigmatizing and (except in Ireland) applying tapered withdrawal in respect of other

Table 13.1 Comparing the structure of pensions in six liberal welfare states

	(a) Statutory		(b) Mandatory		(c) Voluntary
	Flat-rate Social insurance (Redistributive, poverty prevention)	Needs-tested Social assistance (Poverty relief)	Earnings-related Public (Income replacement)	Earnings-related Private (Income replacement)	Earnings-related Private (Income replacement)
UK	BP (contributory)	MIG (claimed top-up)	SERPS (DB)	OP; APP (DC) (contracted out of SERPS)	OP; APP (DC)
US	–	SSI (claimed top-up)	SS (DB) (redistributive)	–	IRA (DC); 401K (DC)
IR	OAP (contributory)	NP (received if no OAP)	–	–	OP; personal pensions
CA	OAS (clawback possible)	GIS (automatic top-up)	C/QPP (DB)	–	RRSP (DC); RPP (DB)
AU	–	AP (universal)	–	SGC (DC) (only employer contribs)	OP; personal pensions
NZ	NZS	–	–	–	OP; personal pensions (no tax relief)

Note: DB: defined benefit
DC: defined contribution

income. These programmes contrast with the residual safety nets of Britain and the US, which must be claimed using complex, intrusive procedures to determine absolute need based on both income and assets, are stigmatized as poor relief, and have a 100 per cent withdrawal rate which creates a severe poverty trap. There is thus a spectrum of social assistance programmes, ranging from a universal pension which is gradually withdrawn from the better off (Canada and Australia) to punitive poverty relief at the other extreme (Britain and the US).

Mandatory earnings related pensions

Three countries (Britain, the US and Canada) have mandatory state earnings-related pensions (see Table 13.1b). These all provide defined benefits (DB) for those covered under the schemes, which have the advantage of providing a risk-free retirement income for life. The US Social Security scheme (SS) is unusual in combining an earnings-related element with some redistribution in favour of the low paid, thus performing the dual function of poverty prevention and income replacement.

Britain is unique among the six countries in encouraging contracting out from the State Earnings Related Pensions Scheme (SERPS) into occupational (OP) or personal pensions (APPs) which satisfy certain requirements. People who opt out of SERPS in favour of an APP exchange a secure state DB entitlement for an unpredictable private DC pension, with all its disadvantages. Australia mandates private defined contribution (DC) pensions through the Superannuation Guarantee Charge (SGC) which is financed solely by employers and whose benefits can be taken as lump sums.

Despite neo-liberal preferences for mandated DC individual schemes, compelling employers to provide them does not lessen a country's pension tax burden. Contributions to mandated private pensions are logically identical to social security contributions (that is, a fixed labour cost), although the security of benefits is less and the potential for women-friendly provisions such as childcare credits is lost.

Voluntary private pensions

The third tier of voluntary private pensions exists in all six countries (see Table 13.1c) but their contribution to overall pension provision varies markedly among these countries, in terms of pensioners' income and of fund assets held. For example, nearly half of British pensioners received some private pension compared with less than 15 per cent in Australia and New Zealand. Private pensions are becoming predominantly DC in the US, whereas in Britain DB occupational pension schemes are most common. In most countries, DB coverage is declining and DC schemes are spreading, transferring the investment risk from employers to employees and reducing the employer's contribution relative to that usually paid into DB schemes. All the countries except New Zealand provide tax incentives for contributions to voluntary private pensions, thus subsidizing private pensions. The greatest benefit from such tax spending goes to those contributing the most to private pensions – men and the highest paid employees. British pension fund assets were nearly 80 per cent of GDP in 1993 compared with 60 per cent in the US and 40 per cent in Ireland (PPG 1998).

The relatively high level of resources devoted to private pension provision in Britain, the US, Canada and Ireland benefits men at the expense of women in so far as it diverts resources into tax relief, limiting resources available for public provision. Ireland's public pensions are more redistributive towards the low paid than in Britain, having no earnings-related component. In the remaining two countries, Australia has tax-privileged voluntary private provision, so that New Zealand redistributes more strongly towards those with low lifetime earnings.

Comparing pension system quality for women

The quality of a pension system for women depends on both ease of access to pension schemes and features which ensure that the value of pensions is adequate for those whose lifetime earnings, because of their caring responsibilities, are low relative to the average lifetime earnings of men.

Following the framework set out in Chapter 1 (see Figure 1.1), we focus on aspects of pension schemes that are particularly relevant to women with caring responsibilities. Table 13.2 compares conditions governing access to membership of each pension scheme and the amount of benefit to which a woman could expect entitlement as an individual or as a spouse or widow. Although pension amounts shown do not all relate to the same year they do provide a rough guide to relative generosity in the six countries. For convenience of comparing amounts, local currencies have been converted to pounds sterling using Purchasing Power Parities (PPPs) for 1998 (OECD 2000). PPPs reflect the number of monetary units needed to buy the same representative basket of consumer goods and services, thus avoiding the distortion that occurs when exchange rates are used to convert to sterling, due to the substantial overvaluation of the pound relative to Australian, New Zealand and Canadian dollars. Table 13.2 also shows amounts of pensions expressed as a percentage of average earnings. To simplify cross-country comparison,

Table 13.2 Gender-sensitive comparison of pension system quality in six liberal welfare states, late 1990s

	UK	US	IR	CAN	AUS	NZ
Purchasing Power Parity (for conversion to £)	1.00	1.52	1.06	1.78	2.01	2.25
State pension age: Women	60[1]	65[2]	66[5]	65	61[3]	64[4]
Men	65	65[2]	66[5]	65	65	64[4]
(a) State pensions, entitlement in own right						
Tax-funded flat-rate universal	–	–	–	OAS	–	NZS
Full weekly amount (lone pensioner)	–	–	–	£54(C$97)	–	£100.4(NZ$226)
Full amount as per cent national average earnings	–	–	–	14.7%[16]	–	44%[6]
Years' residence required for full	–	–	–	40	–	10[7]
Contributory flat-rate	BP	–	OAP	–	–	–
Full weekly amount (lone pensioner)	£67	–	£91(I£96)	–	–	–
Full amount as per cent national average earnings	15%[16]	–	28.5%	–	–	–
Years required for full amount	39[8]	–	20 from 1979	–	–	–
Allowance for years of caring	HRP	–	HS	–	–	–
Contributory earnings-related	SERPS	SS	–	C/QPP	–	–
Maximum as per cent individual's average earnings	25%[9]	41%	–	25%	–	–
Years required for full amount	39[8]	35	–	40	–	–
Allowance for years of caring	No	No	–	Yes	–	–
(b) State pension entitlements as dependant						
Pensioner wife (per cent of husband's)	60% BP	50% SS	None	[10]	–	–
Pensioner widow (per cent of dead husband's)	100% BP	100% SS	93%	60% C/QPP	–	–
Pensioner divorcee	[11]	50% SS[12]	~	[11]	–	–

	MIG	SSI	NP	GIS	AP	
(c) State needs-tested pensions						
Basis of needs-test	means	means	means	income	means[13]	–
Minimum income/week (lone pensioner)	£75	£76($115)	£79(↑£84)	£65($115)	£88($177)	–
Minimum as per cent national average earnings	17%[16]	16%[16]	25%	18%[16]	25%[16]	–
Unit for needs-test (in shared households)	Md/cohab	Household	Md/cohab	Md/cohab	Md/cohab	–
Tapered withdrawal	No	No	No	Yes	Yes	–
Per cent receiving: Women	15%[14]	4.3%	24%	47%	81%	–
Men	7%[14]	1.7%	24%	36%	81%	–
(d) Private pensions (occupational/personal)						
Mandatory	No	No	No	No	Yes[15]	No
Widow's pension (as per cent of husband's)	50%	66%	variable	60%	~	~
Tax relief on employee contributions	Yes	Yes	Yes	Yes	Yes	No
Public pension transfers as per cent GDP (1990s)	4.4%	3.9%	4.8%	5.2%	3.1%	4.0%
Tax spending on private pensions as % GDP[17]	2.8%	1.0%	2.1%	2.2%	1.9%	0

Notes: Purchasing Power Parities (PPPs) quoted by OECD (2000) have been used to convert local currencies into British pounds. PPPs can be understood as exchange rates that have been adjusted to take account of the undervaluation (in terms of goods and services which can be bought) of each local currency relative to the pound

– not applicable; ~ not available;

1 65 by 2020;
2 67 in 2020;
3 62 in 2000;
4 65 by 2001;
5 65 if retired;
6 % of net average earnings 34% for a married person;
7 or 5+ years from age 50 and current resident;
8 44 by 2020;
9 will reduce to 20% by 2010;
10 C/QPP benefits of spouses can be combined, then split equally;
11 divorced woman may use ex-husband's contribution record;
12 100% if divorced husband is dead;
13 generously means-tested;
14 non-married;
15 many take benefits as a lump sum to invest;
16 % of average male earnings; 'Md/cohab' refers to couples living as man and wife.
17 Adema (2000)

and because older women's poverty is concentrated among those without a partner, benefit amounts are given for non-married individuals.

(a) State pensions, entitlement in the individual's own right

In all six countries women are more reliant on state pensions than men since most women have little or no private pension income. Therefore the level of state pensions is particularly important in preventing poverty among older women. The tax-funded pensions of Canada and New Zealand are available to each older individual, irrespective of past employment and earnings or current marital status. This type of pension is potentially an effective means of ensuring that women's caring roles only minimally reduce their later life income relative to childless women or men, providing that benefit levels are set at a high enough level. However, New Zealand Superannuation (NZS) is a more generous pension than Old Age Security (OAS) both in access and amount. The NZS has less stringent residence conditions and provides 44 per cent of the net average wage, for a person living alone (see Table 13.2a).

The Canadian OAS provides a very low amount, only £54 (C$97) per week and is subject to reduction (or clawback) at the rate of C$1 for every C$2 of other income of the individual above a threshold that is over £20,000 per annum. However all low income Canadians also automatically receive the income-tested Guaranteed Income Supplement (GIS), administered through the tax system, yielding a guaranteed minimum income, discussed in more detail below.

The full amount of the Irish Old Age Pension (OAP) is £91 (I£96) per week, a third higher than the British BP at £67 per week (28.5 and 15 per cent respectively of national average male earnings). Both these pension schemes have the advantage, for women, of disregarding a number of years of family caring, through Home Responsibilities Protection (HRP) in Britain and the Homemakers Scheme (HS) in Ireland. Despite this, many women currently do not meet the qualifying conditions for a full pension (39 years in Britain and 20 years since 1979 in Ireland). In Britain, women's fewer years of employment have been compounded by a history, until 1978, of disincentives for married women to contribute to social insurance pensions and by an earnings threshold for contributions. Thus both restricted access and a low amount undermine the potential for Britain's BP to redistribute towards women who have spent years in family caring.

Mandatory state earnings-related pension schemes, such as Britain's SERPS, Canada's C/QPP and Social Security (SS) in the US, are potentially more helpful than private pensions in boosting women's pension income, for several reasons. First, they can allow for some years of low/

zero earnings to be disregarded, as in SS and C/QPP (seven years each) and in SERPS as originally formulated. C/QPP additionally disregards years of low or no earnings for primary carers of children under age 7. Second, as DB schemes, these programmes provide a predictable pension for life, with no reduction for women's greater longevity as occurs in private DC pensions. Third, benefits can be skewed towards the low paid, to the advantage of women. Thus SS replaces 41 per cent of earnings over the working life for average earners, but 57 per cent for the low paid. The upper earnings limit for C/QPP contributions means the benefit covers a larger proportion of women's lower average earnings. Fourth, state second-tier pensions are easily portable without loss across jobs and gaps in employment and incur no charges to contributors. In Canada and the US, the state earnings-related scheme includes the self-employed as well as employees. Those with very low earnings are excluded from the schemes in Britain, Canada and the US.

(b) State pension entitlements as a dependant

Wives over state pension age may receive a derived pension as a proportion of their husband's entitlement in Britain (60 per cent of the BP) and the US (50 per cent of SS) (Table 13.2b). Although such spouse pensions benefit married women by ensuring some personal income in later life, they discriminate against dual-earner couples because married women entitled to a small pension in their own right receive no more than a lifelong homemaker wife. In Canada there is no spousal pension, per se, but couples can choose to split their combined C/QPP benefit equally between them, an arrangement that is far more satisfactory for women. In Ireland the OAP carries no spouse benefit as such although additional benefits for dependants may be paid to the OAP recipient. Australian older women require no spousal state benefits, since the Age Pension (AP) is split equally between spouses, while in New Zealand there is no need for any derived state benefits for older women, because they receive a citizen's pension in their own right, irrespective of marital status.

Widows receive all of their husband's state pension in Britain (BP and SERPS) and in the US (SS), 93 per cent in Ireland (OAP) and 60 per cent in Canada (C/QPP). For Australian women whose husbands' high income deprived them of the AP during marriage, widowhood may increase their personal income as they become eligible for AP. Divorced women in Britain may use their ex-husband's contribution record for the duration of the marriage to improve their entitlement to the BP, and in most Canadian provinces C/QPP pension credits are split upon divorce. In the US, women divorced after ten years of marriage receive derived benefits at 50 per cent of their ex-husbands' rates.

(c) State needs-tested benefits

All the countries except New Zealand have a needs-tested programme
for older people (see Table 13.2c). Reliance on needs-tested benefits is
itself an indicator of poverty and in all the countries except Ireland,
women are more likely than men to receive such benefits. For example,
in Britain twice the proportion of non-married women as men receive
the Minimum Income Guarantee (MIG). The maximum weekly amounts
(also the level of the minimum safety net) for a non-married older
person in the late 1990s were £75 in Britain (MIG), £79 (I£84) in
Ireland (NP) and £88 (A$177) in Australia (AP); the US has no guar-
anteed minimum, although destitute seniors can apply for SSI with
maximum benefits of £76 (US$115) per week. In Canada, a maximum of
£65 (C$115) per week is added to the OAS, making a guaranteed min-
imum income of £119 (C$212) per week for a lone pensioner. In both
Britain and Canada, the full amount of the flat rate pension is less than
the level of the needs-tested safety net, although these two countries'
method of dealing with the low rate of the basic pension is strikingly
different. In contrast to Britain's stringent, complex and stigmatizing
means-test, which deters many British pensioners from claiming the MIG,
Canada bases GIS eligibility on the previous year's income tax return,
delivering benefits automatically to all eligible low income pensioners.
Women predominate among the oldest old, who are most likely to find
the process of claiming means-tested benefits difficult and distressing.
Women are also more likely than men to fall foul of the pensions poverty
trap, because of their typically modest amounts of private income.

In all five countries, the needs test for couples is based on their joint
resources, leaving married women vulnerable to lose access to benefits if
their husband has a high income or assets. In the US the whole household's resources are taken into account, further reducing women's likelihood of qualifying for benefits. Where married women with low personal
incomes are rendered ineligible for needs-tested benefits, they must depend financially on their partner. Thus pension systems which rely heavily
on a needs-tested element (Australia, Canada and Ireland) may reinforce many older women's subordinate status in marriage, denying them
the autonomy and dignity of an independent income.

On the other hand, the ease of claiming and wide coverage of needs-
tested pensions in Australia, Canada and Ireland, together with tapered
withdrawal of benefits in Canada and Australia, mitigate some of the
adverse effects of needs-testing. Canada is unusual in applying only an
income test, leaving assets out of consideration.

In Britain, however, a pernicious situation exists in which the full
amount of the contributory BP is much lower (£11 per week for a non-
married pensioner in 2000) than the means-tested MIG. This creates a

severe poverty trap where a second-tier pension bringing income up to the amount of the MIG is 'wasted', since MIG is withdrawn pound for pound. For example, a woman with a partial BP of £58 per week (three-quarters of the full amount) and a modest second-tier pension of £20 per week would see no financial gain from her contributions to the second-tier pension. Thus the relationship of the BP and MIG is a perverse one, especially for those, mainly women, who have an incomplete employment record and a relatively small second-tier pension. In the US, the means test for SSI is even more restrictive than for MIG in Britain, accompanied by an even deeper poverty trap for women with any alternative source of income, or with assets in excess of US$2000. Thus Canada's and Australia's form of needs-testing is more women-friendly than that in Britain, Ireland and the US.

(d) Private pensions

Private pensions link benefits more closely to lifetime earnings than do state earnings-related pensions, to the disadvantage of most women. Moreover, private pensions are often defined contribution (DC), exposing women to high charges, investment risk and discriminatory annuity rates (see Chapters 4 and 8). DC schemes also have the disadvantage for women that contributions made early in the working life, when women are likely to be raising children, have a disproportionate effect on the amount of the fund at retirement. Australian private pensions may be taken as lump sums, avoiding the annuity problem but women's greater average longevity means they are at higher risk than men of using up their capital before death.

   The choice, unique to Britain, of contracting out of the state scheme (SERPS) into a personal pension (APP) is a dubious benefit, especially for women where such a switch is likely to leave them worse off in later life. Lack of adequate uprating of private pensions to keep pace with inflation and rising standards of living is a more serious problem for women than for men. Since retirement often spans 15 years for men but 20 years or more for women, the decline in relative value of even inflation-proofed pensions is considerable. Widows' benefits in private pensions are generally a lower proportion of the original pension than is the case in state pensions, so that increasing privatization of pensions will tend to leave widows less well-protected.

   Tax relief on private pension contributions and on investment gains can amount to a considerable loss of tax revenue, limiting the resources available to improve the public pensions on which women rely more heavily than men. The main beneficiaries of tax relief are higher paid men of working age. Thus such tax spending operates to counter the redistribution in favour of women performed by flat-rate state pensions. New Zealand is unusual in not providing privileged tax treatment to private pensions, releasing resources to finance a universal citizen's pension.

In terms of poverty prevention, none of the six countries provides state pensions at an adequate amount by European standards, although New Zealand, providing a lone pensioner with 44 per cent of the net average wage, has the best claim to adequacy and Britain the worst (15 per cent of average male earnings). The level of the needs-tested safety net for a lone pensioner is highest in Canada (equivalent to £119 per week), followed by Britain and Ireland, then Australia and the US. Thus, in the first tier of basic and needs-tested pensions, New Zealand and Canadian women fare best; but an important distinction is that the pensions amount is linked only to prices in Canada, whereas in New Zealand the pension is linked to a wage band so that wage indexation replaces price indexation when the floor of the wage band is reached. Consequently, among women receiving only first-tier pensions, New Zealand women will share in productivity gains in their economy, while Canadian women will not. While the effectiveness of pension systems in preventing poverty among older women can be assessed by looking at the overall structure and the levels of benefits, pension regimes' performance can also be compared in terms of gender inequality of outcomes.

Outcomes: extent of gender inequality in pensioners' income

Gender inequality of later life income indicates how far pension systems take account of women's lesser earning power over the life course – or alternatively how far they discriminate against those with family caring commitments. Drawing on information in the previous chapters allows some comparison of the relationship between older women's and men's incomes, although the form of the data is not the same for each country. For Britain and Ireland, where individual incomes were analysed and the US and Canada, where statistics on individual income are available, it is possible to compare all men and women pensioners. For Australia and New Zealand, gender inequality can be gauged by comparing incomes of older non-married men and women.

Gender disparity is greatest in the US and Britain. For example in the US, older women's median income from SS and occupational pensions was only 60 per cent of men's, among those with income from these sources, while in Britain older women's median gross total income was 62 per cent of men's. In contrast, older women's and men's incomes were more equal in the other four countries. Among low income non-married older Canadians (42 per cent of non-married older women and 27 per cent of equivalent men), incomes were very similar and among the remainder of non-married older Canadians, women's average income was 78 per cent of men's. Older Irish women's (equivalized) average incomes were 87 per cent of men's. The gender difference in lone pensioner income is small in Australia and New Zealand. Among older non-married Australians, women's average net income was 94 per cent of men's. In New Zealand the near-universality of a pension at one-third of the net average wage (44 per cent for those living alone) and the low receipt of private pensions ensures gender similarity of pensioner incomes; among those aged over 65, women's median income was 98 per cent of men's in 1996.

Thus countries where private pensions play the largest role (Britain and the US) show the greatest gender inequality in retirement incomes. Evidence from the six countries suggests that this is not only because men are better able than women to obtain good private pensions but also because tax spending to subsidize private pensions reduces the resources needed to provide redistributive state pensions at an adequate level to all older people. In both Britain and the US, women receive significantly smaller state pensions than men, due to their contributory nature, despite an element of redistribution towards women through childcare drop-out years (HRP in Britain) and a progressive benefit structure. In contrast, flat-rate universal pensions equalize incomes between men and women, but usually at levels insufficiently high to prevent poverty. While needs-tested pensions are critical in all countries (except New Zealand) to ensure women's income adequacy in old age, they often deprive married women of financial independence by relating the amount of benefit to joint resources.

For the majority of women, who have gaps in employment and periods of low pay, flat-rate pensions set at a generous level are most important, although redistributive features in state second-tier defined benefit (DB) pensions can also help prevent poverty in later life. Private pensions, however, translate low lifetime earnings into low pensions. DC schemes provide particularly poor value for money to most women.

Pension reforms trends

In Britain and the US, pressure for shifting the balance of pension provision from Pay-As-You-Go (public) towards funded pensions (generally private) has been intense, resulting in far-reaching changes in Britain in the 1980s. It is striking that although Britain will experience only a modest ageing of its population and faces no fiscal crisis, a more radical shift towards private pension provision was made in the 1980s than in any other country except Chile. This trend in Britain continues into the twenty-first century, with plans to reduce state pension provision still further as a proportion of GDP and to expand private pensions in the form of personal (Stakeholder) pensions. The likely outcome of the reforms, as Chapter 5 clearly demonstrated, will be to draw even more lone women pensioners into stigmatized means-testing, as the value of the Basic Pension declines, and to increase the financial dependence of married women pensioners on their husbands.

Plans to privatize Social Security (SS) in the US, if implemented, will also have detrimental effects on women's income in later life, replacing a secure income for life with unpredictable income from an annuity. Privatization initiatives would replace redistributive SS benefits with first-tier residual benefits set well below poverty level, topped up by annuitized individual benefits that favour the well-paid, and reduce spouses' and widows' pensions. Unless some as yet unanticipated women-friendly features are included in privatization plans, the likely outcome for US women of SS privatization as currently proposed would mirror detrimental processes that have already occurred for women in Britain.

Canada's public pension reforms have stabilized contribution rates and achieved a modest level of pre-funding for C/QPP and cut first-tier costs (OAS/GIS) by placing a surtax on the previously universal OAS pension. The government recently withdrew its controversial plan to combine OAS and GIS into a single Senior Benefit, which would have withdrawn first-tier benefits from all but older Canadians with low or very modest incomes. Had the Senior Benefit been enacted, many married Canadian women would have lost entitlement to pensions in their own right since the income test was based on couples' incomes. Concern over cost to the public purse has not extended to withdrawing generous tax relief for private pensions, from which Canadian women gain little benefit. Consequently, the Canadian pension system has become more selective, increasingly basing receipt of public pensions on need rather than citizenship, and income adequacy on receipt of subsidized private pensions.

The extension of private pensions in Australia has both advantages and disadvantages for women. On the one hand, almost all employed women are included in a second-tier pension through the Superannuation Guarantee Charge (SGC) for which they make no direct contributions. Moreover, benefits may be taken as a lump sum, avoiding the annuity problem for women. On the other hand, employers' contributions arguably reduce wages paid, a trade-off which may not be desirable for low paid women. Gender inequality of pension income may increase, first because more Australians will in future receive earnings-related pensions and second because expansion of private pensions may erode popular support for maintaining the level of the state pension.

Ireland is unusual in promoting the expansion of social insurance. An increasing proportion of women will receive a full contributory pension in their own right, with the amounts currently being uprated by more than price inflation. At the same time, however, private provision is also being promoted. It remains to be seen whether state provision will be cut back, to the detriment of women, as men's income from private pensions increases. Perhaps Ireland can avoid following Britain in this respect, pursuing an independent, and more women-friendly, pension policy.

New Zealand has seen a roller-coaster series of reforms so that predicting a consistent trend is difficult. Yet if the present pension system is maintained, with a citizen's pension tied to average earnings (at over 40 per cent for a lone pensioner) the pension outlook for New Zealand women is more positive than in any of the other five countries. A relatively generous basic pension that is not needs-tested, and that is payable to each individual in her own right, provides a secure platform on which additional sources of income can be added. This system contrasts sharply with Britain, where a pensions poverty trap operates, penalizing those with small additional income or assets. If the New Zealand pension system is stable, it will be a beacon of hope to women in other countries, demonstrating the viability of a women-friendly model of pension provision operating in a liberal welfare state.

Pension privatization (that is, reforms which expand private provision at the expense of state pensions) has been justified by neo-liberal rhetoric which brands collective social insurance as 'welfare dependency' while approving private funded pensions as 'individuals taking responsibility for themselves'. Such a dichotomy skates over the fact that these are merely two different mechanisms for transferring resources over the life course, although the former counts non-financial contributions to society as well as financial. Reform proposals have also been justified as necessary to curb escalating state spending or to prevent intergenerational inequity. However, as Chapter 3 has shown, these arguments are flawed in numerous ways. Their weakness has led some analysts to conclude that a crisis has been socially constructed in order to present a political choice as an economic imperative (Walker 1990; Vincent 1999). According to these writers, an ideological opposition to public welfare by neo-liberal governments, rather than economic reasons or the danger of intergenerational conflict has motivated welfare retrenchment: 'Political ideology has distorted and amplified the macroeconomic consequences of population ageing in order to legitimate anti-welfare policies' (Walker 1990: 377). Another driver of pension privatization may be the commercial gains for the finance sector of industry from the expansion of personal pensions.

Prospects for later cohorts of women

Employment trends as well as pension reforms have a bearing on women's pension prospects. There is no clear upward trend in women's full time employment, despite the rise in their employment participation in the six liberal welfare states considered. Nor is the gender gap in pay set to disappear, in spite of women's increased educational levels. Both gender discrimination and women's caring roles continue to limit their career opportunities and pay, although more in some countries than in others.

Workfare initiatives (illiberal policies in that they aim to influence mothers' employment, yet framed to appear consistent with liberal values), may serve to contain public spending. Yet they seem unlikely to lead to an increase in well-paid permanent full time jobs for women. The alternative of providing infrastructural childcare support, as in the social democratic Nordic countries, may be more successful by support-ing women in coping with their dual commitments to paid and unpaid work. Subsidized state childcare services and legislation to promote family-friendly employment, however, run counter to neo-liberal ideo-logy. Consequently, women in liberal welfare states who have children have reduced employment and earnings due to both a gender gap and a family gap (the difference between similar women with and without children at home). Although the extent of the loss of earnings due to being female and to motherhood varies across the six countries (being relatively high in Britain and low in Australia) the contrast with Swed-ish mothers, who experience minimal losses, is striking (Harkness and Waldfogel 1999; Rake 2000).

Most women in liberal welfare states will continue to be disadvan-taged relative to men in building independent pension rights, to the extent that the pension system as a whole relates pension income more closely to individuals' lifetime earnings. This link is tightened by reforms which expand private provision at the expense of state pensions. Such reforms threaten to magnify gender inequality of later life income, erod-ing the benefit of women-friendly features in state pensions such as childcare drop-out provisions and redistributive benefit formulas.

However, such pension privatization will also widen differentials among women. Those who are highly qualified and childless will be well-placed to emulate men's employment patterns, as will women who have chil-dren but who, with their partners, have household incomes high enough to purchase comprehensive childcare and domestic support. Although such women will typically still have lower earnings than equivalent men, their pensions are likely to be substantial.

The greatest losers from pension privatization will be women who are disadvantaged in the labour market for any reason. One important group is women who have children, or spend a number of years caring for frail relatives, and lack a partner to share the caring or to help pay for childcare and eldercare services. In Britain, the number of lone parents has tripled in the last 30 years, with over one in five families now headed by a lone parent, mirroring trends in other industrialized societies. Lone mothers, including widows and divorcees as well as never-married mothers, will be least able to maintain their employment record and to rebuild their earning capacity on return to paid employment. They already face a difficult pension future in all the six countries except New Zealand, and this will worsen if state pensions are reduced.

Other groups of women who stand to lose disproportionately from pension privatization are those with few educational qualifications and those from minority ethnic groups, in so far as their earnings are depressed. A decline in the value of state pensions means that women will not only receive lower state pensions in their own right but also lower derived pensions from social insurance schemes (spouse benefits, survivors' benefits and divorcees' rights).

Policies to improve women's prospects

In countries with a relatively redistributive pension system, such as New Zealand, the pension effects of women's disadvantages in the labour market due to their caring responsibilities are minimized. However, where pension income is closely linked to lifetime earnings, as in countries with high reliance on private pensions, it is especially important that those with caring commitments are enabled to maintain well-paid employment.

State provisions to assist women in combining paid and unpaid work, or requirements placed on employers, are often condemned by neoliberals as 'burdens on business' or 'interference with the market'. However the laissez-faire ideal is often ignored or relaxed in liberal welfare states, for example in subsidizing private pensions through tax spending. Moreover, a liberal concern for women's equality as citizens implies that women should have equal rights in all social institutions, not only formally but in practice. If liberal welfare states aim to provide equal opportunities for men and women to obtain an adequate pension income, there are several types of policy that could be adopted.

Equality legislation

Explicitly pro-equality employment policies such as equal pay legislation and prohibition of sex discrimination have had limited effects on sex equality, first because of women's domestic and caring responsibilities.

Imagine a race with equal starting times and distance but where one group of runners must carry children while the other runs freely. Inevitably the encumbered group will trail behind. As long as the bulk of family care work is performed by women, treating them equally leaves them disadvantaged. Second, the persistence of gender ideology concerning appropriate roles of men and women, held by both employers and colleagues, creates barriers to women's opportunities in paid work. Attitudes and longstanding practices are resistant to change through equal opportunities policies, in spite of dramatic increases in women's qualifications in developed societies.

Legislation improving workers' rights

Pro-worker reforms such as a minimum wage, shorter working week, rights to paid leave for family needs (paid parental leave while children are young, paid compassionate leave for family crises such as illness or death) have a disproportionately beneficial effect for women, as they relieve the most acute conflicts between family needs and employment. Because women have lower hourly earnings on average than men, the minimum wage helps women most. Thus ostensibly gender-neutral policies in favour of workers can have gendered effects. Flexible work hours, where employees have a large measure of control, make it easier for women to manage their family commitments. Limiting employers' right to require changes in working hours, especially at short notice, would also protect women unable to rearrange their family commitments to fit new working schedules.

Legislation improving parents' rights at work

Improving rights specifically for mothers (extending paid maternity leave, ensuring mothers' right to return to the same or an equivalent job at reduced hours and allowing mothers to work a shorter day) all help women to maintain their employment after childbearing and to prevent loss of occupational status. However, there is a danger that 'mommy-track' jobs or occupational niches predominantly occupied by women (and attracting lower pay and prestige) may develop as employers and colleagues react to legislative rights for mothers. Enabling fathers to take paid family-related leave reinforces the message that fathers have equal responsibilities, even if take-up by fathers lags behind that of mothers (as in the Swedish experience). Better quality part time jobs would help women returning to employment to move later into full time better-paid employment, when their caring responsibilities become less onerous.

Childcare and eldercare policies

State provision of childcare and eldercare services, while formally gender-neutral, is of greater benefit to women than men as long as women shoulder the bulk of unpaid domestic and caring work. Where the state takes responsibility for part of the task of caring for the vulnerable, women are to this extent defamilized, freed from private patriarchy. Although such policies may be partly concerned with the welfare of children and the frail elderly, and not explicitly designed to enable women's employment, the effect is profoundly gendered. Women's handicaps in the running race are substantially lifted, allowing a more equal outcome.

State policy can do much to reconcile the conflict between gendered family responsibilities and the liberal ideal of sex equality of opportunity in the labour market. Yet liberal states tend to minimize their intervention in both family and employment, leaving the conflict to be played out in each family and each workplace. If something has to 'give' it is usually the woman's employment participation, with adverse effect on her earnings and ultimately her pension. States can also, through the design of the pension system, substantially reduce the pension penalties incurred by women with short employment records, periods of part time employment and low earnings.

Conclusions

This chapter has compared pension systems in the six liberal welfare states, from a gender-sensitive perspective, analysing how pension income is affected by women's family-related disadvantages in the labour market. Although broadly neo-liberal in orientation, the six pension systems have varying effects on women's pension acquisition. Britain and the US differ strikingly in the rate of full time employment of women. Yet these two countries both stand out as having a large gender gap in later life income and as providing a particularly harsh pensions environment for many working-age women. Ireland's pension system is somewhat more women-friendly than Britain's, while Canada's is more egalitarian than that of the US. New Zealand and Australia, in different ways, have ensured the greatest gender and class equality of pensions.

Pension reform trends that shift resources away from state pensions towards funded private pensions are evident, especially in Britain and to a lesser extent in Canada and Australia. Privatization of public pensions is also under consideration in the US. Since both women's full time employment rate and the gender gap in pay are stagnant, gender convergence of lifetime earnings is not on the horizon. It is therefore likely that gender inequality of later life income, and increased reliance of lone women on means-tested benefits, will result from pension privatization, since pensions are thereby tied more closely to lifetime earnings. A further effect will be increasing differentiation among older women, with those who were lone mothers especially disadvantaged.

Given the instability of financial markets, the wisdom of placing pension investment risk increasingly upon individuals is questionable and suggests that trends in pension reform are driven by neo-liberal ideology and the interests of the finance sector of industry, rather than by the aim of ensuring a reliable and adequate source of income in later life. While it is clear that longer life must mean higher contributions to pensions, the case for using the vehicle of private funded DC pensions rather than a public PAYG mechanism (social insurance or citizen's pension) is flimsy. There is little evidence that the needs of women for a secure independent income in later life has exercised the minds of policymakers when considering pension reforms.

A gender-sensitive analysis of pension systems is relevant not only to women. As labour markets are further deregulated with growth of contingent work, insecure and part time employment, the features of pension systems which tend to benefit women become more important for men as well, especially those who are low paid.

Although the six countries vary somewhat, they each manifest a conflict between policies based on the Protestant work ethic and a rhetoric of approval for 'family values'. Liberal capitalist countries tend to encourage individualism, opposing the cooperative ethos of family life. As Beck (1992: 116) put it, 'the ultimate market society is a childless society – unless the children grow up with mobile, single fathers and mothers'. Yet societies depend on the family to reproduce the next generation, to nurture and socialize the young and to perform a myriad of supportive roles for kin. Over much of the world people regard children as the chief means of providing for their old age, whereas for many women in industrialized countries parenthood is a predictor of poverty in later life. Families and their needs are relegated to the private sphere, with the difficulties of reconciling full time employment with family caring responsibilities falling overwhelmingly on women. If women behave in accordance with economic rationality, maximizing their earnings through full time continuous employment, other changes must follow. Women's availability to care for husbands and ageing parents may lessen and fertility (already below replacement rate in Britain) may continue to decline. Thus economic rationality, if widely adopted, could render pension schemes of all types unviable.

Societies have choices to make concerning women's (and men's) unpaid work of caring for others. Is such work to be regarded as a purely private matter, or recognized as a vital contribution to the welfare and ultimately the survival of society? If caring is acknowledged as work, policies are needed to support those who provide care, rewarding their unpaid as well as their paid work. For women, and increasingly for men too, this will mean challenging the fashionable but flawed arguments for pension privatization and reversing the tide of state welfare retrenchment.

Glossary of technical terms and abbreviations

accrual rate	rate at which pension contributions earn benefits, per year
accrued rights	entitlements to pension benefits at a particular date
AP	Age Pension; flat-rate means-tested, near universal, pension (Aus)
annuity	regular income for remaining life, bought with fund from DC pension
annuity rate	annuity income as a percentage of fund used for purchase
APP	Appropriate Personal Pension (UK); approved for contracting out of SERPS
BP	Basic Pension (UK); flat rate NI pension, depends on age and NICs
citizen's pension	flat-rate pension paid to older individuals by virtue of residence
clawback	withdrawal of pension benefits above a certain income level (Can)
contract out	forgo rights to SERPS; NIC reduced but balance is paid to APP/OP
contracted out rebate	reduction in NI contributions; paid into private pension scheme
C/QPP	Canada/Quebec Pension Plan, mandatory state earnings related pension
DB	defined benefit formula, based on years in pension scheme and earnings
DC	defined contribution; benefits vary with amount and investment returns
derived benefits	benefits paid to individuals other than scheme members
dually entitled	wives whose derived SS entitlement exceeds their own SS (US)

EU	European Union
final salary scheme	OP in which pension is based on salary in last or last few years
401K	DC occupational pension (US)
FT	full time
funded pension	pension paid from a fund made up of contributions and investment returns
FYFT	full-year, full time employment
GIS	Guaranteed Income Supplement (Can); income-tested pensioner benefit
GRI	Guaranteed Retirement Income (NZ); alternative name for basic pension
HRP	Home Responsibilities Protection (UK); protects BP for carers
HS	Homemaker Scheme (Ire); protects OAP for carers
income replacement	relationship of pension amount to previous earnings
indexation	automatic uprating of benefit amounts in line with prices or earnings
inflation proofing	indexing to prices
IRA	Individual Retirement Account (US); personal pension
IS	Income Support (UK); means-tested income supplement
LEL	Lower Earnings Limit (UK); minimum earnings for liability for NICs
LICO	low-income cut-off
lump sum	part of private pension that can be taken as cash, usually at retirement
means test	test of income and assets; for couples, usually based on joint income
MIG	Minimum Income Guarantee (UK); Income Support for pensioners
mis-selling	selling APPs to those for whom they were likely to be unsuitable
money purchase scheme	DC pension scheme; can be occupational, group-based or individual
National Superannuation	flat-rate residence-based universal basic pension (NZ)
needs test	test of income, assets or both; includes income tests and means tests
neo-liberal	pertaining to ideas and policies hostile to collective state provision
NZS	New Zealand Superannuation; alternative name for basic pension
NI	National Insurance (UK); state social insurance scheme
NIC	National Insurance Contributions (UK), compulsory for all employed

NI fund	Holding fund into which NICs are paid (UK); finances NI benefits
NP	Non-contributory Pension (Ire); means-tested pension, payable at 65
OAP	Old Age Pension (Ire); flat-rate social insurance pension, payable at 66
OAS	Old Age Security (Can); flat-rate residence-based pension
OECD	Organization for Economic Cooperation and Development
OP	occupational pension, operated on a group basis by employer
PAYG	Pay-As-You-Go; current contributions are paid out immediately as benefits
personal pension	DC scheme purchased by an individual; includes APPs
PHYLIS	Pensions and Hypothetical Lifetime Income Simulation model
portability	the ability to transfer accrued pension rights between schemes
private pension	Occupational or personal (individual) pension
PT	part time
Retirement Pension	flat-rate social insurance pension (Ire), payable at 65 if retired
retrenchment	cuts in public insurance programmes that are hard to reverse
RRSP	Registered Retirement Savings Plan (Can); individual retirement savings
RPP	Registered Pension Plan (Can); occupational pension scheme
SERPS	State Earnings Related Pension Scheme (UK); part of NI scheme from 1978
social insurance	state collective welfare scheme financed by contributions on PAYG basis
SGC	Superannuation Guarantee Charge (Aus); mandatory private pension
SA	Spouse Allowance (Can)
social assistance	state financial support for those with low incomes, needs-tested
SS	Social Security (US); state social insurance scheme
SSI	Supplemental Security Income (US); means-tested income for pensioners
SHP	Stakeholder Pension (UK); type of personal pension with limited charges
S2P	State Second Pension (UK); planned to replace SERPS by 2010
Superannuation	occupational pension (Aus)

support ratio	ratio of working-age population to population over state pension age
surcharge	withdrawal of benefits above an income threshold (NZ)
survivors' benefits	benefits paid to other individuals after the scheme member's death
Theil index	index relating between-group and within-group income inequalities
take up	proportion of people claiming a benefit, among those entitled to do so
taper	gradual reduction of a needs-tested benefit as income rises; not pound for pound
tax spending	tax reliefs on pension contributions, which reduce tax revenue
UEL	Upper Earnings Limit (UK) for employee NICs (set at seven times LEL)
unisex annuity rates	annuity rates that are equal for men and women
vesting period	duration of plan membership required to secure pension entitlement

References

Adema, W. (2000) Revisiting social spending across countries: a brief note, *OECD Economic Studies*, 30: 191–7.

Advisory Council on Social Security (1997) *Report on the 1994–1996 Advisory Council on Social Security. Volume 1: Findings and Recommendations.* Washington, DC: Social Security Administration.

Akyeampong, E. (2000) RRSPs in the 1990s, *Perspectives*. Ottawa: Statistics Canada, spring: 1–7.

Aldridge, A. (1998) *Habitus* and cultural capital in the field of personal finance, *The Sociological Review*, 46(1): 1–23.

Allison, P. (1978) Measures of inequality, *American Sociological Review*, 43(6): 865–79.

Alwin, D., Braun, M. and Scott, J. (1992) The separation of work and the family: attitudes towards women's labour force participation in Germany, Great Britain and the United States, *European Sociological Review*, 8(1): 13–37.

Arber, S. (1989) Class and the elderly, *Social Studies Review*, 4(3): 90–5.

Arber, S. and Ginn, J. (1991) *Gender and Later Life: A Sociological Analysis of Resources and Constraints.* London: Sage.

Arber, S. and Ginn, J. (1995) Gender differences in the relationship between paid employment and informal care, *Work, Employment and Society*, 9(3): 445–71.

Attias-Donfut, C. and Arber, S. (2000) Equity and solidarity across the generations, in S. Arber and C. Attias-Donfut (eds) *The Myth of Generational Conflict.* London: Routledge.

Australian Bureau of Statistics (ABS) (1995) *Superannuation Australia*, November, Cat. no. 6319.0, Canberra: ABS.

Australian Bureau of Statistics (ABS) (1996) *Census of Population and Housing, Aboriginal and Torres Strait Islander People*, Cat. no. 2034.0, Canberra: ABS.

Australian Bureau of Statistics (ABS) (1998) *Labour Force*, June, Cat. No. 6203.0, Canberra: ABS.

Australian Bureau of Statistics (ABS), Social Statistics Branch (1992) *Labour Market and Employment Characteristics of Immigrant Women in Australia.* Canberra:

Australian Government Publishing Service for the Bureau of Immigration Research.

Bacon, B. and Gallagher, P. (1995) Early retirees: trends and their use of super-annuation benefits and social security payments. Paper presented to Department of Social Security Seminar on Early Retirement, Canberra, 14 December.

Baker, D. (1995) *Robbing the Cradle: A Critical Assessment of Generational Accounting.* Washington, DC: Economic Policy Institute.

Baker, D. (1998) *Unequal Sacrifice: The Impact of Changes Proposed by the Advisory Council on Social Security.* Washington, DC: Preamble Center.

Bakker, I. (1998) *Unpaid Work and Macroeconomics: New Discussions, New Tools for Action.* Ottawa: Status of Women Canada, Research Directorate.

Barrientos, A. and Firinguetti, L. (1995) Individual capitalisation pension plans and old-age pension benefits for low-paid workers in Chile, *International Contributions Labour Studies*, 5: 27–43.

Bateman, H. and Piggott, J. (1998) Mandatory retirement saving in Australia, *Annals of Public and Cooperative Economics*, 69(4): 547–69.

Battle, K. (1997) Pension reform in Canada, *Canadian Journal on Aging*, 16(3): 519–52.

Bauman, Z. (1998) *Work, Consumerism and the New Poor.* Buckingham: Open University Press.

Baxter, D. (1992) Domestic labour and income inequality, *Work, Employment and Society*, 6(2): 229–49.

Beck, U. (1992) *Risk Society.* London: Sage.

Becker, G. (1981) *A Treatise on the Family.* Cambridge, MA: Harvard University Press.

Beedon, L. (1991) Women and Social Security: challenges facing the American system of social insurance, *Issue Brief 2.* Washington, DC: AARP.

Bengston, V. and Harootyan, R. (1994) *Intergenerational Linkages: Hidden Connections in American Society.* New York: Springer.

Bianchi, S. (1995) Changing economic roles of women and men, in R. Farley (ed.) *State of the Union – America in the 1990s. Volume One: Economic Trends.* New York: Russell Sage.

Binstock, R. (1983) The aged as scapegoat, *The Gerontologist*, 23: 136–43.

Binstock, R. (1994) Transcending intergenerational equity, in T. Marmor, T. Smeeding, and V. Greene (eds) *Economic Security and Intergenerational Justice: A Look at North America.* Washington, DC: Urban Institute.

Birch, R., Hancock, R., Legrys, D. and Roberts, R. (1999) *Paying for Age in the 21st Century. The Millennium Papers.* London: Age Concern England.

Blau, F. (1998) Trends in the well-being of American women, 1970–1995, *Journal of Economic Literature*, 36: 112–65.

Blossfeld, H-P. and Hakim, C. (eds) (1997) *Between Equalization and Marginalization: Women Working Part Time in Europe and the United States.* Oxford: Oxford University Press.

Borzi, P. (1995) Women and their retirement income: will it be enough? *Government Finance Review*, 11(5): 46–8.

Bos, E., Vu, M., Massiah, E. and Bulatao, R. (1994) *World Population Projections, 1994–95.* Washington, DC: The International Bank for Reconstruction and Development/The World Bank.

Boyd, S. and Treas, J. (1996) Family care of the frail elderly: a new look at women in the middle, in J. Quadagno and D. Street (eds) *Aging for the Twenty-First Century*. New York: St. Martin's Press.

Bradshaw, J. and Chen, J. (1996) *Poverty in the UK: A Comparison with Nineteen Other Countries*, working paper no. 147. Walferdange: The Luxembourg Income Study, CEPS/INSTEAD.

Brannen, J. and Moss, P. (1991) *Managing Mothers: Dual Earner Households after Maternity Leave*. London: Macmillan.

Brannen, J. and Wilson, G. (eds) (1987) *Give and Take in Families*. London: Allen & Unwin.

Braun, M., Alwin, D. and Scott, J. (1998) Generational change in gender roles: western industrialized and former socialist countries compared. Paper presented to International Sociological Association Conference, Montreal, 26 July–2 August.

Brayfield, A. (1995) A bargain at any price? Child care costs and women's employment, *Social Science Research*, 24: 188–214.

Brooks, N. (1993) Gender pay gap found among top executives, *Los Angeles Times*, 30 June: D1.

Bruegel, I. (1996) Whose myths are they anyway? A comment, *British Journal of Sociology*, 47(1): 175–7.

Bureau of Labor Statistics (BLS) (1992) *Work and Family: Child-Care Arrangements of Young Working Mothers*. Report 820, Washington, DC: US Department of Labor.

Bureau of Labor Statistics (BLS) (1997) *1997 Annual Averages*, Table 5. Washington DC: US Department of Labor.

Burkhauser, R. and Smeeding, T. (1994) *Social Security Reform: A Budget Neutral Approach to Reducing Older Women's Disproportionate Risk of Poverty*. Syracuse, NY: Center for Policy Research, Syracuse University.

Buti, M., Franco, D. and Pench, L. (1999) Reconciling the welfare state with sound public finances and high employment, in M. Buti, D. Franco and L. Pench (eds) *The Welfare State in Europe. Challenges and Reforms*. Cheltenham: Edward Elgar.

Canadian Council on Social Development (CCSD) (1996) *Women and Pensions Fact Sheets*. Ottawa: CCSD.

Carney, C. (1983) A case study in social policy – the non-contributory old age pension, *Administration*, 33(4): 483–529.

Castles, F. (1985) *The Working Class and Welfare: Reflections on the Political Development of the Welfare State in Australia and New Zealand, 1890–1980*. Wellington: Allen & Unwin.

Castles, F. (2000) Population Ageing and the Public Purse: How real is the problem? Paper presented to the international conference, What Future for Social Security? Stirling University, Scotland, 15–17 June.

Castles, F. and Shirley, I. (1996) Labour and social policy: gravediggers or refurbishers of the welfare state, in F. Castles, R. Gerritsen, and J. Vowles (eds) *The Great Experiment*. Wellington: Allen & Unwin.

Castro, I. (1998) *Equal Pay: A Thirty-five Year Perspective*. Washington, DC: US Department of Labor.

Census Bureau (1997) *Money Income in the United States: 1996*. Washington, DC: USGPO.

Census Bureau (1998) *Statistical Abstract of the United States*. Washington, DC: USGPO.

Census Bureau (1999) *Statistical Abstract of the United States*. Washington, DC: USGPO.

Census Bureau (2000) *Income of the Population 55 and Older, 1998*. Washington, DC: USGPO.

Chappell, N. (1993) Implications of shifting health care policy for care-giving in Canada, *Journal of Aging and Social Policy*, 5(1–2): 39–55.

Clare, R. (1994) Women and superannuation, in *Women and Superannuation*, background paper no. 41. Economic Planning Advisory Council (EPAC) and Office of the Status of Women (OSW). Canberra: AGPS.

Clark, P. (1993) Moral discourse and public policy in aging: framing problems, seeking solutions, and public ethics, *Canadian Journal on Aging*, 12(4): 485–508.

Clark, R. and Quinn, J. (1999) *The Economic Status of the Elderly*, Medicare Brief No. 4. Washington, DC: National Academy of Social Insurance.

Cleveland, G. and Krashinsky, M. (1998) *The Benefits and Costs of Good Child Care: The Economic Rationale for Public Investment in Young Children*. Toronto: University of Toronto.

Coder, J., Smeeding, T. and Torrey, B. (1990) *The Change in the Economic Status of the Low-Income Elderly in Three Industrial Countries: Circa 1979–1985*, working paper no. 47. Walferdange: The Luxembourg Income Study, CEPS/INSTEAD.

Commission of Inquiry into Poverty (1975) *Poverty in Australia*, First Main Report (Prof. R.F. Henderson, Chairman), Vol. 1. Canberra: AGPS.

Commonwealth Department of Family and Community Services (FaCS) (1998) *Customers: A Statistical Overview*. Canberra: Commonwealth Department of Family and Community Services.

Commonwealth Department of Family and Community Services (FaCS) (1999) *Research FaCS Sheet*, no. 3. Canberra: Commonwealth Department of Family and Community Services.

Congressional Budget Office (CBO) (1987) *Tax Policy for Pensions and Other Retirement Savings*. Washington, DC: USGPO.

Connell, R. (1987) *Gender and Power. Society, the Person and Sexual Politics*. Cambridge: Polity Press.

Cook, L. (1997) Retirement in the 21st century. Do we have an option? Unpublished paper, Wellington: Statistics NZ.

Corcoran, M., Datcher, L. and Duncan, G. (1984) The economic fortunes of women and children: lessons from the panel study of income dynamics, *Signs*, 10: 232–8.

Costello, P. (1997) *Budget Speech 1997–8*. Canberra: Parliament of Australia.

Courchene, T. (1994) *Social Canada in the Millennium: Reform Imperatives and Restructuring Principles*. Toronto: C.D. Howe Institute.

Cousins, C. (1994) A comparison of the labour market position of women in Spain and the UK with reference to the flexible labour debate, *Work, Employment and Society*, 8(1): 45–67.

Cox, E. (1994) Super for unwaged and low waged women, in *Women and Superannuation*, background paper no. 41. Economic Planning Advisory Council (EPAC) and Office of the Status of Women (OSW). Canberra: AGPS.

Crompton, R. and Harris, F. (1998) Explaining women's employment patterns: orientations to work revisited, *British Journal of Sociology*, 49(1): 118–36.

Crompton, S. (1993) Facing retirement, *Perspectives*. Ottawa: Statistics Canada, spring: 31–38.

Crystal, S. and Shea, D. (1990) Cumulative advantage, cumulative disadvantage, and inequality among elderly people, *The Gerontologist*, 30: 437–43.

Current Population Survey (1999) *March Supplement*. Washington, DC: US Department of Labor, Bureau of Labor Statistics.

Cuvillier, R. (1979) The housewife: an unjustifiable burden on the community, *Journal of Social Policy*, 8(1): 1–26.

Dailey, N. (1998) *When Baby Boom Women Retire*. Westport, CT: Praeger.

Daly, A. (1991) *The Participation of Aboriginal People in the Australian Labour Market*, working paper no. 6. Canberra: Centre for Aboriginal Economic Policy Research, Australian National University.

Daly, M. (1999) The functioning family: Catholicism and social policy in Germany and the Republic of Ireland, *Comparative Social Research*, 18: 105–33.

Daly, M. and Yeates, N. (1999) The influence of social and political institutions on welfare state adaptation and change in Britain and Ireland. Paper presented at the Fourth European Sociological Association Conference, Amsterdam, 18–21 August.

Davies, B. and Ward, S. (1992) *Women and Personal Pensions*. London: EOC.

Department of Social, Community and Family Affairs (1992) *Statistical Information on Social Welfare Services*. Dublin: The Stationery Office.

Department of Social, Community and Family Affairs (1996) *Statistical Information on Social Welfare Services*. Dublin: The Stationery Office.

Department of Social, Community and Family Affairs (1997) *Statistical Information on Social Welfare Services*. Dublin: The Stationery Office.

Department of Social, Community and Family Affairs (1999) *Statistical Information on Social Welfare Services*. Dublin: The Stationery Office.

Department of Social, Community and Family Affairs (2000) *Statistical Information on Social Welfare Services*. Dublin: The Stationery Office.

Department of Social Security (DSS) (1994) *Personal Pension Statistics 1992/3*, rev. edn. London: Government Statistical Services.

Department of Social Security (DSS) (1997) *Home Responsibilities Protection Statistics*. Newcastle: Government Statistical Services.

Department of Social Security (DSS) (1998a) *A New Contract for Welfare: Partnership in Pensions*, Cm 4179. London: The Stationery Office.

Department of Social Security (DSS) (1998b) *Social Security Statistics 1998*. London: The Stationery Office.

Department of Social Security (DSS) (2000a) *The Changing Welfare State: Pensioners' Incomes*, DSS Paper No. 2. London: DSS.

Department of Social Security (DSS) (2000b) *Are You Just Getting By When You Could Be Getting More?* Press Release 00/088, 29 March.

Desai, S. and Waite, L. (1991) Women's employment during pregnancy and after the first birth: occupational characteristics and work commitment, *American Sociological Review*, 56: 551–66.

Dex, S. (1987) *Women's Occupational Mobility: A Lifetime Perspective*. Basingstoke: Macmillan.

Dex, S. (1990) Occupational mobility over women's lifetime, in G. Payne and P. Abbott (eds) *The Social Mobility of Women: Beyond Male Models*. Basingstoke: Falmer.

Dex, S., Joshi, H. and Macran, S. (1996) A widening gulf among British mothers, *Oxford Review of Economic Policy*, 12(1): 65–75.

Dex, S. and Shaw, L. (1986) *British and American Women at Work: Do Equal Opportunities Policies Matter?* London: Macmillan.

Dilnot, A., Disney, R., Johnson, P. and Whitehouse, E. (1994) *Pensions Policy in the UK. An Economic Analysis*. London: Institute of Fiscal Studies.

Disney, R. (1996) *Can We Afford to Grow Older?* London: MIT Press.

Disney, R., Grundy, E. and Johnson, P. (1997) *The Dynamics of Retirement*. London: The Stationery Office.

Doering, D., Hauser, R., Rolf, G. and Tibitanzl, F. (1994) Old-age security for women in the twelve EC countries, *Journal of European Social Policy*, 4(1): 1–18.

Dominelli, L. (1991) *Women Across Continents: Feminist Comparative Social Policy*. Hemel Hempstead: Harvester Wheatsheaf.

Drobnic, S. and Wittig, I. (1997) Part time work in the United States of America, in H-P. Blossfeld and C. Hakim (eds) *Between Equalization and Marginalization: Women Working Part Time in Europe and the United States of America*. Oxford: Oxford University Press.

Drolet, M. (1999) *The Persistent Gap: New Evidence on the Canadian Gender Wage Gap*. Ottawa: Statistics Canada, Income Statistics Division.

Durham, P. (1994) Millions will lose money on private pensions, *Independent*, 28 March.

Edelman, M. (1977) *Political Language: Words that Succeed and Policies that Fail*. New York: Academic Press.

Edelman, M. (1988) *Constructing the Political Spectacle*. Chicago, IL: University of Chicago Press.

Eller, J. and Fraser, W. (1995) *Asset Ownership of Households, 1993*. US Census Bureau, Current Population Reports P70–47, Washington, DC.

Employee Benefits Research Institute (EBRI) (1997) *Women in Retirement. Facts From EBRI*. 19 November. www.ebri.org/facts/1197fact.htm

Ermisch, J. (1990a) Women's economic activity and fertility in the UK, in PA Cambridge Consultants (ed.) *Study on the Relationship Between Female Activity and Fertility, Vol 2*. Brussels: EC(DGV).

Ermisch, J. (1990b) *Fewer Babies, Longer Lives*. York: Joseph Rowntree Foundation.

Esping-Andersen, G. (1990) *The Three Worlds of Welfare Capitalism*. Cambridge: Polity.

Esping-Andersen, G. (1999) *Social Foundations of Postindustrial Economics*. Oxford: Oxford University Press.

Evandrou, M. and Falkingham, J. (1993) Social Security and the life course: developing sensitive policy alternatives, in S. Arber and M. Evandrou (eds) *Ageing, Independence and the Life Course*. London: Jessica Kingsley.

Evans, M. and Falkingham, J. (1997) *Minimum Pensions and Safety Nets in Old Age: A Comparative Analysis*, WSP/131. London: LSE/STICERD.

Even, W. and Macpherson, D. (1990) The gender gap in pensions and wages, *Review of Economics and Statistics*, 72(2): 259–65.

Falkingham, J. (1998) Financial (in)security in later life, in M. Bernard and J. Phillips (eds) *The Social Policy of Old Age: Moving into the 21st Century*. London: Centre for Policy on Ageing.

Falkingham, J. and Rake, K. (1999) 'Partnership in Pensions' – delivering a secure retirement for women? *Benefits*, September/October: 11–15.

Falkingham, J. and Victor, C. (1991) *The Myth of the Woopie? Incomes, the Elderly and Targetting Welfare*, WSP/55. London: LSE/STICERD.

Family Resources Surveys (1994–6) Computer files held at the Data Archive, Essex University.

Farkas, J. and O'Rand, A. (1998) The pension mix for women in middle and late life: The changing employment relationship, *Social Forces*, 76(3): 1007–32.

Feldstein, M. (1974) Social Security, induced retirement, and aggregate capital accumulation, *Journal of Political Economy*, 82(5): 905–26.

Feldstein, M. (1982) Social Security and private saving: reply, *Journal of Political Economy*, 90(4): 630–42.

Ferrara, P. (ed.) (1985) *Social Security: Prospects for Real Reform*. Washington, DC: Cato Institute.

Ferri, E. and Smith, K. (1997) *Parenting in the 1990s*. London: Family Policy Study Centre.

Field, J. and Farrant, G. (1993) Public perceptions of occupational schemes, in R. Goode (ed.) *Pension Law Reform: The Report of the Pension Law Reform Committee, Vol. 2, The Research*. London: HMSO.

Finch, J. (1989) *Family Obligations and Social Change*. Cambridge, MA: Basil Blackwell (Polity Press).

Frenken, H. and Maser, K. (1992) Employer-sponsored pension plans – who is covered, *Perspectives*. Ottawa: Statistics Canada, Winter: 27–35.

Friedman, M. (1962) *Capitalism and Freedom*. Chicago, IL: University of Chicago Press.

Friedman, M. and Friedman, R. (1980) *Free to Choose*. London: Secker & Warburg.

Gabriel, Y. and Lang, T. (1995) *The Unmanageable Consumer: Contemporary Consumption and its Fragmentations*. London: Sage.

General Household Surveys (1993–4) Computer files held at the Data Archive, Essex University.

Gershuny, J., Godwin, M. and Jones, S. (1994) The domestic labour revolution: a process of lagged adaptation?, in M. Anderson, F. Bechofer and J. Gershuny (eds) *The Social and Political Economy of the Household*. Oxford: Oxford University Press.

Gershuny, J. and Robinson, J. (1988) Historical changes in the household division of labour, *Demography*, 25(4): 537–52.

Ghilarducci, T. (1997) Testimony before the Subcommittee on Social Security of the US House Committee on Ways and Means, 18 September.

Gibson, R. (1996) The Black American retirement experience, in J. Quadagno and D. Street (eds) *Aging for the Twenty-First Century*. New York: St. Martin's Press.

Giddens, A. (1991) *Modernity and Self-Identity: Self and Society in the Late Modern Age*. Cambridge: Polity Press.

Gignac, M., Kelloway, K. and Gottlieb, B. (1996) The impact of caregiving on employment: a mediation model of work–family conflict, *Canadian Journal on Aging*, 15(4): 525–42.

Ginn, J. and Arber, S. (1991) Gender, class and income inequalities in later life, *British Journal of Sociology*, 42(3): 369–96.

Ginn, J. and Arber, S. (1992) Towards women's independence: pension systems in three contrasting European welfare states, *Journal of European Social Policy*, 2(4): 255–77.

Ginn, J. and Arber, S. (1993) Pension penalties: the gendered division of occupational welfare, *Work, Employment and Society*, 7(1): 47–70.

Ginn, J. and Arber, S. (1994) Heading for hardship: how the British pension system has failed women, in S. Baldwin and J. Falkingham (eds) *Social Security and Social Change: New Challenges to the Beveridge Model*. Hemel Hempstead: Harvester Wheatsheaf.

Ginn, J. and Arber, S. (1996) Patterns of employment, pensions and gender: the effect of work history on older women's non-state pensions, *Work Employment and Society*, 10(3): 469–90.

Ginn, J. and Arber, S. (1998) How does part time work lead to low pension income?, in J. O'Reilly and C. Fagan (eds) *Part Time Prospects*. London: Routledge.

Ginn, J. and Arber, S. (1999) Changing patterns of pension inequality: the shift from state to private sources, *Ageing and Society*, 19(3): 319–42.

Ginn, J. and Arber, S. (2000a) Gender, the generational contract and pension privatisation, in S. Arber and C. Attias-Donfut (eds) *The Myth of Intergenerational Conflict: The State and Family Across Cultures*. London: Routledge.

Ginn, J. and Arber, S. (2000b) Personal pension take-up in the 1990s in relation to position in the labour market, *Journal of Social Policy*, 29(2): 205–28.

Ginn, J. and Sandell, J. (1996) Balancing home and employment: Stress experienced by social services staff, *Work, Employment and Society*, 11(3): 413–34.

Ginn, J., Arber, S., Brannen, J. *et al*. (1996) Feminist fallacies: A reply to Hakim on women's employment, *British Journal of Sociology*, 47(1): 167–74.

Glennerster, H. and Hills, J. (1998) *The State of Welfare: the Economics of Social Spending*. Oxford: Oxford University Press.

Globe and Mail (1999) Ottawa saves 2.4 billion as judge defers to MPPs' will, 5 November: A1.

Glover, J. and Arber, S. (1995) Polarisation in mothers' employment, *Gender, Work and Organisation*, 2(4): 165–79.

Goldin, C. (1990) *Understanding the Gender Gap: An Economic History of American Women*. Oxford: Oxford University Press.

Gordon, M., Mitchell, O. and Twinney, M. (1997) *Positioning Pensions for the Twenty-First Century*. Pennsylvania: The Pension Research Council, University of Pennsylvania Press.

Government Actuary Department (GAD) (2000) *Drafts on the Social Security Benefits Uprating Order*, Cm 4587, Feb. London: The Stationery Office.

Grace, M. (1998) The work of caring for young children: priceless or worthless? *Women's Studies International Forum*, 21(4): 401–13.

Graebner, W. (1980) *A History of Retirement*. New Haven, CT: Yale University Press.

Groves, D. (1987) Occupational pension provision and women's poverty in old age, in C. Glendinning and J. Millar (eds) *Women and Poverty in Britain*. Brighton: Wheatsheaf.

Groves, D. (1991) Financial provision for women in retirement, in M. Maclean and D. Groves (eds) *Women's Issues in Social Policy*. London: Routledge.

Gunasekera, M. and Powlay, J. (1987) *Occupational Superannuation Arrangements in Australia*, background/discussion paper no. 21. Canberra: Social Security Review, Department of Social Security.

Gunderson, M. (1998) *Women and the Canadian Labour Market: Transition Towards the Future*. Ottawa: Statistics Canada.

Hakim, C. (1991) Grateful slaves and self-made women: fact and fantasy in women's work orientations, *European Sociological Review*, 7: 101–21.

Hakim, C. (1995) Five feminist myths about women's employment, *British Journal of Sociology*, 46(3): 429–55.

Hakim, C. (1996) *Key Issues in Women's Work*. London: The Athlone Press.

Hakim, C. (1997) A sociological perspective on part time work, in H-P. Blossfeld and C. Hakim (eds) *Between Equalization and Marginalization: Women Working Part Time in Europe and the United States of America*. Oxford: Oxford University Press.

Hakim, C. (1998) Developing a sociology for the twenty-first century: preference theory, *British Journal of Sociology*, 49(1): 137–43.

Hancock, R. and Sutherland, H. (1997) *Costs and Distributional Effects of Increasing the Basic Pension*. London: Age Concern England.

Hannah, L. (1986) *Inventing Retirement: The Development of Occupational Pensions in Britain*. Cambridge: Cambridge University Press.

Hardy, M. and Hazelrigg, L. (1995) Gender, race/ethnicity, and poverty in later life, *Journal of Aging Studies*, 9(1): 43–63.

Harkness, S. and Waldfogel, J. (1999) *The Family Gap in Pay: Evidence from Seven Industrialised Countries*, CASE paper 29. London: Centre for Analysis of Social Exclusion.

Harrington Meyer, M. (1990) Family status and poverty among older women: the gendered distribution of retirement income in the United States, *Social Problems*, 37: 551–63.

Harrington Meyer, M., Street, D. and Quadagno, J. (1994) The impact of family status on income security and health care in old age: a comparison of western nations, *International Journal of Sociology and Social Policy*, 14(1–2): 53–83.

Hauser, R. (1997) *Adequacy and Poverty Among the Retired*. Paris: OECD.

Hawkes, C. and Garman, A. (1995) *Perceptions of Non-State Pensions*, In-house report 8. London: Social Research Branch, Department of Social Security.

Hayek, F. (1960) *The Constitution of Liberty*. London: Routledge & Kegan Paul.

Hayek, F. (1982) *Law, Legislation and Liberty: A New Statement of the Liberal Principles of Justice and Political Economy*. London: Routledge & Kegan Paul.

Hernes, H. (1984) Women and the welfare state. The transition from private to public dependence, in H. Holter (ed.) *Patriarchy in a Welfare Society*. Oslo: Universitetsforlaget.

Hewitt, P. (1993) *About Time: The Revolution in Work and Family Life*. London: IPPR.

Himmelweit, S. (1998) Accounting for caring, *Radical Statistics*, 70: 3–7.

Hill, D. and Tigges, L. (1995) Gendering welfare state theory: a cross national study of women's public pension quality, *Gender and Society*, 9(1): 99–119.

Hills, J. (1993) *The Future of Welfare. A Guide to the Debate*. York: Joseph Rowntree Foundation.

Hills, J. (1995) The welfare state and redistribution between generations, in J. Falkingham and J. Hills (eds) *The Dynamic of Welfare. Social Policy and the Life Cycle*. Hemel Hempstead: Harvester Wheatsheaf.

Hinz, R., McCarthy, D. and Turner, J. (1997) Are women conservative investors? Gender differences in participant directed pension investments, in M. Gordon, O. Mitchell and M. Twinney (eds) *Positioning Pensions for the Year 2000*. Philadelphia, PA: University of Pennsylvania Press.

Hochschild, A.R. (1989) *The Second Shift: Working Parents and the Revolution at Home*. New York: Viking.

Hochschild, A. (1990) *The Second Shift: Working Parents and the Revolution at Home*. London: Piatkus.

Hochschild, A. (1997) *The Time Bind: When Work Becomes Home and Home Becomes Work*. New York: Metropolitan Books.

Holtz-Eakin, D. and Smeeding, T. (1994) Income, wealth, and intergenerational economic relations of the aged, in L. Martin and S. Preston (eds) *Demography of Aging*. Washington, DC: National Academy Press.

Hughes, G. and Whelan, B.J. (1996) *Occupational and Personal Pension Coverage 1995*. Dublin: Economic and Social Research Institute.

Human Resources Development Canada (HRDC) (1999) *Fact Sheet on Credit Splitting Upon Divorce or Separation*. Ottawa: HRDC.

Hutton, S., Kennedy, S. and Whiteford, P. (1995) *Equalization of State Pension Ages: The Gender Impact*. Manchester EOC.

Hutton, S. and Whiteford, P. (1994) Gender and retirement incomes: A comparative analysis, in S. Baldwin and J. Falkingham (eds) *Social Security and Social Change. New Challenges to the Beveridge Model*. Hemel Hempstead: Harvester Wheatsheaf.

Institute for Women's Policy Research (1993) *State Pay Equity Programs Raise Women's Wages*, News release, 20 May, Washington, DC: IWPR.

Itzin, C. and Phillipson, C. (1993) *Age Barriers at Work: Maximising the Potential of Mature and Older Workers*. Solihull: Metropolitan Authorities Recruitment Agency.

Jacobs, L. and Shapiro, R. (1995) *The News Media's Coverage of Social Security*. Washington, DC: National Academy of Social Insurance.

Jacobs, S. (1999) Trends in women's career patterns and in gender occupational mobility in Britain, *Gender, Work and Organisation*, 6(1): 32–46.

Johnsen, J. (1922) *Selected Articles on Social Insurance*. New York: The H.W. Wilson Company.

Johnson, P. and Falkingham, J. (1992) *Ageing and Economic Welfare*. London: Sage.

Johnson, P. and Rake, K. (1998) Comparative social policy research in Europe, *Social Policy Review*, 10: 257–78.

Johnson, P., Conrad, C. and Thomson, D. (eds) (1989) *Workers versus Pensioners: Intergenerational Conflict in an Ageing World*. Manchester: Manchester University Press.

Johnson, P., Disney, R. and Stears, G. (1996) *Pensions: 2000 and Beyond. Volume 2*. London: Retirement Income Inquiry.

Johnson, R. and Lo Sasso, A. (2000) *The Trade-off Between Hours of Employment and Time Assistance to Elderly Parents at Midlife*. Washington, DC: Urban Institute.

Joshi, H. and Davies, H. (1992) *Childcare and Mothers' Lifetime Earnings: Some European Contrasts*. London: Centre for Economic Policy Research.

Joshi, H. and Davies, H. (1994) The paid and unpaid roles of women: how should social security adapt?, in S. Baldwin and J. Falkingham (eds) *Social Security and Social Change. New Challenges to the Beveridge Model*. Hemel Hempstead: Harvester Wheatsheaf.

Joshi, H. and Verropoulou, G. (2000) *Maternal Employment and Child Outcomes*. London: Smith Institute.

Kaden, J. and McDaniel, S. (1990) Care giving and care receiving: A double bind for women in Canada's aging society, *Journal of Women and Aging*, 2(3): 3–26.

Kangas, O. and Palme, J. (1992) The private–public mix in pension policy, in J.E. Kolberg (ed.) *The Study of Welfare State Regimes*. Armonk, NY: M.E. Sharpe.

King, A. (1998) Income poverty since the early 1970s, in R. Fincher and J. Nieuwenhuysen (eds) *Australian Poverty: Then and Now*. Melbourne: Melbourne University Press.

King, A., Bakgaard, H. and Harding, A. (1999) *Australian Retirement Incomes*, discussion paper no. 43. Canberra: National Centre for Social and Economic Modelling, University of Canberra.

Kingson, E., Hirshorn, B. and Cornman, J. (1986) *Ties that Bind: The Interdependence of Generations*. Washington, DC: Seven Locks Press.

Knox, D.M. (1994) The relationship between the age pension and superannuation benefits, particularly for women, in *Women and Superannuation*, background paper no. 41. Economic Planning Advisory Council (EPAC) and Office of the Status of Women (OSW). Canberra: AGPS.

Kotlikoff, L. (1992) *Generational Accounting: Knowing Who Pays, and When, for What We Spend*. New York: Free Press.

Labour Party (1992) Social security and poverty (section 6), in *Policy Briefing Handbook*. London: Labour Party.

Land, H. (1989) The construction of dependency, in M. Bulmer, J. Lewis and D. Piachaud (eds) *The Goals of Social Policy*. London: Unwin & Hyman.

Land, H. (1994) The demise of the male breadwinner – in practice but not in theory: a challenge for social security systems, in S. Baldwin and J. Falkingham (eds) *Social Security and Social Change. New Challenges to the Beveridge Model*. Hemel Hempstead: Harvester Wheatsheaf.

Langan, M. and Ostner, I. (1991) Gender and welfare, in G. Room (ed.) *Towards a European Welfare State?* Bristol: School for Advanced Urban Studies.

Larkin, J. (1994) Occupational link – eligibility and the 'two year rule', in *Women and Superannuation*, background paper no. 41. Economic Planning Advisory Council (EPAC) and Office of the Status of Women (OSW). Canberra: AGPS.

Lazear, E. and Rosen, S. (1987) Pension inequality, in Z. Bodie, J. Shoven and D. Wise (eds) *Issues in Pension Economics*. Chicago, IL: University of Chicago for NBER.

Levy, F. (1998) *The New Dollars and Dreams: American Incomes and Economic Change*. New York: Russell Sage.

Lewis, C. (1982) The observation of father–infant relationships: an 'attachment' to outmoded concepts, in L. McKee and M. O'Brien (eds) *The Father Figure*. London: Tavistock Publications.

Lewis, J. (1992) Gender and the development of welfare regimes, *Journal of European Social Policy*, 2(3): 31–48.

Lichtenstein, J. and Wu, K. (2000) *Pension and IRA coverage Among Boomer, Pre-Boomer and Older Workers*. Washington, DC: AARP Public Policy Institute.

Lister, R. (1992) *Women's Economic Dependency and Social Security*. Manchester: Equal Opportunities Commission.

Lister, R. (1994) 'She has other duties' – Women, citizenship and social security, in S. Baldwin and J. Falkingham (eds) *Social Security and Social Change. New Challenges to the Beveridge Model*. Hemel Hempstead: Harvester Wheatsheaf.

Longman, P. (1987) *Born to Pay: The New Politics of Aging in America*. Boston, MA: Houghton Mifflin Company.

Lowe, J. (1997) *The Which? Guide to Pensions: How to Maximise your Retirement Income*. London: Which? Books/The Consumers Association.

Lusk, H. (1913) *Social Welfare in New Zealand*. London: William Heinemann.

Mabbett, D. (1997) *Pension Funding: Economic Imperative or Political Strategy*, Discussion Paper 97/1. Uxbridge: Brunel University.

McClure, M. (1998) *A Civilised Community: A History of Social Security in New Zealand*. Auckland: Auckland University Press.

McDonald, L. (1997) The invisible poor: Canada's retired widows, *Canadian Journal on Aging*, 16(3): 553–83.

McDonald, L. (2000) Alarmist economics and women's pensions: a case of 'semanticide', in E. Gee and G. Gutman (eds) *The Overselling of Population Aging: Apocalyptic Demography, Intergenerational Challenges, and Social Policy*. Oxford: Oxford University Press.

McKnight, A., Elias, P. and Wilson, R. (1998) *Low Pay and the National Insurance System: A Statistical Picture*. Manchester: EOC.

McQuaig, L. (1993) *The Wealthy Banker's Wife: The Assault on Equality in Canada*. Toronto: Penguin Books.

McRae, S. (1993) Returning to work after childbearing: opportunities and inequalities, *European Sociological Review*, 9(2): 125–37.

Marmor, T., Smeeding, T. and Greene, V. (eds) (1994) *Economic Security and Intergenerational Justice: A Look at North America*. Washington, DC: Urban Institute.

Marshall, V. (1993) A critique of Canadian aging and health policy, *Journal of Canadian Studies*, 28(1): 153–65.

Martin Matthews, A. and Campbell, L. (1995) Gender roles, employment and family care, in S. Arber and J. Ginn (eds) *Connecting Gender and Ageing*. Buckingham: Open University Press.

Martin Matthews, A. and Rosenthal, C. (1993) Balancing work and family in an aging society, in G. Maddox and P. Lawton (eds) *Annual Review of Gerontology and Geriatrics*, 13: 96–122. New York: Springer.

Minkler, M. (1991) Generational equity and the new victim blaming, in M. Minkler and C. Estes (eds) *Critical Perspectives on Aging: The Political and Moral Economy of Growing Old*. Amityville, NY: Baywood.

Mitchell, D. (1991) *Income Transfers in Ten Welfare States*. Aldershot: Avebury.

Mitchell, D. (1993) *Income Security for Old Age: Evidence from Eight OECD Countries*. Research School of Social Sciences Working Paper. Canberra: Australian National University.

Modood, T. and Berthoud, R. (1997) *Ethnic Minorities in Britain: Diversity and Disadvantage*. London: Policy Studies Institute.

Moon, M. and Mulvey, J. (1996) *Entitlements and the Elderly: Protecting Promises, Recognizing Realities.* Washington, DC: The Urban Institute Press.

Morgan, E. (1984) *Choice in Pensions: The Political Economy of Saving for Retirement.* London: Institute for Economic Affairs.

Morissette, R. (1997) The declining labour market status of young men, in M. Corak (ed.) *Labour Markets, Social Institutions, and the Future of Canada's Children.* Ottawa: Statistics Canada.

Morissette, R. and Drolet, M. (1999) *The Evolution of Pension Coverage of Young and Prime-Aged Workers in Canada.* Ottawa: Statistics Canada.

Morris, M., Robinson, J. and Simpson, J. (1999) *The Changing Nature of Home Care and Its Impact on Women's Vulnerability to Poverty.* Ottawa: Status of Women Canada.

Mullan, P. (2000) *The Imaginary Time Bomb: Why an Ageing Population is not a Social Problem.* London: I.B. Tauris.

Murgatroyd, L. and Neuberger, H. (1997) *A Household Satellite Account for the UK.* London: The Stationery Office.

Murthi, M., Orszag, M. and Orszag, P. (2001) Administrative costs under a decentralised approach to individual accounts: lessons from the United Kingdom, in R. Holzmann and J. Stiglitz (eds) *New Ideas About Old Age Security.* Washington, DC: World Bank/Oxford University Press.

Myles, J. (1988) Decline or impasse? The current state of the welfare state, *Studies in Political Economy,* 26: 73–107.

Myles, J. (1989) *Old Age in the Welfare State: The Political Economy of Public Pensions.* Lawrence, KS: University Press of Kansas.

Myles, J. (2000) *The Maturation of Canada's Retirement Income System: Income level, Income Inequality and Low Income Among the Elderly.* Ottawa: Statistics Canada.

Myles, J. and Street, D. (1995) Should the economic life course be redesigned? old age security in a time of transition, *Canadian Journal on Aging,* 14(2): 335–59.

National Audit Office (1990) *The Elderly: Information Requirements for Supporting the Implications of Personal Pensions for the National Insurance Fund,* HC 55. London: HMSO.

National Council of Welfare (NCW) (1989) *A Pension Primer.* Ottawa: NCW.

National Council of Welfare (NCW) (1999) *A Pension Primer.* Ottawa: NCW.

National Council of Women of Great Britain (1998) *Securing our Future: Women and the Economics of Later Life.* London: The National Council of Women of Great Britain.

National Council on Ageing and Older People (1999) *Income, Deprivation and Well-Being Among Older Irish People.* Dublin: National Council on Ageing and Older People.

National Economic Council (NEC) (1998) *Women and Retirement Security.* Washington, DC: National Economics Council.

Newell, S. (1993) The Superwoman Syndrome: gender differences of attitudes towards equal opportunities at work and towards domestic responsibilities at home, *Work, Employment and Society,* 7(2): 275–89.

Nolan, B. and Watson, D. (1999) *Women and Poverty in Ireland.* Dublin: Oak Tree Press/Combat Poverty Agency.

O'Connor, S., Orloff, A. and Shaver, S. (1999) *States, Markets, Families: Gender, Liberalism and Social Policy in Australia, Canada, Great Britain and the United States*. Cambridge: Cambridge University Press.

Office for National Statistics (ONS) (1995) *Social Trends 25*, London: HMSO.

Office for National Statistics (ONS) (1996) *Living in Britain. Results for the 1994 GHS*. London: HMSO.

Office for National Statistics (ONS) (1997) *Social Security Statistics 1997*. London: The Stationery Office.

Office for National Statistics (ONS) (1998a) *New Earnings Survey 1998*, London: The Stationery Office.

Office for National Statistics (ONS) (1998b) *Labour Force Survey, Spring 1998*. London: The Stationery Office.

Office for National Statistics (ONS) (1998c) *Birth Statistics 1997. Series FM1, no. 26*. London: The Stationery Office.

Office for National Statistics (ONS) (1999a) *Social Trends 29*, London: The Stationery Office.

Office for National Statistics (ONS) (1999b) *New Earnings Survey 1998, Part A*. London: The Stationery Office.

Office of Management and Budget (OMB) (1998) *Budget of the President*, Washington, DC: Office of Management and Budget.

Olsberg, D. (1997) *Ageing and Money*. Sydney: Allen & Unwin.

O'Rand, A. (1986) The hidden payroll: employee benefits and the structure of workplace inequality, *Sociological Forum*, 1: 657–83.

O'Rand, A. (1994) *The Vulnerable Majority: Older Women in Transition*. The Advisory Panel on Older Women of the National Academy on Aging. Syracuse, NY: Syracuse University.

O'Rand, A. (2000) Risk, rationality and modernity: social policy and the ageing self, in K. Schaie and J. Hendricks (eds) *The Evolution of the Ageing Self: Societal Impact on the Ageing Process*. New York: Springer.

O'Rand, A. and Henretta, J. (1999) *Age and Inequality: Diverse Pathways Through Later Life*. Boulder, CO: Westview Press.

O'Reilly, J. and Fagan, C. (1998) *Part Time Prospects*. London: Routledge.

Organization for Economic Cooperation and Development (OECD) (1981) *Labour Force Statistics*. Paris: OECD.

Organization for Economic Cooperation and Development (OECD) (1988) *Reforming Public Pensions*. Paris: OECD.

Organization for Economic Cooperation and Development (OECD) (1995) *Private Pensions in OECD Countries: Canada*. Paris: OECD.

Organization for Economic Cooperation and Development (OECD) (1996) *Employment Outlook*. Paris: OECD.

Organization for Economic Cooperation and Development (OECD) (1997) *Aging in OECD Countries*. Paris: OECD.

Organization for Economic Cooperation and Development (OECD) (1998a) *The Future of Female Dominated Occupations*. Paris: OECD.

Organization for Economic Cooperation and Development (OECD) (1998b) *OECD Social Expenditure Database 1980–1986*. Paris: OECD.

Organization for Economic Cooperation and Development (OECD) (1999) *Employment Outlook*. Paris: OECD.

Organization for Economic Cooperation and Development (OECD) (2000) www.oecd.org/std/ppp/pps.htm (accessed June 2000).

Orloff, A. (1993) Gender and the social rights of citizenship: the comparative analysis of gender relations and welfare states, *American Sociological Review*, 58: 303–28.

Orszag, P., Lav, I. and Greenstein, R. (1999) *Exacerbating Inequities in Pension Benefits: An Analysis of the Pension Provisions in the Tax Bill*. Washington, DC: Center on Budget and Policy Priorities.

Pahl, J. (1989) *Money and Marriage*. London: Macmillan Education.

Palme, J. (1990) Models of old age pensions, in A. Ware and R.E. Goodin (eds) *Needs and Welfare*. Sage: London.

Parker, H. (ed.) (2000) *Low Cost But Acceptable Incomes for Older People. A Minimum Income standard for households aged 65–74 years in the UK*. Bristol: The Policy Press.

Peggs, K. (1995) Women and pensions. Unpublished PhD thesis, University of Surrey.

Peggs, K. (2000) Which Pension? Women, risk and pension choice, *The Sociological Review*, 48(3): 349–64.

Pensions Board (1998) *Securing Retirement Income*. Dublin: Pensions Board.

Pensions Provision Group (PPG) (1998) *We All Need Pensions – the Prospects for Pension Provision*. London: The Stationery Office.

Periodic Report Group (PRG) (1997a) *1997 Retirement Income Report: A Review of the Current Framework, Interim Report*, 31 July. Wellington: GP Print.

Periodic Report Group (PRG) (1997b) *Concluding Report*, 18 December. Wellington: GP Print.

Peterson, P. (1993) *Facing Up: How to Rescue the Economy from Crushing Debt and Rescue the American Dream*. New York: Simon & Schuster.

Pfau-Effinger, B. (1998) Part time work between family and employment in cross-national perspective, in J. O'Reilly and C. Fagan (eds) *Part Time Prospects*. London: Routledge.

Phillips, L. (1998) Hegemony and political discourse: the lasting impact of Thatcherism, *Sociology*, 32(4): 847–67.

Phillipson, C., Bernard, M. and Strang, P. (eds) (1986) *Dependency and Interdependency in Old Age*. London: Croom Helm.

Pierson, P. (1994) *Dismantling the Welfare State? Reagan, Thatcher and the Politics of Retrenchment*. Cambridge: Cambridge University Press.

Pre-Retirement Association (PRA) and Help the Aged (HtA) (1997) *Women and Pensions*. London: Help the Aged.

Procter, I. and Padfield, M. (1998) *Young Adult Women, Work and Family: Living a Contradiction*. London: Mansell.

Quadagno, J. (1988) *The Transformation of Old Age Security: Class and Politics in the American Welfare State*. Chicago, IL: University of Chicago Press.

Quadagno, J. (1989) Generational equity and the politics of the welfare state, *Politics & Society*, 17: 353–76.

Quadagno, J. (1996) Social security and the myth of the entitlement crisis, *The Gerontologist*, 36: 391–99.

Rake, K. (1999) Accumulated disadvantage? Welfare state provision and the incomes of older women and men in Britain, France and Germany, in J. Clasen (ed.) *Comparative Social Policy Concepts, Theories and Methods*. Oxford: Blackwell.

Rake, K. (ed.) (2000) *Women's Incomes over the Lifetime*. London: The Stationery Office.

Rake, K., Falkingham, J. and Evans, M. (1999) *Tightropes and Tripwires: New Labour's Proposals and Means-testing in Old Age*, CASE paper 23. London: Centre for Analysis of Social Exclusion.

Rappaport, A. (1997) Money, sex, and pensions: why retirement policy reforms are truly women's issues, *Contingencies*, 9(4): 34–9.

RCSS (1972) *Social Security in New Zealand*. Wellington: Royal Commission on Social Security.

Rees, T. (1992) *Women and the Labour Market*. London: Routledge.

Reich, R. (1997) *Financial Times*, 3 March, cited in M. Buti, D. Franco and L. Pench (eds) *The Welfare State in Europe. Challenges and Reforms*. Cheltenham: Edward Elgar.

Reno, V. and Friedland, R. (1997) Strong support but low confidence: what explains the contradiction?, in E. Kingson and J. Schulz (eds) *Social Security in the 21st Century*. New York: Oxford University Press.

Reskin, B. and Hartmann, H. (eds) (1986) *Women's Work, Men's Work: Sex Segregation on the Job*. Washington, DC: National Academy Press.

Reskin, B. and Padavic, I. (1994) *Women and Men At Work*. London: Pine Forge Press.

Rix, S. and Williamson, J. (1998) *Social Security Reform: How Might Women Fare?* Washington, DC: AARP Public Policy Institute.

Robertson, A. (1991) The politics of Alzheimer's Disease: a case study in apocalyptic demography, in M. Minkler and C. Estes (eds) *Critical Perspectives on Aging: The Political and Moral Economy of Growing Old*. Amityville, NY: Baywood.

Rosenman, L. (1997) The social assistance approach and retirement pensions in Australia, in J. Midgley and M. Sherraden (eds) *Alternatives to Social Security: An International Inquiry*. Westport, CT: Auburn House.

Rossi, A. (1993) Intergenerational relations: gender, norms and behavior, in V. Bengtson and A. Achenbaum (eds) *The Changing Contract Across Generations*. New York: Aldine de Gruyter.

Ruane, F.P. and Sutherland, J.M. (1999) *Women in the Labour Force*. Dublin: Employment Equality Agency.

Sainsbury, D. (1994) *Gendering Welfare States*. London: Sage.

Sainsbury, D. (1996) *Gender, Equality and Welfare States*. Cambridge: Cambridge University Press.

Saunders, P. (1994) *Welfare and Inequality: National and International Perspectives on the Australian Welfare State*. Cambridge: Cambridge University Press.

Scheiwe, K. (1994) German pension insurance, gendered times and stratification, in D. Sainsbury (ed.) *Gendering Welfare States*. London: Sage.

Schellenberg, G. (1994) *The Road to Retirement: Demographic and Economic Change in the 90s*. Ottawa: Canadian Council on Social Development.

Scott, J. (2000) European attitudes towards maternal employment, *International Sociology and Social Policy*, 19: 151–86.

Secretary of State for Social Security (1998) *A New Contract for Welfare: Partnership in Pensions*, Cm 4179. London: The Stationery Office.

Select Committee on Aging (1992) *How Do Women Fare Under the Nation's Retirement Policies?* Committee Print 102–879. Washington, DC: US Government Printing Office.

Sen, A. (1984) Rights and capabilities, *Resources, Values and Development*. Oxford: Blackwell.

Sharp, R. (1995) Women and superannuation: super bargain or raw deal?, in A. Edwards and S. Magarey (eds*) Women in a Restructuring Australia: Work and Welfare*. Sydney: Allen & Unwin.

Shaver, S. (1991) 'Considerations of mere logic': the Australian age pension and the politics of means testing, in J. Myles and J. Quadagno (eds) *States, Labor Markets and the Future of Old-Age Policy*. Philadelphia, PA: Temple University Press.

Shaver, S. (1997) *Universality and Selectivity in Income Support: An Assessment of the Issues*. Aldershot: Ashgate.

Shelton, B. (1992) *Women, Men and Time*. New York: Greenwood.

Shirley, E. and Spiegler, P. (1998) *The Benefits of Social Security Privatization for Women*. Washington, DC: The Cato Institute Project on Social Security Privatization.

Shragge, E. (1984) *Pensions Policy in Britain: A Socialist Analysis*. London: Routledge & Kegan Paul.

Shutt, H. (1998) *The Trouble with Capitalism: An Enquiry into the Causes of Global Economic Failure*. London: Zed Books.

Sinfield, A. (1978) Analyses in the social division of welfare, *Journal of Social Policy*, 72: 129–56.

Sinfield, A. (1993) Reverse targeting and upside down benefits: How perverse policies perpetuate poverty, in A. Sinfield (ed.) *Poverty, Inequality and Justice*. University of Edinburgh.

Sloane, P. (1990) Use of Equal Opportunities legislation and earnings differentials: a comparative study, *Industrial Relations Journal*, 21(3): 221–9.

Smart, B. (1999) *Facing Modernity: Ambivalence, Reflexivity and Morality*. London: Sage.

Smeeding, T. (1997) *Reshuffling Responsibilities in Old Age: The United States in Comparative Perspective*, working paper no. 153, Luxembourg Income Study. Syracuse, NY: Maxwell School of Citizenship and Public Affairs.

Smeeding, T., Torrey, B. and Rainwater, L. (1993) *Going to Extremes: An International Perspective on the Economic Status of the U.S. Aged*, working paper no. 87. Walferdange: The Luxembourg Income Study, CEPS/INSTEAD.

Smith, J. (1997) *The Changing Economic Circumstances of the Elderly: Income, Wealth and Social Security*. Policy Brief No. 8/1997. Center for Policy Research, Syracuse University.

Snell, J. (1993) The gendered construction of elderly marriage, 1900–1950, *Canadian Journal on Aging*, 12(4): 509–23.

Social Security Administration (SSA) (1998a) *Management of the Supplemental Security Income Program*. Washington, DC: USGPO.

Social Security Administration (SSA) (1998b) *Income of the Aged Chartbook, 1996*. Washington, DC: USGPO.

Social Security Administration (SSA) (1999a) *How Does Social Security Benefit Women?* Washington, DC: USGPO.

Social Security Administration (SSA) (1999b) *Facts and Figures about Social Security*. Washington, DC: USGPO.

Social Security Administration (SSA) (2000) *2000 Annual Report of the Board of Trustees*. Washington, DC: USGPO.

St John, S. (1992) Superannuation: How not to make policy, in J. Boston and P. Dalziel (eds) *The Decent Society*. Auckland: Oxford University Press.

St John, S. (1999) Superannuation in the 1990s: where angels fear to tread?, in P. Dalziel, J. Boston, and S. St John (eds) *Redesigning the Welfare State in New Zealand: Problems, policies prospects*. Auckland: Oxford University Press.

St John, S. and Ashton, T. (1993) *Private Pensions in New Zealand. Can they avert the crisis?* Wellington: Institute of Policy Studies.

Statistics Canada (1995) *Women in Canada: A Statistical Report*, 3rd edn. Catalogue 89-503-XPE. Ottawa: Statistics Canada.

Statistics Canada (1998) 1996 Census, *The Daily*, Catalogue 11-001-XIE, 17 March. Ottawa: Statistics Canada.

Statistics Canada (1999a) *A Portrait of Seniors in Canada*, 3rd edn. Catalogue 89-519-XPE. Ottawa: Statistics Canada.

Statistics Canada (1999b) Employer-sponsored pension plans, *The Daily*, Catalogue 11-001-XIE, 22 November. Ottawa: Statistics Canada.

Statistics Canada (1999c) Proportion of labour force and paid workers covered by a Registered Pension Plan. *Canadian Statistics*. www.statcan.ca/english/Pgdb/People/Labour/labor26.htm

Statistics Canada (1999d) *Retirement Savings Through RPPs and RRSPs, 1991–1997*, Catalogue 740002XPB. Ottawa: Statistics Canada.

Statistics Canada (1999e) Employment after childbirth, *The Daily*, Catalogue 11-001-XIE, 1 September. Ottawa: Statistics Canada.

Statistics New Zealand (1997) *Ageing and Retirement in New Zealand*. Wellington: Statistics New Zealand.

Statistics New Zealand (1998a) *New Zealand Now Incomes*. Wellington: Statistics New Zealand.

Statistics New Zealand (1998b) *New Zealand Now Women*. Wellington: Statistics New Zealand.

Stephens, R., Frater, P. and Waldegrave, C. (2000) *Below the line: an analysis of income poverty in New Zealand, 1984–1998*. Working Paper 2/00 Graduate School of Business and Economic Management, Victoria University of Wellington, Wellington.

Steuerle, C. and Bakija, J. (1994) *Retooling Social Security for the 21st Century*, Washington, DC: Urban Institute.

Stone, R., Cafferata, G. and Sangl, J. (1987) Caregivers of the frail elderly: A national profile, *The Gerontologist*, 27: 616–26.

Street, D. (1995) The public life of private pensions. Paper presented at the Annual Meeting of the Society for the Study of Social Problems, Washington, DC, August.

Street, D. (1996) The politics of pensions in Canada, Great Britain, and the United States. PhD dissertation, Florida State University, Tallahassee, FL.

Street, D. and Quadagno, J. (1993) The state, the elderly, and the intergenerational contract: Toward a new political economy of aging, in K.W. Schaie and W.A. Achenbaum (eds) *Societal Impact on Aging: Historical Perspectives*. New York: Springer.

Task Force (1991) *Interim Report of the Task Force on Private Provision for Retirement: The Issues*. Wellington: Task Force.

Task Force (1992) *Report of The Taskforce on Private Provision for Retirement (1992) Private Provision for Retirement: The Options*. Wellington: Task Force.

Taylor-Gooby, P. (1991) Welfare state regimes and welfare citizenship, *Journal of European Social Policy*, 1(2): 93–105.

Thatcher, M. (1993) *Margaret Thatcher: The Downing Street Years*. New York: HarperCollins.

Thomson, D. (1991) *Selfish Generations? How Welfare States Grow Old*. Wellington: Bridget Williams Books.

Thomson, D. (1998) *A World Without Welfare: New Zealand's Colonial Experiment*. Auckland: Auckland University Press.

Tilly, C. (1992) Two faces of part time work: Good and bad part time jobs in the US service industries, in B. Warme, K. Lundy and L. Lundy (eds) *Working Part time: Risks and Opportunities*. New York: Praeger.

Titmuss, R. (1974) *Social Policy*. London: Allen & Unwin.

Toporowski, J. (2000) *The End of Finance*. London: Routledge.

Townson, M. (1995) *Mid-life Financial Futures: Women's Prospects for a Secure Retirement*. Ottawa: Canadian Advisory Council on the Status of Women.

Treasury (1973) *White Paper on New Zealand Superannuation Scheme*. Wellington: Government Printer.

Turner, J. and Beller, D. (1992) *Trends in Pensions, 1992*. Washington, DC: USGPO.

United Nations (1991) *The World's Women: Trends and Statistics 1970–1990*. New York: UN Publications.

Urban Institute (1988) *Earnings Sharing under Social Security: A Model for Reform*. Washington, DC: Center for Women Policy Studies.

US Bureau of the Census (1996) *Poverty in the United States: 1995*, Current Population Reports, Series P60–194. Washington, DC: US Government Printing Office.

US Bureau of Labor Statistics (1991) *Employment and Earnings* 38 (January). Washington, DC: US Department of Labor.

US Bureau of Labor Statistics (1992) *Employment and Earnings* 39 (January). Washington, DC: US Department of Labor.

US Bureau of Labor Statistics (1993) *Employment and Earnings* 40 (January). Washington, DC: US Department of Labor.

US Department of Labor (DOL) (1994) *Pension and Health Benefits of American Workers*, Table B11, Washington, DC: US DOL.

US Department of Labor (DOL) (1997) *Private Pension Plan Bulletin: Abstract of 1994 Form 5500 Annual Reports*. Washington, DC: GPO.

US Department of Labor (DOL) (1999a) *Current Population Survey March Supplement*. Washington, DC: US DOL.

US Department of Labor (DOL) (1999b) *Report on the American Workforce*. Washington, DC: US DOL.

US House of Representatives (1996) *1996 Green Book: Background Material and Data on Programs Within the Jurisdiction of the Committee on Ways and Means*, WMCP: 104–14. Washington, DC: USGPO.

US House of Representatives (1998) *1998 Green Book: Background Material and Data on Programs Within the Jurisdiction of the Committee on Ways and Means*, WCMP: 105–7. Washington, DC: USGPO.

Van Drenth, A., Knijn, T. and Lewis, J. (1999) Sources of income for lone mother families: policy changes in Britain and the Netherlands and the experiences of divorced women, *Journal of Social Policy*, 28(4): 619–42.

Vezina, A. and Roy, J. (1996) State–family relations in Quebec from the perspective of intensive home care services for the elderly, *Journal of Gerontological Social Work*, 24(3–4): 149–64.

Vincent, J. (1995) *Inequality and Old Age*. London: UCL Press.

Vincent, J. (1996) Who's afraid of an ageing population? *Critical Social Policy*, 16(2): 3–44.

Vincent, J. (1999) *Politics, Power and Old Age*. Buckingham: Open University Press.

Waine, B. (1995) A disaster foretold? The case of the personal pension, *Social Policy and Administration*, 29(4): 317–34.

Walby, S. (1986) *Patriarchy at Work: Patriarchal and Capitalist Relations in Employment*. Cambridge: Polity Press.

Walby, S. (1997) *Gender Transformations*. London: Routledge.

Walker, A. (1986) The politics of ageing in Britain, in C. Phillipson, M. Bernard and P. Strang (eds) *Dependency and Inter-dependency in Old Age*. London: Croom Helm.

Walker, A. (1990) The economic 'burden' of ageing and the prospect of intergenerational conflict, *Ageing and Society*, 10: 377–96.

Walker, A. (1992) The poor relation: poverty among older women, in C. Glendinning and J. Millar (eds) *Women and Poverty in Britain: The 1990s*. Brighton: Wheatsheaf.

Walker, A. (1999) The third way for pensioners (by way of Thatcherism and avoiding today's pensioners), *Critical Social Policy*, 19(4): 511–27.

Walker, R. and Huby, M. (1989) Escaping financial dependency in old age, *Ageing and Society*, 9(1): 17–41.

Walker, R., Heaver, C. and McKay, S. (2000) *Building Up Pension Rights*. London: Department of Social Security.

Ward, C., Dale, A. and Joshi, H. (1996) Combining employment with children: an escape from dependence? *Journal of Social Policy*, 25(2): 223–48.

Ward, P. (1996) *The Great British Pensions Robbery*. Preston: Waterfall Books.

Warde, A. and Hetherington, K. (1993) A changing domestic division of labour? issues of measurement and interpretation, *Work, Employment and Society*, 7(1): 23–45.

Waring, M. (1988) *Counting for Nothing: What Men Value and What Women are Worth*. Wellington: Allen & Unwin.

Weitz, H. (1992) *The Pension Promise: The Past and Future of Canada's Private Pension System*. Scarborough: Thomson Canada Ltd.

Wheelock, J. (1990) *Husbands at Home. The Domestic Economy in a Post-Industrial Society*. London: Routledge.

Wilkinson, M. (1993) British tax policy 1979–90: equity and efficiency, *Policy and Politics*, 213: 207–17.

Williams, L. and Batrouney, T. (1998) Immigrants and poverty, in R. Fincher and J. Nieuwenhuysen (eds) *Australian Poverty: Then and Now*. Melbourne: Melbourne University Press.

Williams, T. and Field, J. (1993) *Pension Choices: A Survey on Personal Pensions in Comparison with other Options*. London: HMSO.

Williamson, J. (1997) A critique of the case for privatizing Social Security, *The Gerontologist*, 37(5): 561–71.

Wilmoth, J. (1998) Marital dissolution, remarriage and wealth in later life. Paper presented at the Gerontological Society of America Annual Meeting, Philadelphia, PA, November.

Wilmoth, J. and Koso, G. (2000) Does marital history matter? The effect of marital histories on wealth outcomes among pre-retirement aged adults. Unpublished manuscript.

Wolfson, M. (1997) Divergent inequalities: theory and empirical results, *Review of Income and Wealth*, 43: 401–21.

World Bank (1994) *Averting the Old Age Crisis*. New York: Oxford University Press.

Zimmerman, L. (1998) *Canada Pension Plan Reforms: Issues for Women*. Burnaby, BC: Simon Fraser University Gerontology Research Centre.

Index